DATE DUE

Secret Chromatic Art
in the Netherlands Motet

NUMBER SIX OF THE COLUMBIA
UNIVERSITY STUDIES IN MUSICOLOGY

Secret Chromatic Art in the Netherlands Motet

by Edward E. Lowinsky

TRANSLATED FROM THE GERMAN BY
CARL BUCHMAN

NEW YORK / RUSSELL & RUSSELL

TO THE MEMORY OF
MY PARENTS

Columbia University Studies in Musicology

Board of Editors

PREFACE

MUSICAL NOTATION has never done more than to hint at the sounds which the composer had in mind when he wrote down the symbols. This is more true the farther we delve into the past. Every age has its "self-evident" rules of performance, not marked in the notation. One of the major efforts of musicology is directed toward uncovering these unwritten laws and reconstructing the real music merely suggested by the notation, whether we are dealing with an organum by Perotin, a motet by Orlando di Lasso, or the Well Tempered Clavier by Bach.

One of the main obstacles to reliable interpretation of sixteenth-century polyphonic music is the uncertainty concerning the application of the old rules for singers in regard to the flattening and sharpening of tones, as embedded in the system of *musica ficta*. This uncertainty in itself is annoying enough. It causes every editor of early polyphonic music to adopt his own policy in regard to the supplementing of accidentals. It causes bewilderment and insecurity among the choral directors who want to perform the music. It causes confusion in the vital question of modality and tonality of early polyphony. But add for a moment to all of this the possibility that the composers of that time intentionally developed a technique devised to hide the true extent to which they applied chromatic alterations in their works—and the picture of confusion is complete.

The present book deals with exactly this situation. Nine years ago I stumbled for the first time upon an example of the secret chromatic art. At that time I thought I had to do with an isolated instance of a strange procedure. But the evidence to the effect that we are here confronted with a technique developed systematically and used in a number of great works kept on mounting slowly but surely. Yet I wonder whether I should have written down the whole story, strange and incredible as it seemed, if it had not been for the friendship, the encouragement, and the constructive criticism of Dr. Charles van den Borren, Professor of Musicology at the University of Brussels. In a correspondence that extended over many years I have submitted every example of secret chromaticism to him, and his agreement, his criticism, and his suggestions have been a source of continued inspiration to me. (While I write these lines Belgium has been freed by Allied armies, and I cherish the hope that this book will find Dr. van den Borren among the survivors of this frightful war.)

I should not be surprised if the reader, at first, is unwilling to accept my thesis of the existence of a secret chromatic art. I myself was puzzled and doubtful at the outset. However, I may be allowed to say a word about what the reader may expect from the book and what this book may well expect from its reader. The reader will find an attempt at answering two basic questions: What is the technique and the meaning of the secret chromatic art? and What are the reasons for the secrecy employed? The book, on the other hand, hopes for a reader who is willing to read and judge it, not piece by piece, chapter by chapter, but as a whole. The total evidence of music, theoretical sources, religious and cultural background is needed to explain what seems to be the only genuinely secret technique known in the history of music.

The book has not been written for the historians of music alone. On the contrary, I hope that it may find its way to the musician, and among the musicians particularly to the composer. In the long chain from composer to performer, theorist, and historian the widest gulf seems to be that between the historian and the composer. The historian, absorbed in the study of a dim past, seems to lose contact with contemporary music. Little has it been realized that the historian may actually grapple with the same problems and fight the same battles as does the composer—only on another plane. The historian may provide not only a powerful stimulus for the composer, he may actually open new vistas and new roads to the creative artist. A later age may realize that the historians who rediscovered the greatness of Bach's *Kunst der Fuge* or of medieval and Renaissance polyphony have contributed substantially toward the music of the present as well as of the future. It is time that we recognize the inevitable unity and interdependence of our work. All of us, whether we compose or perform, analyze or write history, are weaving the great pattern of our music of today and of tomorrow.

I have had the good fortune to meet a number of composers who have shown a deep interest in the music and the problems dealt with in this book. I have had long and absorbing discussions with Mark Brunswick, who gave me the benefit of his criticism. Ernst Křenek helped me not only by reading the proofs but also by making a number of most valuable suggestions and keen observations. I am deeply indebted to Hugo Kauder, with whom I had many long evenings of good conversation on music in general and the secret chromatic art in particular. His singular devotion to his work, done in solitary remoteness from the highways of modern publicity, his deep insight into the essentials of music combined with an encyclopedic knowledge of it, have been a great inspiration to me.

This book is also directed to the student of the Renaissance. Since the times of Burckhardt music has always been—with a few notable exceptions —the stepchild in the numerous studies on the culture of that period. I feel confident that the study of Renaissance music is called upon to make a real contribution to the long and heated debate, which has been going on for decades, on the problem of the Renaissance. The present book, I hope, will make a small step in this direction. The reader who is more familiar with other cultural aspects of the Renaissance than with music may find it easier to start with the last two chapters on the religious and the cultural background of the secret chromatic art, to go from there to the discussion of the aesthetical problem of the *musica reservata*, the relation of the secret chromatic art to the Netherlands artifices, and to end up with the study of Chapters III, II, and I on the music itself.

In my attempt to relate the secret chromatic art to the religious and cultural aspects of its time, I was aided by a number of outstanding scholars in the field of Renaissance research. Dr. Robert Bainton has been kind enough to read the chapter on "The Religious Background." I profited greatly from his patient and detailed criticism. The last chapter owes a great deal to the very great help I received from Dr. Rosemond Tuve, Dr. Erwin Panofsky, and Dr. Paul Oskar Kristeller.

I wish to acknowledge gratefully the debt which this book owes to my colleagues. Dr. Alfred Einstein, Dr. Gustave Reese, and Dr. Gerhard Herz gave generously of their time to read the manuscript and to suggest a number of improvements. I shall not forget how Dr. Einstein, during his visit to the Second Music Institute of Black Mountain College, insisted on helping me with reading the page proofs and the index. I received help and encouragement from Dr. Curt Sachs, Dr. Paul Henry Láng, Dr. Carleton Sprague Smith, and many others, whom I wish to thank here.

It is perhaps not superfluous to point out that none of those who helped me so generously with criticism and advice identify themselves necessarily with any position taken in this book. The responsibility for any statement or interpretation is solely mine.

For permission to quote from books and periodicals I am indebted to the following publishers:

Columbia University Press, New York: E. Rosen, *Three Copernican Treatises*, and R. H. Bainton, *Concerning Heretics*.

The Macmillan Company, New York: H. O. Taylor, *Thought and Expression in the Sixteenth Century*, and A. Wolf, *A History of Science, Technology and Philosophy in the Sixteenth and Seventeenth Centuries.*

Oxford University Press, New York: Erwin Panofsky, *Studies in Iconology.*

Princeton University Press, Princeton, New Jersey: Desiderius Erasmus, *The Praise of Folly*, translated by Hoyt H. Hudson.

G. Schirmer, Inc., New York: passages from articles by J. S. Levitan and E. E. Lowinsky, published in *The Musical Quarterly.*

Charles Scribner's Sons, New York: G. Vasari, *Lives of Seventy of the Most Eminent Painters*, edited by E. H. Blashfield, E. W. Blashfield, and A. A. Hopkins.

Moreover, I wish to thank Mr. W. H. Hay II for permission to quote from his translation of Petrus Pomponatius, *Tractatus de immortalitate animae*, published by Haverford College Press, Haverford, Pa.

It is my privilege to acknowledge the help of the staff of Columbia University Press, particularly of Miss Ida M. Lynn, who went over the text of this book with the greatest care.

In fairness to the translator it should be said that in addition to a number of passages throughout the book the last three chapters have been written in English by the author himself.

I remember with deep gratitude the kind interest which the late Bernard Flexner took in the publication of this work. Upon his recommendation the Emergency Committee in Aid of Displaced Foreign Scholars financed the translation.

I feel unable to express adequately the measure of debt which this book owes to the infinite patience, understanding, and ever resourceful help of my wife. She has not only shared with me the burden of writing it; she has also carried alone, and with admirable humor, the burden caused by a husband devoted to scholarship. The initiated know what this means.

EDWARD E. LOWINSKY

Black Mountain College, N.C.
October, 1945

CONTENTS

Contents

Contents

———

MUSIC EXAMPLES   *Following page* 184

INTRODUCTION

THE FIRST HALF of the sixteenth century was one of the most brilliant epochs in the history of European music. Scarcely any other has exerted so decisive an influence upon the subsequent development of the art. Molded by great geniuses, however, it was not. The star of Josquin des Prez still dominated its musical firmament, but not so much as to obliterate the constellation of younger masters who had arisen alongside him, particularly the antipodes Nicolas Gombert and Adrian Willaert. Both were outstanding, not only by virtue of their great talent, but even more because of the problems which they set themselves, because of the unflinching tenacity and singleness of purpose with which they devoted lives of unremitting labor solely to the solution of these problems. What is true of these two men likewise holds for the entire generation: it was pregnant with the seed of future development because of the problems it posed; it was great by reason of the courage, the tenacity, the sheer volume of the labor it performed in the service of new ideas.

During this period we find the free creative concept adopted as guiding principle. The technique of composition is liberated from its dependence upon the *cantus firmus;* the several voices are no longer conceived sequentially (one after another), but simultaneously; polyphonic imitation undergoes its first consistent development; the concept of an organic whole, unified despite linear multiplicity, attains to its first realization; the ecclesiastical system of modes begins to approximate the major-minor tonality of later epochs, and the groundwork of a tonal system of harmony is laid. By and large, it is the new relation of music to the word which is responsible for the transformation in the technique of composition. Not only for its spiritual significance but also as a sensuous phenomenon, as sound and rhythm, the word is now accepted at its full value by the composer. For the first time in the history of music the *word* becomes the chief source of creative inspiration. There arise new melodics and rhythmics, born out of the spirit of language; in the search for new media of expression, chromaticism and modulation are discovered, and with them a new harmonic world. Of secular significance are the upheavals here enacted: they call forth a conflict between old and new, which in turn endows the theory of music with fresh ideas and with a new sense of direction.

Existing research is still far from having fully revealed the magnificence of the period. In the present work we shall attempt to decipher the riddle of a secret art, of a new facet in the history of the chromatic movement. Accepted by most authorities as established fact is a cool indifference, on the part of the Netherlands school of that generation, to Italian innovations in the field of chromaticism. The Netherlanders cultivated with astonishing consistency the one large, free form held in universal esteem —the motet—but thus far most investigators have found even in this form no sign of an approach to chromaticism. This is scarcely to be wondered at. Chromaticism is a child of secular art, while the motet belongs essentially to sacred music, despite the existence of a certain number of secular works in motet style. Originally a set form of definitely ecclesiastical character, the motet of this period moves consistently in the direction of free expression of religious feeling and experience, a development which prompts the Netherlanders to seek new media of expression for their new religious world. Discussed at some length in the authors' book on Lasso [1] are the strong ties linking the Italian and Netherlands composers of this epoch. There is ample proof that Antwerp and Venice enjoyed an active exchange not only of official, commercial, and general cultural enterprises but of musical activities as well. The Antwerp publisher Susato reprinted works from the publications of his Venetian colleague Gardane, while Gardane included in his own editions a series of Netherlands masterworks. Around 1550 the art of the motet in the Netherlands underwent a change of style which placed its entire structure on new foundations. Of central importance in these new efforts are the text itself; a setting whose rhythm corresponds with the rhythm of the words; a musical realization of its pictorial and expressive content. As the composer yields to a growing preoccupation with the text, he tends to soften the hitherto prevailing strictness of the contrapuntal art and endeavors to enrich his harmonic palette —particularly through the new art of modulation. The closely-knit web of contrapuntal imitation is loosened more and more, through cleavage of the chorus into high registers and low or into antiphonal groups of the same combination of voices. Examination of the Venetian motet literature reveals that in Venice this new style attained complete maturity as early as 1540. The actual exchange of published works between Antwerp and Venice, together with the undeniable relationship between the Netherlands music and its Venetian counterparts, is sufficient evidence that the

[1] Lowinsky, *Das Antwerpener Motettenbuch Orlando di Lasso's und seine Beziehungen zum Motettenschaffen der niederländischen Zeitgenossen;* See the chapter "Beziehungen zwischen den niederländischen und Venezianer Motettendrucken." This study will hereafter be referred to as A. Mb.

change of style which took place in the Netherlands motet around 1550 was to a great extent inspired by Venetian models.

These facts stand witness to the living unity of the music of the Netherlands throughout all its epochs. For the reciprocal influence of Italy and the Netherlands is an essential element in the history of European music of this era. The relationship is obvious enough in the music of the Burgundian period, in that of Ockeghem's time, of Josquin's, and later of Lasso's, only in the case of the generation of Clemens non Papa and Crecquillon has its existence been not only not recognized, but specifically denied. The present investigation, which is devoted exclusively to the problem of chromaticism, will demonstrate in detail what was indicated only in broad outline in the monograph on Lasso, namely, the Italian orientation of the younger Netherlands school. All these tendencies are tied up with the rebirth of the secret character of music as we know it from the celebrated "artifices" of the older Netherlands school: a rebirth, however, in an entirely new sphere, which renders the problem more fascinating, as well as more involved.

Secret Chromatic Art
in the Netherlands Motet

I: THE NETHERLANDS MOTET ON THE
ROAD TO CHROMATICISM

BEFORE we take up our actual subject, the secret chromatic art, we must determine what obvious chromatic or prechromatic phenomena were present in the Netherlands motet around 1550.

SHARPS AND FLATS

Key Signatures

Sharps and flats are the first and most conspicuous messengers of a chromatic alteration in the diatonic system. It is a well-known fact that in the Netherlands vocal music there was, by and large, no use of the sharp sign, that is, no transposition of the church modes to the fifth above, the F sharp thereby being necessitated, but only the transposition to the fourth above, with one flat, or, at the very most, the transposition of the transposition, with a signature of two flats. This observation likewise holds for the motet repertoire now under consideration.[1] Here we find a series of works with partial or, what is far rarer, with total transposition to the major second below and a resulting key signature of two flats.

It is characteristic of almost all these works that they belong to a certain sphere of expression, being composed for texts of grief and lamentation, of contrition and desperation, of entreaty and longing. Most of the compositions with a key signature of two flats are by Clemens non Papa. Worthy of mention are his four-part motets "Conserva me domine" (two flats in the three lower voices),[2] "Jesus Nazarenus . . . defendat nos ab

---

[1] The present discussion is based on the same sources as the book on Lasso: on the motet publications, between 1546 and 1557, of the three great Netherlands editors Tieleman Susato, Pierre Phalèse, and Hubert Waelrant (see the chapter "Das Antwerpener Motettenrepertoire," in the study of Lasso, pp. 47–52). Of these thirty-two books of motets, twenty-eight contain motets for five voices or more, while only four books contain four-voice works. Hence, I have also drawn, for the purposes of this discussion, upon the seven books of four-part motets which Phalèse published in the year 1559: *Liber I–VI cantionum sacrarum vulgo moteta vocant, quatuor vocum autore D. Clemente non Papa.* The seventh book ". . . Autore Thomas Cricquillon," gives us the four-part motets of Clemens non Papa's foremost contemporary. Special mention will be made in the text of the use of any other handwritten or non-Netherlands sources.

[2] Phalèse 1559, Lib. III, No. 14. Concerning the use of different key signatures in different voices see the author's article on "The Function of Conflicting Signatures in Early Polyphonic Music," *The Musical Quarterly*, Vol. XXXI (April, 1945), 227–260.

omnibus malis" (two flats in the three lower voices),[3] "Ne abscondas me"
(bass, two flats),[4] "Rex autem David . . . lugebat filium" (bass, two flats),[5]
"Videns Jacob vestimenta Joseph scidit vestimenta sua" (bass, two flats),[6]
"O Thoma didime . . . succurre nobis miseris" (bass, two flats),[7] "Jerusalem cito veniet salus tua quare dolore consumaris" (bass, two flats),[8] "Tollite jugum meum" (bass, two flats),[9] "Ve tibi Babylon et Syria" (bass, two
flats);[10] the six-part motet "Fremuit spiritu Jesum" (two basses, two
flats).[11] Clemens is, furthermore, the only composer in the Antwerp repertoire to write works with complete transposition, that is, with key signatures of two flats in all the voices. Examples of this are the four-part
"Tristicia et anxietas,"[12] the five-voice "Job tonso capite,"[13] and "O quam
moesta dies."[14] He is also the only one who wrote a work with three flats,
the five-voice "Qui consolabatur me" (in the Susato edition, with three
flats in all five voices; in the Phalèse edition, with three flats in the three
lower voices).[15] Crecquillon, in his four-voice legend of Susanna, "Ingemuit
Susanna,"[16] writes two flats only in the alto and bass parts; in the six-part
"Congregati sunt inimici," only in the bass part;[17] in the four-part "Servus
tuus ego sum," again only in the bass part.[18] A composer called by Susato[19]
"incertus autor," who on the basis of other sources[20] can be identified as
Benedictus Appenzeller, writes the motet "Peccantem me et non poenitentem timor mortis perturbat" for four voices, and indicates a signature of
two flats in the soprano, alto, and bass. We find the same signature in
Benedictus's five-voice motet, based on the Song of Songs, "Surge
aquilo";[21] his five-voice motet of mourning, "Aperi domine . . . et vide afflictionem nostram"[22] also has the transposition to the major second below.
Although this list of works with key signatures of more than one flat lays
no claim to completeness, it already reveals a substantial number of trans-

[3] *Ibid.*, Lib. IV, No. 17.
[4] *Ibid.*, Lib. II, No. 13. In the bass part the two flats are found only in the margin
of the first line. Apparently this is the result of an oversight, inasmuch as a signature of two flats is justified by the leading of the bass line throughout.
[5] *Ibid.*, Lib. I, No. 11.   [6] *Ibid.*, No. 8.   [7] *Ibid.*, No. 5.   [8] *Ibid.*, No. 2.
[9] *Ibid.*, Lib. IV, No. 11.   [10] Susato 1553, Lib. II, No. 17.
[11] Phalèse 1553, Lib. II, No. 15.
[12] Susato 1553, Lib. I, No. 5, and Phalèse, 1559, Lib. V, No. 2.
[13] Susato 1554, Lib. IX, No. 10.
[14] Phalèse 1554, Lib. IV, No. 7 (Commer, *Collectio operum musicorum Batavorum*,
Vol. X, No. 9).
[15] Susato 1557, Lib. XIV, No. 18, and Phalèse 1554, Lib. I, No. 16.
[16] Susato 1547, Lib. III, No. 17, and Phalèse 1559, Lib. VII, No. 13.
[17] Phalèse 1555, Lib. VII, No. 12.   [18] Phalèse 1559, Lib. VII, No. 3.
[19] Susato 1553, Lib. II, No. 10.
[20] Ulhard 1545; Montanus 1556; see also Bartha, *Benedictus Ducis und Appenzeller.*
[21] Phalèse 1554, Lib. IV, No. 8.   [22] Susato 1553, Lib. VII, No. 12.

positions, viewed in the perspective of the infrequence of this phenomenon in the music of that period.[23] The key signature of two flats for single voices often obviates the writing of E flat even in those voices which have a signature of one flat; beyond that it makes possible, through the hexachord on B flat, the use of A flat—as *supra la*—without the express use of an accidental. But before we go into the subject of unspecified accidentals as they exist in the *musica ficta*, we must first look into the matter of written accidentals as distinguished from written key signatures.

Accidentals

Here, likewise, surprises await us. The Netherlanders in general, particularly those of that generation, enjoyed a reputation for economy in the use of flats, all question of sharps aside; considered against this background, the growing number of accidentals in the publications of 1550 and thereabouts stands out in symptomatic fashion. The greatest number of accidentals occur in motets with a key signature of one flat. For the most part, the accidentals have to do with the lowering of E to E flat. The use of an accidental to produce A flat is very rare, as is likewise the use of sharps. In Clemens's four-voice "Venit ergo rex" [24] (signature of one flat) we find ten instances of a flat on E and one of a sharp on B flat (the sharp also functions at times as a natural-sign); in his four-voice "Angelus domini ad pastores" [25] (signature of one flat) we find twelve instances of a flat on E. In Crecquillon's four-voice "Domine Deus exercituum" [26] (signature of one flat) we find thirteen instances of a flat on E; in Baston's six-voice "Congregati sunt inimici" [27] (signature of one flat) we likewise find thirteen instances of a flat on E; in Clemens's four-voice Song of Songs motet "In lectulo meo" [28] (signature of one flat) there are nineteen instances of a flat on E; of these, characteristically enough, we find fifteen in Part 1, where the Shulamite searches for her beloved, and only four in Part 2, where she finds him. In Clemens's four-voice Job motet, "Quare de vulva" [29] (no key signature) there are eight instances of a flat on B and three of a sharp written below B; in his lament of Jacob for Joseph "Videns Jacob" [30] (signature of one flat; bass, two flats), there are twelve instances

[23] See Schmidt-Görg, *Nicolas Gombert*, p. 146: "We do, however, find pieces with key signatures of two flats, i. e., with transpositions to the major second below, e. g. the motet 'Dignare me laudare te.' Examples of such *musica ficta* are scarce in the work of that epoch; worthy of mention is an 'Ave Regina coelorum' of Robert Naich, which appeared in the fourth book of the 'Motetti del fiore' of Jakobus Modernus."
[24] Waelrant 1556 (Cf. A. Mb., p. 48*n*), Lib. I, No. 7.
[25] Phalèse 1559, Lib. I, No. 6.   [26] Waelrant 1556, Lib. II, No. 8.
[27] Phalèse 1555, Lib. VIII, No. 9.   [28] Phalèse 1559, Lib. IV, No. 10.
[29] *Ibid.*, Lib. IV, No. 12.   [30] *Ibid.*, Lib. I, No. 8.

of a flat on E and five of a sharp on E. In his five-voice Psalm motet, "Domine probasti me" [31] (signature of one flat), there are as many as thirty-two flats on E and one sharp on E. Except where Clemens uses a key signature of three flats, there is only one instance of an A flat: in the above-mentioned four-voice motet of Benedictus Appenzeller "Peccantem me" [32] (three voices, two flats). Here, to be sure, the A flat exists only as an accidental. It occurs four times: twice in the bass, once in the soprano, and once in the tenor, and the last has a signature of one flat only. All four instances occur toward the end of Part 2, on the words "miserere mei deus" (Ex. 10b).

A revolution in the use of accidentals is disclosed in the publications of Waelrant, especially in his own compositions. He not only uses flats in key signatures and as accidentals, but is, moreover, the only composer to make systematic use of the sharp.[33] Unlike Susato and Phalèse, in the infrequent cases where they make use of a sharp, he places it, not under the note, but in front of it. Mention has already been made in the author's book on Lasso [34] of the fact that his coördination of text and music was incomparably more painstaking than that of either of his Netherlands competitors. A count of the accidentals in the seven works of his own composition which he publishes in his collections of Netherlands motets will demonstrate the difference. In his edition of five- and six-voice motets he publishes three of his works with the following accidentals: in the six-voice "Confiteor tibi Domine" [35] (signature of one flat), ten instances of a flat on E and three of a sharp on B flat; in the five-voice "Afflictus sum" [36] (signature of one flat) twelve instances of a flat on E, ten of a sharp on F, four of a sharp on C, and two of a sharp on B flat; in the five-voice "Et veniat super me misericordia" [37] (signature of one flat) twenty-three instances

---

[31] Waelrant 1555, Lib. II, No. 3.

[32] Quoted from the version of Susato 1553, Lib. II, No. 10.

[33] Always in the case of Waelrant, as a rule in the case of the other Netherlands publishers, the sharp is used to symbolize raised pitch. Nonetheless, there are in Phalèse's collection of four-voice motets of 1559 a few places in which the sharp functions as a kind of warning signal; this is the way the Italian madrigalists used it. In Clemens's motet "Jesus Nazarenus" (Lib. IV, No. 17) we find, for example, three instances of a sharp on E flat—the latter demanded by the key signature—which are to be interpreted purely as warning signals or reminders of the key signature. Two other instances, however, in the same motet and likewise on E flat, are clearly cases of the use of the sharp as sign of raised pitch, or, in the language of today, as a natural sign.

[34] Page 52. These typographical innovations alone must have been reason enough for Waelrant to get in touch with a printer and to establish a new music publishing house.

[35] Waelrant 1556, Lib. V, No. 11.   [36] *Ibid.*, Lib. V, No. 3.

[37] *Ibid.*, Lib. IV, No. 10.

of a flat on E, six of a sharp on F, seven of a sharp on C, five of a sharp on B flat, and one of a sharp on E. In his two books of four-voice motets he publishes four of his own works with the following accidentals: in the "Videntes autem stellam" [38] (signature of one flat) nine instances of a flat on E, one of a sharp on E, four of a sharp on B flat, five of a sharp on F, and four of a sharp on C; in "Si peccaverit in te frater tuus" [39] (signature of one flat) ten instances of a flat on E, two of a sharp on B flat, five of a sharp on F, and two of a sharp on C; in "Venit fortior post me" [40] (signature of one flat) thirteen instances of a flat on E, six of a sharp on B flat, three of a sharp on F, two of a sharp on C; in "Recumbentibus undecim discipulis" [41] (signature of one flat) fifteen instances of a flat on E, eighteen of a sharp on B flat, two of a sharp on E, twenty of a sharp on F, and seven of a sharp on C.

CHROMATICISM INDICATED THROUGH NOTATION

What is the practical result of this unusually free disposition of accidentals? (1) It assures, through written stipulation, the execution of the concluding melodic phrases known as the clausulas,[42] which previously had been given no indication of accidentals in the Netherlands motet. We shall take up this matter presently. (2) By broadening the scope of the church modes and eventually disrupting them altogether, it makes possible an entirely new and multi-colored harmonic structure, the essential features of which are discussed in the book on Lasso.[43] (3) It brings about—to follow Kroyer's definition [44]—"direct" and "indirect" chromatic phenomena. An example of direct chromaticism is the following passage in the tenor part of the motet "Afflictus sum" (Ex. 1). Similar is a passage in the soprano part of "Et veniat super me misericordia tua" (Ex. 2). One might be led to suppose that the sharp in front of the second C likewise affects the preced-

[38] *Ibid.*, Lib. I, No. 3.
[40] *Ibid.*, No. 9.
[39] Waelrant 1556, Lib. II, No. 2.
[41] *Ibid.*, Lib. I, No. 5.
[42] In this matter Waelrant is, however, inconsistent. In some of the least doubtful of the clausulas he often indicates the accidentals, while in others he omits them altogether.
[43] See A. Mb. pp. 75–77, where attention is drawn to Waelrant's tendency "to let sounds overflow into each other as though they were colors, and to render dubious their basic function. It is typical that many of the cadences . . . terminate as deceptive cadences, and that interchange of major and minor keys of the same name was a favorite device. Instead of a logical harmonic development there are often sudden and unexpected twists: from B major to A major with descending columns of resonant parallel fifths and parallel octaves; from A minor to F-sharp minor; and from D Major to F-sharp major."
[44] See *Die Anfänge der Chromatik im italienischen Madrigal des 16. Jahrhunderts.*

ing C, as is often the case in the works of the Italian madrigalists.[45] Quite apart from the circumstance that in the year 1555 this usage peculiar to the early madrigalists had already been abandoned, it should also be taken into account that Waelrant never elsewhere makes use of it. He has a definite reason, moreover, for using the sharp only on the second C: had a sharp been placed before the first C, a chord of the augmented fifth (F-A-C♯) would have resulted.

The variety of signatures which Waelrant assigns to his clausulas shows that it is precisely these augmented chords in the cadence that he wants to avoid. In the same motet we find the following clausulas (Ex. 3). In the first clausula the sharp is used only on the second C; if the first C were sharpened, a diminished fourth (C♯-F) would result. In the second clausula the first C is raised because it brings about a normal triad. In the third clausula we have the same case as in the first: here, likewise, the raising of the first B flat would bring about a chord of the augmented fifth (E♭-G-B) and hence is avoided. In the fourth clausula the sharp might have stood before the first B flat; here it was purely melodic considerations which led Waelrant to do without the leading tone until the end of the cadence. In the fifth clausula Waelrant again puts a sharp only before the second B flat, even though this gives the interval E-B♭; here, however, we are dealing with the more customary dissonance of the diminished fifth, sounded, at that, in a scarcely perceptible fusa—as passing note on the weak beat.

This comparison must not lead us to suppose that Waelrant would not use an augmented fifth or a diminished fourth. In every respect he has recourse to the most unconventional media conceivable, but he never works with unusual colors unless there is inner motivation. In the four-part motet "Si peccaverit frater tuus" he uses the harshest sort of false relations, forbidden parallel intervals, piercing and irregularly resolved dissonances, as well as a chord of the augmented fifth and one of the diminished fifth, in order to give to the mood of repentance and atonement as striking a musical realization as possible. What he permits himself, however, in order to express human emotions, he avoids in a simple cadence devoid of pictorial content. Considered from the standpoint of melodic construction, the clausulas show—especially the first, third, and fifth—that the progression D-C-C♯-D lay well within the scope of Waelrant's development, since all those cited are, as a matter of fact, variants of this chromatic progression.

We have examined the questionable passage from every standpoint—

---

[45] See Von Ficker's essay, *Beiträge zur Chromatik des 14.-16. Jahrhunderts.*

from that of notation, of harmony, and of melody. All evidence speaks in favor of accepting the notation prescribed by Waelrant: D-C-C♯-D, whence the harmonic sequence in Ex. 4.

In the work of Clemens non Papa we likewise find evidence of indicated direct chromaticism. Twice he specifies through the use of accidentals two successive falling steps of a half tone.[46] The first time this occurs, the second step is separated from the first by a rest; the second time, however, it immediately follows upon the first step (Ex. 5). The first example we find in the alto part of the Song of Songs motet "In lectulo meo per noctes quesivi quem diligit anima mea quesivi illum *et non inveni.*" The second example we find in the alto part of the Job lamentation: "Quare de vulva eduxisti me? Utinam essem consumptus ne oculus me videret: *Fuissem, quasi non essem.*" While the text alone shows that this chromatic progression can fully be understood only with reference to the whole, the musical setting itself brings out the fact even more clearly. Chromaticism is always but one medium among the many used to represent in tones the meaning of the words. Among other media almost always found in the company of chromaticism are (1) good declamation (this is striking in the two examples of Waelrant, as well as in those of Clemens just cited; the words are sung, one note to a syllable, with accents faithful to those of speech; the first example especially is moving in its static and almost stammering delivery of "et non—et non inveni"); (2) homophonic or half-homophonic style; (3) special harmonic colors (by their very nature intimately connected with chromaticism); (4) unusual dissonances. We soon become aware of the fact that almost without exception every chromatic license is prepared. In the two preceding motets, for instance, the half-tone progres-

[46] Theoretical writings of the period make a distinction between the larger and the smaller half tone. The smaller half tone is the one between C sharp and D, between F sharp and G, and between A and B flat; it corresponds to our leading-tone. The larger half-tone is the one between C and C sharp, between F and F sharp, and between B flat and B. This larger half tone is unanimously and specifically forbidden by theorists as being an interval running counter to the laws of the diatonic system. A composer who disregards this prohibition consciously aligns his work outside the diatonic system. *Semitonium majus ad genus diatonicum ineptum est.* "The larger step of the half tone is not suitable to the uses of the diatonic system," says Glareanus in his *Isagoge in Musicen,* and his is only one voice among many. It is important to bear this in mind from the very outset. The secret chromatic art represents a radical departure from the diatonic system as conceived in the Middle Ages. The use of the larger half tone proves beyond a doubt that the boundaries of the diatonic system have been surmounted. It is no coincidence that we find these chromatic innovations only in the works of Clemens non Papa and Hubert Waelrant. For these two composers will ultimately reveal themselves as the chief exponents of the secret chromatic art.

sions F-E-Eb and C-B-Bb-A are at first disguised and only later allowed to appear one directly following the other in the manner quoted.[47] All these details are fully as significant as the chromatic phenomenon itself. Since in isolation the latter can never be correctly understood, we give both examples in their context (Ex. 6 and 7). In both works the chromatic passages prove to be the climax of a sharply delineated upward curve of *espressivo* writing. In both cases the text is set with particular felicity and effectiveness; in both there is a perceptible effort toward homophony. There are differences, however, in the harmonic materials used. In the Song of Songs motet Clemens works with dissonances—especially with that of the major seventh—which are handled in a rather free manner; thanks to their abundance, and also to the fact that their effect is emphasized by the use of drawn-out rhythms and of dissonant passing-notes in a melody of portamento character, they are well calculated to express with utmost realism the full measure of the Shulamite's grief.

In the Job Lamentation, Clemens uses no dissonances. What he is trying to express here is, not the violence of love's pain, but the mood of one who is broken in spirit and tired of living, of one who wishes he had never been born. How wonderfully Clemens evokes this mood with the falling faux-bourdon and the merging colors of the chromatic passage! What ingenuity in this find! The four-voice episode on the words "fuissem quasi non essem" is repeated, as is the antecedent three-voice faux-bourdon. But the first time Clemens leads us from A minor—via C major, G major, B *flat major*, F major, and A minor—to E minor; the second time he goes from A minor—via C major, G major, B *minor*, G major, and A minor— to E major. To be sure, this passage takes us squarely into the realm of *musica ficta*, inasmuch as the F sharp and G sharp, for B minor and E major, respectively, are not indicated. The twice-repeated use of a sharp on B,[48] however, invalidates the possibility of lowering this note to B flat, so that the only way of avoiding the diminished triad on the leading-tone is to sharpen the F. The justification for raising G to G sharp is furnished by the cadential character of this passage, by its relation to the

[47] The Song of Songs motet has in its second section motifs which derive from the chromatic passage of the first section, e.g., on the words "stipate me malis": D-F-E-C-Eb-D. This time the E flat is not indicated, but from the sound of the ensemble its presence according to the rules of *musica ficta* is unmistakable.
[48] The threefold insertion of a sharp at one and the same spot is most significant, especially since in the entire work there are no more sharps to be found. It is well known that in the notation prevalent during this era a note with a flat in front of it was construed as *fa*, while a note with a sharp was taken to be a *mi*. The threefold use of the sharp on B-*mi* serves the purpose of establishing beyond question the G-*ut*, thus legalizing the use of F sharp.

E major closing phrases of the motet as a whole—which is in the Phrygian mode—and, above all, by the various motifs already introduced whose cadence is on A. These consequently present the G sharp as *subsemitonium modi;* the cadence, furthermore, is immediately followed by another such motif B-C-B-A-G(♯)-A, which is imitated in all the voices, so that the construction of a cadence on E major is fully motivated by the context. The repetition of a harmonic episode incorporating an interchange of the harmonies of B flat major and B minor is out of the ordinary and bold; the entire motet, in fact, is notable for its well-conceived and intensely felt setting of the text. Indeed, Clemens does not shy at the use of utterly realistic media of expression; he allows the words "paucitas dierum finietur brevi," for instance, suddenly to be interrupted on a minima (half note), whereupon they virtually fall into a breve rest. With a kind of note symbolism, he sets the syllables of the word "brevi" by using breve values in the various voices.[49] All such devices must of necessity come under consideration in our present inquiry, since it is only a comprehensive view of the whole that can bring home to us the tremendous urge toward expression which animated Clemens's generation, an urge so compelling that in the end it shattered the traditional system of church modes.

In addition to the cases of direct chromaticism already quoted, we also find in the works of Clemens and Waelrant a whole series of examples of "indirect" chromaticism. These include: frequent interchange between fundamental tones and chromatic tones; modified progressions of steps of a half tone (for instance, the following modification of a progression

---

[49] In *Das Antwerpener Motettenbuch Orlando di Lasso's*, p. 56, I pointed out a similar case of symbolic representation. Johann Crespel ends his motet "Vox in rama" on minims, in order to lend point and vividness to the words of the close, "quia non sunt." "This ending," I wrote at that time, "breaking off on minims instead of on the customary final longa, as though in its last gasp, is in all likelihood unique in the Netherlands motet-literature." In this connection Van Crevel remarks (*Adrianus Petit Coclico*, p. 58): "Bold as this ending is, it can scarcely stand as the only example of such a phenomenon. Coclico two years earlier anticipated this procedure with an example which is perhaps even bolder; it occurs in the last motet (No. 41) of his Musica Reservata." The motet in question is the "Vidi impium," in which the words "et transivi, et ecce non erat" suddenly break off on a minim and fall, so to speak, into a rest. If, however, the reader examines the work, which is reproduced in its entirety on p. 424 of the Coclico monograph, he will notice that the passage referred to by Van Crevel stands, not at the end, but in the middle of the piece and that hence it can hardly be compared with the analogous passage in Crespel's composition. There is a motet susceptible of classification alongside Crespel's, but it occurs several decades later. Anna Amalie Abert. (*Die stilistischen Voraussetzungen der "Cantiones sacrae" von Heinrich Schütz*, p. 102) has pointed out that in the motet "O quam suavis est, Domine, spiritus tuus," Leonhard Lechner, the great pupil of Lasso, renounces the construction of a musical ending, illustrating the words "dimittis inanes" by letting the voices break off one after the other (here, likewise, on minims).

of five half tones: F#-G-G-F-E-D-Eb-D in the tenor part of Waelrant's motet "Si peccaverit frater tuus," measure 11); motifs with emphasis on the major third in tonalities whose characteristic is the minor third, just as Kroyer found them in the work of the madrigalists and as we find them particularly in evidence in Waelrant's motets, as for instance in the four-voice "Videntes autem stellam" (soprano, measure 1, Ex. 8) or in the four-voice "Recumbentibus undecim discipulis" (soprano, measure 1; soprano, measure 8 of Part 2; tenor, measure 8 of Part 2; Ex. 9). There are many other motifs of this nature. The material here discussed, which could be greatly augmented, is of particular significance, since the chromaticism is indicated in the notation itself and hence is beyond dispute.

UNSPECIFIED CHROMATICISM

Unspecified A Flat

Our examination of chromatic phenomena now leads us one step farther —to the realm of *musica ficta*, where such phenomena exist without written indication. First of all, we find a number of examples of an A flat unspecified, but nonetheless unmistakable by virtue of the disposition of the voices. Three such occur in Part 1 of the motet "Peccantem me" of Benedictus; it was Part 2 of this motet which furnished the only four examples of a specified A flat in the entire repertoire examined. The unspecified A flats are part of the setting of the words "timor mortis perturbat me" ("fear of death fills me with terror"), which prepares the "miserere" in Part 2 (Ex. 10 a and 10 b). In the legend of Susanna, "Ingemuit autem Susanna," Crecquillon uses on the words "incidere in manus hominum" ("to fall into the hands of men") an A flat in the bass, which already has a signature of two flats (Ex. 11). While in both these examples there are two flats in the signature, and while the A flat is reached either through a progression of a fourth or through a leap of a fourth, there is but one flat in the signature of Clemens non Papa's five-voice "Domine non est exaltatum cor meum." Here, too, the A flat is reached through a leap of a fourth, from E flat; the E flat is explicitly noted three times in the preceding measures. But Clemens employs still another device, that of motif transposition. The motif *mi-ut-fa* is started on A, then transposed a fourth higher (the *fa* landing on E flat, specified by the use of an accidental), then, finally, transposed still a fourth higher, starting on G (this time the *fa* lands on A flat, but the flat is *not* specified). The A flat is designed to convey the thought image "wondrous" and comes on the first syllable of the word "mirabilis" (Ex. 12). This motet was printed as early as 1546 in Susato's second book of motets.[50] The use of an A flat is, in this case, as in that of the two other works, still hesitant and unaccompanied by modulations or bold combinations of harmonies.[51] The use of motif-transposition, however, is in this connection very significant. Clemens here has recourse to an effective means of making possible the use of chromaticism without explicit notation; even the notation of the E flat might in this case have been dispensed with. This approach to chromaticism is destined to make a firm place for itself and to exert a far-reaching influence. Examination of it belongs, properly speaking, in the next chapter.

THE CHROMATIC CLAUSULA

Before proceeding farther we must draw to the reader's attention a very significant phenomenon, which still belongs to *musica ficta*, namely, the chromatic clausula. The elevation of the next-to-last tone of the cadence to the estate of leading tone, in which role it is known as *subsemitonium modi*, is an old story to those familiar with the *musica ficta*. Thus far unknown, however, is the fact that to the subsemitone the Netherlanders added a suprasemitone, and in this fashion transformed B-A-G♯-A into B♭-A-G♯-A, E-D-C♯-D into E♭-D-C♯-D, and even A-G-F♯-G into A♭-G-F♯-G. In some cases the suprasemitone was specified; in others it was left unspecified and hence was handled like the subsemitone, the presence of which was to be deduced from the context. We shall first consider those cases which, being clearly specified, offer us the surest point of departure. In the four-voice motet "Caligaverunt oculi mei" of Clemens non Papa [52] there are three chromatic clausulas, the first on the words "qui consolabatur me," the second on the words "si est dolor similis," both of them in Part 1 of the motet; the third occurs in Part 2 and is identical with the second clausula of Part 1, with the difference that the one in Part 2 leaves the suprasemitone unspecified (Ex. 14). Each time, the sequence in question is B♭-A-G♯-A.

[50] Susato prints the motet a second time in 1553, as No. 2 in Lib. VII of his *ecclesiasticae cantiones*.
[51] In the interest of completeness I should like to point out the use of the A flat in the four-voice motet "Conserva me domine" of Clemens non Papa (Phalèse 1559, Lib. III, No. 14). In the three lower voices two flats are indicated in the signature. The A flat is again reached through the progression of a fourth—this time from A (flat) to E flat and from E flat by leap back to A (flat)—and is composed to the words "parce peccatis" (Ex. 13).
[52] Phalèse 1559, Lib. II, No. 5.

The technique of the chromatic clausula is simple. The cadential formula IV-V-I, in this case d-E-a,[53] is adorned with portamento notes or suspensions, so that the chromatic clausula db^{65}-E^{43}-a is inevitable. The suprasemitone is indicated. By the restoration, in one of the other voices, of the note from which the suprasemitone is derived (in this case, B) and the suspension A-G#-A the subsemitone becomes, not simply possible, but obligatory.

In the four-voice motet "Vox in rama audita est" [54] we find the same chromatic clausulas on the word "ululatus" ("cry of pain") (Ex. 15); in the four-voice motet "Ne abscondas me domine," [55] to which Professor van den Borren drew my attention, we find a series of chromatic clausulas, of which the two most important, in the closing measures common to both Part 1 and Part 2, deserve a more detailed examination (Ex. 16). The modified clausula Eb-C-D-C(#)-D in the tenor followed by the directly chromatic clausula A(b)-G-G-F(#)-G,[56] both on the words "non me terreat" ("may thy strength not frighten me"). Once the presence of the E flat has been firmly established in the most various fashion, through the voice-leading,[57] the A flat is reached by a leap of a fourth from E flat. All doubts concerning this procedure are dispelled by the fact that in Part 2 the E flat is not only repeated but also explicitly specified.

In the four-voice legend of Daniel "Venit ergo rex" [58] Clemens uses a chromatic clausula like the one just described; it occurs on the words "in medio leonum," but this time the suprasemitone is not specified. It is such a typical example of old-Netherlands musical "painting" that it merits being quoted in its entirety (Ex. 17). By the sudden solemn repose on homophonic chords we are first given the picture of Daniel sitting in the lions' den, whereupon the descent of the lions upon him is represented by the imitation of one motif in stretto and in all the voices, while the ominousness of the situation is suggested by the repetition of a chromatic clausula.

[53] In transcribing harmonic progressions, capital letters are used to represent major, small letters, minor harmonies; letters without numbers, the triad in root position, whereas added numbers indicate the intervals other than those belonging to the root position. So the above passage represents the following progression:

$$bb' \; a' - g\#' \; a'$$
$$f' \quad - \; e' - \quad e'$$
$$d' \quad - \; b \; - \quad c'$$
$$d \quad - \; e \; - \quad A$$

[54] Phalèse 1559, Lib. III, No. 9.   [55] *Ibid.*, Lib. II, No. 13.

[56] All accidentals which are not written out in the original, but are provided by this author according to the rules governing *musica ficta*, are placed in parenthesis.

[57] In the original edition, furthermore, the first line of the bass has a signature of two flats, while the remaining lines have but one flat in the signature.

[58] Waelrant 1556, Lib. I, No. 7.

The bass and alto enter on E flat, unavoidable because of the progression of a fourth toward B flat; in addition, the E flat is even specified in the alto. The two E flats already established necessitate the lowering of the E in the tenor, which follows immediately, whereupon the A flat becomes inevitable, since it is approached by a leap of a fourth from E flat. This first chromatic clausula serves as preparation for the still more expressive chromatic cadence which follows.

It is this very scene, incidentally, which is illustrated by a woodcut in a Netherlands Bible of Clemens's time—in Jacobus Giunti, *Biblia*, Lyons, 1546. The composer may well have been influenced by the Bible illustration. It would be interesting to make a comparative study of the texts chosen for graphic illustration and of those adopted for musical setting.

Another achievement of expressive writing is the repeated cry of woe at the end of the "Tristicia et anxietas," [59] the only four-part motet in which Clemens writes a signature of two flats in all the voices (Ex. 18). Here the suprasemitone E flat is made obligatory both by the signature and by the voice leading.

Evidence that Waelrant also used the chromatic clausula is provided by an example from his four-voice motet "Si peccaverit in te frater tuus." Here, too, the suprasemitone is specified, so that there can be no doubt concerning the chromatic character of the clausula, which is composed to the words "demitte illi" ("forgive him"; Ex. 19).

The consistent interrelation between the nature of the text and the use of chromatic passages will at this point doubtless be obvious to the reader, as will also the fact that we here are dealing with an extremely important phenomenon, since the chromatic cadences just described are nothing less than an anticipation of the chord of the Neapolitan sixth, which is later to play so important a part among the various media of expression dear both to classic and to romantic composers. The birth of this famous chord thus antedates by some two centuries the date of birth commonly attributed. Credit for its discovery and for its first systematic use belongs, consequently, not to the Neapolitan school of the eighteenth century, but to the Netherlands school of the sixteenth.[60]

[59] Susato 1553, Lib. I, No. 5, and Phalèse 1559, Lib. V, No. 2.
[60] The earliest instances of chromatic clausulas I found in chansons of the late fifteenth century (see the author's article "The Function of Conflicting Signatures in Early Polyphonic Music," *The Musical Quarterly*, XXXI (April, 1945), 227–260. But there the chromatic clausula is not yet accompanied by the chord of the Neapolitan sixth. Isolated examples of the chromatic clausula occur also in the Italian madrigal.

SUMMARY

Even though a secret chromatic art has not been disclosed, the conclusions drawn from this preliminary inquiry invalidate the opinion, commonly held, that at the outset chromaticism was limited to secular art, that is, to the Italian madrigal, and that Netherlands composers before Lasso, especially of the generation of Clemens non Papa, refrained from any contact with chromaticism. Detailed examination of musical texts alone leads us to the conclusion that it is no longer possible to defend a commentary such as the following on Clemens non Papa's motet style:

The phrase is from beginning to end purely diatonic: there is in all Clemens's music not a single chromatic passage. Specified accidentals are scarcely to be encountered in his works. Even the F sharp is almost nowhere to be found, while the A flat occurs only in the motet "Qui consolabatur me," in the three lowest voices.[61]

It is no coincidence that Bernet-Kempers's conviction that Clemens's style was exclusively diatonic should go hand in hand with his opinion that the latter's motets betray a paucity of expressive resource. The works in which the older master ever more intensively devoted himself to the solution of problems of expression are the ones which escaped Bernet Kempers's attention.

In the material thus far considered we have had to do with the first attempts to hew a path to chromaticism. The tradition of church modes and of *musica ficta*, which imposed limitations on the use of accidentals and above all of sharps, as well as certain conditions of a more general nature, which we shall take up later, were beyond doubt detrimental to the evolution of chromaticism in the Netherlands. This being the case, progressive composers of that period found themselves obliged to seek paths to chromaticism other than those offered by notation. These paths they found in the secret chromatic art.

[61] Bernet-Kempers, *Jacobus Clemens non Papa und seine Motetten*, p. 70.

II: THE SECRET CHROMATIC ART

FOR THE PURPOSES of this study the term "chromaticism" is used to designate not only a succession of half-tone steps but also those departures from the diatonic system that are not provided for by *musica ficta*. This includes the introduction of A flat—which actually is on the borderline between the old *musica ficta* and the new chromaticism —D flat, G flat, C flat; moreover, the use of the tones that change the character of the church mode beyond recognition—as does, for example, the constant interchange of B natural, F sharp, C sharp, and B flat, F, and C in the transposed Dorian mode on G.[1] I speak of "secret" chromaticism in contradistinction to *musica ficta*,[2] because *musica ficta* refers to the flattening or sharpening of one tone only instead of a chain of tones moving in the circle of fifths as in the case of secret chromaticism. In other words, while *musica ficta* results in only transitory changes of single tones, secret chromaticism always effects a modulation.[3] To achieve a modulation, however, without writing down all the necessary accidentals, the Netherlanders developed a new and ingenious technique based on the principles of *musica ficta*. This is why we speak of a secret chromatic "art."

The term "modulation" in modern usage designates "the process of passing out of one key into another" (Grove, *A Dictionary of Music*). As such, its use is restricted to the major and minor mode. The technique of secret chromaticism anticipates, but does not fully establish the prevalence of major and minor over the other modes. Yet we use the term "modulation"

[1] This use of the term "chromaticism" is not new; cf., among others, the studies of Th. Kroyer and of R. v. Ficker, *op. cit.*
[2] "Rules and proscriptions about voice leading were part and parcel of the old polyphony. The theorists of the time confirm this beyond doubt. From their testimony we know that adjusting the clashes between different voices was left to the discretion of the performer. This was done according to an old set of rules producing *musica ficta*, fictive music, so called because 'imagination' had to amend what was written out. These rules required the alteration of augmented or diminished fourths, fifths, and octaves into perfect intervals (usually by flattening one of the two tones in question); the elimination of cross relations between voices (through the same means); and the raising of the seventh in a cadence, thus producing the *subsemitonium modi*." Quoted from the author's "The Goddess Fortuna in Music," The *Musical Quarterly*, XXIX (January, 1943), 1. See also Reese, *Music in the Middle Ages*, pp. 380–382.
[3] There are a few cases where—as in *musica ficta*—only one accidental is to be supplemented. The fact, however, that this accidental lies in the direction of the circle of fifths, that it goes at least two steps beyond the key signature in the circle of fifths, and that it always effects a modulation involving all voices in the polyphonic complex—this is the real touchstone of secret chromaticism as distinguished from ordinary *musica ficta*.

because the processes described below transgress the boundaries of medieval "mutation" at least as much as they fall short of reaching those of its modern counterpart, modulation. Mutation is a tool of *musica ficta*. It is therefore subject to the same limitations outlined above. The term "modulation" is intended to make clear that the secret chromatic art reveals a definite capacity for thinking in chords and a clear understanding of the connections and relationships of chords in the circle of fifths.

CLEMENS NON PAPA

Fremuit spiritu Jesu

As the point of departure for the following inquiry we have chosen one of Clemens non Papa's later works, the magnificent "Fremuit spiritu Jesu,"[4] which a few years ago was the center of a controversy.[5] Does a given passage call for the addition of accidentals, or is it to be sung as it stands? This was the point in question and is, indeed, the principal problem facing us in all the cases here discussed. Familiar enough in discussions of Renaissance music, the question now takes on unexpected implications. For, the consistent insertion of accidentals into a given passage gives rise to something which adds immeasurably to the eloquence of the words— to a magnificent modulation, constructed in such a way that it fits flawlessly into the musical context and returns in the most natural manner to the original key. Hitherto unknown in Renaissance music, this procedure becomes all the more enigmatic because of its double meaning; for although such a passage can also be sung as it stands without sounding at all badly, the literal or diatonic version does not come anywhere near attaining the vividness or power of expression afforded by the chromatic version. It is precisely this double meaning, however, which so strongly demands convincing evidence in favor of accepting the chromatic version, since everything depends on the interpretation of a few notes or, perhaps, of only one. To be correctly interpreted, this note must be considered in relation to the work as a whole—to its notation, its style, its expressive content. The work itself has, then, to be considered in the light of the entire creative effort of the composer, the composer against the background of his musical environment, and the musical environment in the perspective of the general trend, internal and external, of the times.

The first and foremost requirement is to establish the correct reading.

[4] Reprinted in *Uitgave XLVI van de Vereeniging voor Nederlandsche Muziekgeschiedenis.*
[5] *Tijdschrift der Vereeniging voor Nederlandsche Muziekgeschiedenis*, XI, 106–108.

This brings us to the question of sources. There are four known sources of the Lazarus motet of Clemens non Papa: Phalèse, *Liber secundus cantionum sacrarum*, Louvain, 1554; Simon à Bosco, *Tertius liber modulorum . . . ex officina Simonis à Bosco et Guilielmi Gueroult*, n.p., 1555; Montanus and Neuber, *Novum et insigne opus musicum*, Nuremberg, 1558; the Brussels manuscript version in the Cod. Brux. Conserv. 27,088, which Professor van den Borren, expressly for the purposes of this investigation, copied out in score and set at my disposal.

How do these sources compare? The first and the fourth present two independent versions, each incorporating a trustworthy manner of notation. The Brussels manuscript version must be credited with an exceptional conscientiousness and precision; because of its admirable clarity it is to be preferred even to the satisfactory edition of Phalèse. The third, or German, source is clearly a reprint of the first, with the exception that the former contains three printer's errors and an altered embellishment. To the second source I had no access. So far as I can judge on the basis of general acquaintance with Simon à Bosco's motet editions, his version is also a reprint of the earlier version of Phalèse.[6] We shall base our discussion on the first and fourth sources, returning to the initial question, "What reasons are there for a chromatic interpretation of the passage 'et lacrimatus est Jesus'?" (Part 1, measures 63–74; Ex. 20).

Let us begin with the problem of notation. The motet is in the Lydian mode.[7] In the four upper voices Clemens has one flat in the signature, in the two lower voices he has two flats.[8] Noteworthy are the accidentals at the beginning of the modulation. In measures 65 and 66 there are three

[6] The reasons for this are taken up in the discussion of the "Qui consolabatur me" of Clemens non Papa. Cf. with the new edition by E. Reeser of the Lazarus motet. It is to be regretted that this new edition does not present the work in the original key. Since the composers of the Renaissance ascribed a definite expressive character to each mode, as well as to sharps and flats themselves, every arbitrary change of key should be avoided. The change of key in the new edition is all the less justified in the light of the fact that the piece is a vocal work, in which the conductor is free to "tune in" the voices on whatever pitch he desires, if he prefers not to perform it in the original key. Whoever wishes to read the motet from this edition, but in the original Lydian mode, can simplify his task by replacing the treble clef with the soprano clef and the bass clef with the sub-bass clef and, further, by replacing the signature of three sharps by a signature of one flat, the signature in the two lower voices by a signature of two flats.

[7] Hermann Finck quotes the work in his *Practica musica* of 1556 as an example of the Lydian mode (A. Mb., p. 94).

[8] Phalèse specifies two flats in both lower voices, the writer of the Brussels Codex only in the lowest voice. The latter thereby sees himself obliged, in two instances, to use an accidental in order to indicate an E flat, while Phalèse achieves the same result through the key signature.

E flats specified through the use of an accidental, although in not one of these cases is there need of such a direction; in the baritone, the accidental for the E flat is superfluous because of the general context—in addition to which the Phalèse version has the flat in the signature; in the tenor the E flat is self-evident, since the leap of a fourth upward, from B flat, admits only E flat; in the alto, the E flat occurs at exactly the same spot as the E flat twice indicated in the bass, hence it is likewise self-evident. This threefold *superfluous* insertion of the accidental is most significant. I take it to be a signal, a kind of harmonic signpost standing at the beginning of an enigmatic passage.[9]

Certain it is that the E which follows in the alto must be read as E flat, giving Eb-D-C-D-E(b). This gives us C minor,[10] which in turn transforms the A, following in the second soprano, into A flat (C minor, F minor).

This A flat is required, moreover, by the disposition of the voice itself. This is the only place in the entire two-section motet, where the ostinato is transposed, not, as elsewhere, a fourth lower, from the *hexachordum molle* to the *hexachordum naturale*, but a whole tone lower,[11] so that it is sounded, not on C (or G), but on B flat. Since the ostinato (*sol-mi-mi-mi-fa-re-ut*) cannot be changed without losing its ostinato character, the progression Bb-G-G-G-Ab-F-Eb is inevitable.

Was it never permissible to change the ostinato? This is a crucial question, and the answer is decisive in the interpretation of the passage in question. A survey of the ostinato motets of the period is bound to throw light on the subject. We now undertake a comparison of the Antwerp and Venetian repertoires.[12]

The Netherlanders use the ostinato in three different ways: (1) remain-

[9] Professor van den Borren remarks in this connection: "I have often noticed that 'accidentals' of this sort appear at certain places not for the simple purpose of changing the isolated notes to which they are attached, but rather in order to impose upon the polyphonic ensemble a given harmonic order."

[10] Here, at the very beginning of the work of analysis, I should like to observe as a matter of principle that I consider myself in many instances obliged, in this inquiry as in the study of Lasso, to resort to modern terms in order to bring home to the reader certain harmonic concepts. The theoretical writings of the Renaissance had not yet developed a nomenclature adequate to the needs of an evolving harmonic system—indeed, the full development of such a terminology required no less than two centuries of reflection on the part of theorists; this fact should not, however, mislead the contemporary investigator into approaching with inadequate tools the music of a bygone era simply because the era itself had inadequate tools. By the same token, he cannot hope to arrive at a well-balanced picture of the music of that period and of its manifold problems, unless he has made himself familiar with its theoretical concepts.

[11] The ostinato here undergoes a transposition to the fourth-above of the fourth-above —which, when entire works are involved, leads to a signature of two flats.

[12] Cf. the corresponding chapter in the A. Mb.

ing on the same level; (2) ascending and descending stepwise (*pes ascendens et descendens*); (3) transposed a fourth or a fifth (hexachord alternation). In the first and third of these cases the intervals remain immutable; in the second, they change with each transposition. By the middle of the sixteenth century the second type of ostinato had already become very rare. The Antwerp repertoire, for instance, contains seventeen ostinato motets; among them there is not a single example of the *pes ascendens et descendens*, but there are eight of the static variety and nine with hexachord alternation. In the Venetian publications we find four ostinato motets, all of which make use of hexachord alternation.[13] Thus we have a dozen ostinatos with hexachord alternation. In not a single one of these motets are the intervals of the ostinato changed; in not one does the ostinato appear on a level other than the hexachord level. Clemens thus consciously breaks with tradition when in his "Legend of Lazarus's Resurrection" he interrupts the hexachord alternation and sets the ostinato a whole tone lower. Inevitably the question arises, "What considerations prompted Clemens to adopt so extraordinary a procedure?" A satisfactory answer to this question is provided only by the chromatic interpretation; besides, examination of the ostinato pieces of the period reveals that the alteration of an interval forming part of an ostinato is not permitted.[14] If, however, one decided to give the ostinato in this passage a diatonic reading, the following discrepancies would become apparent: (*a*) the unchanging melody of the ostinato would be interrupted; (*b*) a motif built on the perfect fifth—the ostinato being encompassed by the degrees *sol-ut*—would become a motif built on the diminished fifth (Bb-E); (*c*) *sol-mi-mi-mi-fa-re-ut* would become *fa-re-re-re = sol-la-fa-mi;* this is tantamount to mutation in the middle of the ostinato and can be regarded as impracticable.

The main question, however, remains unanswered: on what grounds does Clemens abandon the customary hexachord alternation? Obviously not on melodic grounds, since the melody palpably suffers through the change. On

[13] The hexachord alternation opens up greater harmonic resources than does the ostinato remaining on the same level. It is typical of the Venetians that they used only the transposed ostinato; equally significant is the fact that in the five motets printed by Susato, the conservative Netherlands publisher, only two have hexachord alternation.

[14] Professor van den Borren has drawn my attention to the hitherto unknown motet "Salve crux sancta" of Clemens non Papa in the Brussels Codex (27.088), which likewise has an ostinato with the customary hexachord alternation, and remarks: "I have again re-examined my copies into score of MS. 27.088 to see whether the Codex does not contain, outside of Clemens's motets, other examples of ostinatos, and especially of ostinatos which in certain of their recapitulations do not present a faithful transposition of their expositions. But I have found none."

harmonic grounds? In diatonic reading the passage turns into one of those absolutely conventional harmonic sequences, such as occur frequently throughout the motet.[15] If that was the end in view, obviously it was not necessary to interrupt the traditional hexachord alternation. What, then, could have been the reason? I do not know of one that will bear scrutiny.

The explanation offered by Reeser is based, not on Clemens's motet, but on Lasso's adaptation of it. In the book on Lasso (pp. 92–95) it was established that the motet "Fremuit spiritu Jesu" in Lasso's Antwerp motet book is an adaptation of Clemens's motet. Lasso retains from Clemens's version the "registration" of the voices and the ostinato melody. In the first section of his motet Lasso also transposes this ostinato to the second fourth-above, and at the end of his second section even to the third fourth-above, which brings about a close in F minor. Reeser considers the latter impossible and concludes that Clemens likewise could not have had a chromatic interpretation in mind. Since Lasso does very much as he pleases in the matter of adaptations from other composers, it is an error of method to take the adaptation as a basis for judging the original. On historical grounds alone, however, such a procedure is untenable. Reeser writes, "If we reject the likelihood of a chromatic transposition in Lasso, then it seems to me illogical to suppose that Clemens, though much older, should have used this 'modern' weapon." It is not, however, a question of contrast between two generations, but of one between two countries. Lasso had just come from Italy, where chromaticism was openly indicated, while Clemens lived in the Netherlands, where *musica ficta* was in flower and where the utmost discretion in the use of accidentals was the general rule. Assuming that Lasso did not make use of this "disguised" variety of transposition, his Italian training having given him no opportunity to become acquainted with it, that proves nothing with regard to Clemens.

To be logical, one ought to reverse the evidence. Clemens was the first to set to music "Lazarus's Resurrection"; Lasso took this work as model; on the basis of Clemens's work alone can a decision be made on the question of how the unusual transposition of the ostinato is to be interpreted. Our findings show that in Clemens's version a transposition to the second fourth-above actually is intended. This brings about the opposite question: can we assume that in boldness of concept the extremely advanced young Lasso could have lagged behind his predecessor, that in opposition to Clemens himself he could have placed a diatonic interpretation on the trans-

[15] G^{43}-C-F-B-d-a-C-F-a^{56}-G^{43}-C.

position of the ostinato? That would be conceivable only had he not been thoroughly initiated into the Netherlands practices of those days.

Examination of his Antwerp motet book has, however, revealed that during his stay in that city Lasso made himself abundantly familiar with Netherlands music; the record of his intimate acquaintance with Antwerp musicians, composers, publishers, and friends of music leaves no doubt of his having acquired a complete understanding of the Netherlanders' musical concepts and practices. Of necessity this leads to the conviction that Lasso was fully aware of Clemens's disguised transposition. Since he not only made use of the same transposition, but even carried it one step farther along the circle of fourths, the conclusion is inevitable that he had in mind the same chromatic reading of it as Clemens. Nevertheless, Reeser sees an irreconcilable opposition between the minor close of the Lasso motet, imposed by our interpretation, and the idea of Christ's triumph over death, symbolized by "Lazarus's Resurrection."

Even this objection has no historical foundation. In the monograph on Lasso I repeatedly pointed out that the change of style in motet music around 1550 was the counterpart of a change in the concept of the world as a whole; that while for Gombert's generation the point of departure was the purely religious idea, for young Lasso and his generation, man and his world had captured the center of the stage in creative as in philosophical activity. The avowed aim of the *musica reservata* was *rem quasi actam ante oculos ponere* (Samuel Quickelberg in his famous comment on Lasso's penitential psalms, see below p. 92). This new goal—with musical means to present an event in such a way that the listener sees it before his very eyes, as in a dramatic performance—was pursued by no composer with greater intensity than by Lasso. When he writes the "Resurrection of Lazarus," it is not the abstract idea of Christ's triumph over death that he translates into music, but Christ's actual deed and the way in which it came to pass. Even as did the young Rembrandt eighty years later in his oil painting, "Lazarus's Resurrection" (in the Royal Museum at Amsterdam), Lasso sees the grave open up, sees the gruesomely emaciated Lazarus hearken to Jesus's cry, sees Jesus's outstretched arms lending poignant dramatic emphasis to that cry. He even expresses the emotion of those who witness the scene, an emotion, not of joy, but of divinely inspired fear and terror.

It is true that it had become the general custom to close a piece of music on a major chord. But when it was a question of representing an unaccustomed emotion or an extraordinary event, nothing could keep the young

Lasso from casting aside the rules if he was so disposed. The guiding principle of his creative effort was, first, last, and always, expression—in an
objective sense as well as in a subjective.

There now remain no grounds on which to deny the presence of a true
ostinato transposition in Lasso's adaptation of Clemens's motet. One thing,
however, should constantly be kept in mind—that investigation of Lasso's
composition, and conclusions concerning it, by no means offer a basis on
which to draw conclusions concerning the non Papa composition.

A final argument for the chromatic interpretation is provided by an
examination of the analogous passage in the second section of the motet,
on the same words "Lacrimatus est" (measures 25 ff.; Ex. 21). Here we can
observe what notation Clemens uses when he wants to exclude the possibility of a chromatic interpretation; it should be noted that in this passage
a modulation would have been possible. The bass sings the words "lacrimatus est" on the interval of a fourth: G-C. If one reads the baritone part
in the notation of Phalèse, which has two flats in the signature, this part
would have the same words on the interval of a fourth, Eb-Ab.[16] The
motif which now follows in the bass, A-D, would have to be read Ab-Db,
which would land us squarely in the middle of a modulation. Closer examination, however, and comparison with the analogous passage in the first
section of the motet, clearly show that this time Clemens did not want
the modulation for the following reasons.

1. The accidentals which in the first two sections served as warning
signals are completely missing here, although they could as well have been
used here, too. The first soprano sings g'-d"-d"-e"-d". The E functions as
supra la and has to be changed to E flat, but it has no accidental, while in
the analogous passage in the first section, even the self-evident step of a
fourth, Bb-Eb, was indicated by accidentals. In the baritone, furthermore,
we also find an E flat, which Clemens could have provided for with an
accidental, especially since, two measures before, the E flat has to be sung
as an E (subsemitone). Immediately after, there appears in the same voice
the progression G-F-Eb-D, which once more offered the possibility of
indicating the E flat with an accidental; in Part 1 (measure 66) the same
progression in the alto did have the accidental.

2. Of greater weight, by comparison with the more symptomatic phenomenon of accidentals, is the fact that at the beginning of the passage
in question the ostinato appears in the natural hexachord. This bars any

[16] See p. 17n. This passage shows, furthermore, that likewise in the matter of notation of accidentals the version of the Brussels Codex is better than that of Phalèse;
the former, with its unmistakable E, makes any other reading impossible.

modulation. The above-mentioned E flat in the baritone makes its appearance immediately after we hear the e-*mi* of the ostinato; hence, of necessity it becomes an E, so that the A following right after it, in the bass, cannot possibly be interpreted as an A flat. Not only do all these circumstances prove that we are not justified in assuming the presence of a modulation in this passage: they also confirm our chromatic interpretation of the first section.

At this point one might ask, "Why does Clemens set the same words chromatically in Part 1 and diatonically in Part 2? To provide the answer we must delve into this Renaissance work's psychological subtleties. Clemens sets to music states of mind, not words. Each time Jesus weeps, it is motivated by a different emotional situation. The first time, deeply shaken, he receives the unexpected news of Lazarus's death, whereas the second time his weeping is immediately followed by his call to Lazarus; in his soul now lives a determination to call his departed friend back to life. Like the two wings of an altar, the two parts of the motet represent successive phases of a single development: the first pictures Jesus overcome by the death of Lazarus; the second shows death overcome by Jesus. This is the meaning of Clemens's chromatic and diatonic rendering of the weeping of Jesus.

The problem has now been considered from every angle. All evidence speaks in favor of the chromatic interpretation and against the diatonic, which brings us forthwith to a new problem: is it possible that such a procedure could have been followed but once in the Netherlands music of that period? This question compels us to examine further the motet literature of that time, with Clemens non Papa especially in mind.

A more thorough study of the Lazarus motet already brings us to a new discovery. At the beginning of this work Clemens sets the words "Fremuit spiritu Jesu" to an amazing modulation, which (Ex. 22) glides along through the circle of fifths from F major to G flat major and flows back by way of B flat minor, F minor and C major to the harmonic point of departure.[17] This modulation is likewise not indicated by accidentals. The discovery of the problem passage was in this case more difficult, because there was no ostinato to guide us. The code-note [18] is the first note in the

[17] The return to F major is completely established, both by the harmonic progression (C $^5_{4\ 3}$ -F³) and by the intonation of the ostinato (*sol-mi-mi* . . .), which prepares the a-*mi* for the resolution toward M major.

[18] We have given the name "code-note" to the note on whose interpretation depends the choice between diatonic and chromatic execution of what follows. This note is the key to the meaning of the passage it introduces; in the examples it is inclosed in a circle.

bass at measure 9. Is it to be read as A or as A flat? The following reasons argue in favor of A flat:

a) The progression of the voice itself: E♭-C-A(♭).

b) The motif-transposition: F-D-B♭; E♭-C-A(♭).

c) The notation, which in this case uses as warning-signal the slur binding together the two motifs: F-D-B♭; E♭-C-A♭.

d) The harmonic structure. An A would give us a chord of the diminished fifth on the leading tone, in fundamental position. Both in itself and especially in relation to the surrounding harmonic material, which consists of a unified progression of triads, this chord seems unlikely. To be sure, there could exist still another solution, and I myself was at first in favor of it.[19] The E flat appearing simultaneously in the baritone and alto voices is read as an E; this leads to the very common cross-relation E flat major: C major, which assures a diatonic continuation. The key signature of two flats in the Phalèse edition, however, immediately casts doubt on such an interpretation, while the flat before the E in the alto of the Brussels Codex version makes it utterly impossible.

e) The example of Josquin. A significant indication in favor of the chromatic reading is the fact that we here are dealing with a six-voice adaptation of a four-voice passage in one of Josquin's works. I have already pointed out Josquin's motet "Absalon fili mi" as spiritual ancestor of the Lazarus motet.[20] A thoroughgoing comparison with Josquin's composition brings to light that Clemens's passage is an exact imitation of Josquin's.[21] I have compared three sources of the Josquin motet: Kriesstein, *Selectissimae necnon familiarissimae cantiones*, 1540; Montanus and Neuber, *Tertia pars magni operis musici*, 1559; and the manuscript in the British Museum in London, Royal 8 G VII.[22]

The second source is evidently a reprint of the first; common to both is a set of clefs suitable to high voices. The manuscript version, on the other hand, which in this case offers the most reliable reading, contains a set of clefs suitable to low voices (Ex. 23). In view of the fact that it was a common usage of the times to set texts of lamentation to music for men's voices, this version may be regarded as the original. It contains a most extraordinary key signature: B flat and E flat in the tenor and alto clefs, E flat

---

[19] See A. Mb., p. 71.   [20] *Ibid.*, p. 72*n*.

[21] This comparison was made possible by the friendly coöperation of Professor Smijers, who placed at my disposal photographic reproductions of the above-mentioned sources of Josquin's motet.

[22] For the date of this manuscript see *Werken van Josquin des Pres*, ed. by Prof. A. Smijers Motetten Bundel III, p. vi.

and A flat in the bass clef, and E flat, A flat, and D flat in the sub-bass clef.[23]
In this work, in which A flat, D flat, and G flat occur, we find to the words
"sed descendam in infernum plorans," the very modulation which Clemens imitated. The inner relation is clear. David bemoans the loss of his son
Absalom, Jesus the loss of his friend Lazarus. In order to convey in tones
David's weeping, Josquin has recourse to methods unprecedented in his
time, while Clemens's aim is to paint in music Jesus's weeping. The territory
covered by the modulations is exactly the same, except that Clemens dares
to go one step farther in the circle of fifths. But Clemens takes over from
Josquin not only the harmonic progression but also the bass motif as bearer
of the modulation. The first seven tones—not taking into account the
tone repetitions—are exactly the same in both passages.[24] It was clear to all
the initiated among Clemens's contemporaries that this modulation was a
quotation from Josquin. There is but one difference: Clemens works without accidentals, whereas in the earlier work they are clearly set down by
Josquin himself, who here figures as pioneer in frontier territory.[25] Our

[23] The transposed version of Kriesstein and Montanus has one flat in all voices. Only
in the discant is there a flat before the F, a notation known to be devoid of meaning
in the practical sense; the explanation for this manner of notation is given in the author's article "The Function of Conflicting Signatures in Early Polyphonic Music," *The
Musical Quarterly*, XXXI (April, 1945), 227–260. A work for several voices and with
three different key signatures is a rare occurrence in the music of this period. I know
of but one analogous case—also, significantly enough, a work of Josquin, the "Fortuna
dun gran tempo" in the *Odhecaton* of 1501 (No. 74). This work is for three voices; the
contratenor has two flats in the signature, the tenor has one, the discant has none. In
this case, too, the signature is an advance notice of subsequent modulation. The harmonic compass of this significant work extends from C to D flat, and likewise traverses
the circle of fifths, but it works with *musica ficta*, while the Absalom motet has everything specifically indicated with written-in accidentals. See my essay "The Goddess
Fortuna in Music," *The Musical Quarterly*, XXIX (January, 1943), 1.
[24] This alone should dispose of Van Crevel's doubt (*op. cit.*, p. 98n) as to the existence
of a relation between the two works. Common to both is not only the three-tone motif
sol-mi-ut, which Van Crevel dismisses as stereotyped, but a seven-tone motif with an
unusual mutation (*sol-mi-ut-fa = sol-mi-ut-fa*) and a harmonic progression embodying
an extraordinary modulation. Josquin, furthermore, was the idol of Clemens's generation, and his Absalom motet had received renewed circulation through Kriesstein's
reprint in 1540.
[25] Professor van den Borren went to the trouble of drawing up a "genealogical table"
for this incomparable modulation of Josquin. It starts with Binchois and Dufay and
proceeds by way of Johannes Regis as far as Obrecht (see, *ad* Dufay, Charles van den
Borren, *Guillaume Dufay*, p. 285; *ad* Binchois, *Polyphonia sacra*, ed. by Charles
van den Borren, p. 63; *ad* Regis, C. W. H. Lindenburg, *Het Leven en de Werken
van Johannes Regis*, p. 81; *ad* Obrecht, A. Smijers, "Van Ockeghem tot Sweelinck,"
in *Algemeene Muziekgeschiedenis*, p. 138). All these examples stay within the limits
of chromatic colorings and transitions. The first approach to real modulation is
the chromatic passage written by Obrecht in his "Missa super Maria zart." It is
quite possible, however, that the latter was already under the influence of Josquin,
who still must be credited with having been the first to employ—and with amaz-

investigation gives us further proof that Clemens's Lazarus motet is a work of central importance in the evolution of the Netherlands motet, one in which the leading spirits of three generations—Josquin, Clemens, and Lasso —come together. A most constructive undertaking would be the publication of the original version of Clemens's work, preferably in the reading of the Brussels Codex Cons. 27.088, incorporating the accidentals which assure the intended chromatic reading, together with Josquin's model and Lasso's adaptation.

Rex autem Dávid

In the first book (1559) of Phalèse's collection of four-voice motets,[26] there is also a *Lamentation of David*, by Clemens non Papa. By virtue of its text alone, Clemens's *Lamentation* commands our attention. In Part 1 this motet pictures David weeping for his son Absalom; in Part 2, his grief over Jonathan. Clemens here fuses together, and in reverse order, two completely unrelated events of David's life; in the first he intones the lamentation of the king and father for the son,[27] in the second, that of the adolescent for the friend fallen in battle.[28] Evidence that Parts 1 and 2 were not erroneously coupled in this order is provided not only by the relationship of motifs, but also by the harmonic link between the two *partes:* Part 1 closes on the dominant (C major); Part 2, in answer, begins on the tonic (F major).

What is the significance of this unprecedented procedure on Clemens's part? In answering this question we anticipate the result of the ensuing analysis: it is a tribute to Josquin and to his renowned *Lamentation of David*. Only by pointing to the example of the older master can the otherwise incomprehensible juxtaposition of texts in the later work be accounted for; this is not a self-sufficient composition, but the imitation of a work

---

ingly bold and expressive effect—that logically presented and consistently pursued system of modulation through the circle of fifths which later was to play so important a role in the chromatic style of the Venetians and then migrated by way of northern Italy to other countries. While Reeser thought that "in the time of Clemens so advanced a type of chromaticism was not yet in use," it has now been firmly established that in order to further his efforts toward expression even Josquin had utilized this modern type of chromaticism and that Clemens was only imitating what the older Netherlands master of expressive style had dared to try out a generation earlier.

[26] No. 11; the work was printed for the first time in the year 1549 in the *Cantiones selectissimae quatuor vocum liber secundus . . . Philippus Ulhardus excudebat Augustae Vindelicorum* and appears again in the year 1564 in the collection of Montanus and Neuber, *Thesauri musici tomus quintus et ultimus.*

[27] Second Samuel 19:1.   [28] *Ibid.,* 1:26.

by a master who despite the lapse of a generation still figured among Clemens's contemporaries as the greatest composer of all. Since the reverse chronological order was obviously intentional, it should be plain to the musician that the composer had something quite unusual in mind.

We know from previous investigation that Clemens was acquainted with Josquin's *Absalon fili mi* and had made a thorough study of it. Hence it is reasonable to assume that in setting the same text he was eager not only to equal the older master in power of expression but, if possible, even to surpass him. Comparison of the two works will justify this assumption. At the very beginning Clemens refers to the model he so greatly admired by quoting Josquin's initial imitation (*ut-re-mi-fa-mi*), adapted to his different text.[29] Why, however, with subject matter the same, should the beginning of the text be different? Clemens rightly feels that Josquin's broad initial imitation is not altogether appropriate to the cry of lamentation *Absalon fili mi*. With this in mind he prefaces the exclamation with a few introductory words, chosen to carry the initial imitation: "Rex autem David operto capite incedens lugebat filium suum" (but King David covered his face and mourned for his son). The lamentation which now follows, "Absalon fili mi," is written with free homophonic emphasis on expression.

What Clemens's contemporaries doubtless admired most of all in Josquin's Absalom motet was its harmonic daring; anything so "modern" must have delighted them. When a man of their generation took this work as model he was bound to imitate above all Josquin's chromaticism. At first glance little of this nature is apparent in Clemens's version. The soprano, alto, and tenor each have one flat in the signature, the bass has two flats. In the three upper voices an occasional E flat is required. A more thorough examination soon reveals, however, that the tonality is subject to constant fluctuation. Thematic and contrapuntal association are responsible for the repeated change of E to E flat, of C to C sharp, of F to F sharp; these changes occur, furthermore, with altered tones following close upon the unaltered. In the tenor, measures 6 and 7, we even find two chromatic half-tone steps, one after the other, necessitated by the harmonic context. (Ex. 24; cf. Ex. 1.) Against this labile and as it were glimmering tonal background, small chromatic islands now stand out. Indeed, if we look beneath the surface of the work we make one surprising discovery after the other. Again we find modulations and chromatic progressions smuggled into the score in

[29] Cf. *ad* the peculiar practice of musical quotation in compositions of the period A. Mb. p. 85, note 1. In extenuation it should be remarked, however, that the quotation of the Gregorian lamentation tone occurs rather frequently in motet music of the period.

that enigmatic double language which, taken at its face value, admits of a diatonic reading, but which when seen in the light of structure and style virtually demands a chromatic interpretation.

The first small modulation is on the words "operto capite" (with covered face; Ex. 25). Here the major key takes on the more somber hues of minor. The E in the soprano is the code-note. A chromatic reading of it is suggested by the E flat which precedes it in the alto; the latter also has no accidental, but is necessary because of the transposed initial theme (Bb-C-D-E(b)-D). The influence of this E flat is heightened by the signature-indicated E flat in the bass, which comes in a semibreve later, while the alto's E flat is still sounding. The E flat thus made available in the superius brings about the alteration of the A after it to A flat, and this A flat in the soprano in turn demands an A flat in the alto and the bass. In this manner the alto arrives at the progression Eb-D-C-Ab; since it avoids the diminished fifth Eb-A, it, too, is a factor in favor of the chromatic reading. The harmonic sequence c-f-bb-C^{43}, which terminates on an empty chord of the fifth, on B, constitutes the kernel of the modulation. In order to effect the return from minor to major with as little friction as possible, Clemens has the chromatic episode end on an empty interval of an octave or a fifth and only after this neutral sound (and a rest in the voice concerned) presents the decisive interval of a major third.

Fifteen measures later, the following modulation occurs on the words "Lugebat [30] filium suum" (he mourned for his son; Ex. 26). This modulation is introduced through the note E(flat) in the alto. This E(flat) can be read as E flat: (1) because of the voice-leading: E(b)-D-C-Bb (tritone); (2) because the bass presents its E flat, prescribed by the signature, at the same time as the E(flat) in the alto; (3) because here, likewise, Clemens works with motif-transposition. The motif has E-E-F and is transposed to make D-D-E(b). In the soprano the same motif (A-A-Bb) reacts upon the notes following it to produce a transposition to G-G-A(b). This A flat is prepared by the preceding E flat in the alto and the bass. The motif-transposition extends even farther; it is the framework for the voice-leading in alto and soprano. If we lay this bare, we find in the alto E-F, D-Eb, C-Db; in the soprano A-Bb, G-Ab, F-Gb, E-F. This gives us the following modulation: A-d-g-c-f-Db-b-eb^{65}-Db^4-b-C^{43}-F (empty octave). By comparing the harmonic framework of this modulation with the chromatic episode in Josquin's Absalom motet, we find it to be a free imitation:

[30] In the altus "plangebat."

Josquin (transposed). A-f♯-D-G-e-C-F-B♭ . . .
Clemens: A- d - g - c - f - b♭ . . .

Clemens, however, seeks to outdo his model by presenting this modulation in minor, thus heightening its expression of suffering.

In Part 2 we discover the first unspecified chromatic passage on the words "doleo super te frater mi" (I mourn for you, O my brother; Ex. 27). The two upper voices intone these words in close imitation. The code-note is the E in the alto. The following reasons argue in favor of a chromatic reading:

(1) The consonance $\begin{matrix} b♭ & \searrow & g \\ d & \searrow & e(♭) \end{matrix}$

(2) The canonic imitation of the upper voice, which has preceded with the interval of a minor second;

(3) The motif, which is taken from Part 1, where it likewise demanded a chromatic reading.

The E flat again brings about a chromatic alteration of A in the soprano. Here, too, the A flat is already necessitated through the motif-transposition A-B♭, G-A♭.

While this chromatic reading is the analogue of the second modulation in Part 1, the following modulation on the cry "frater mi Jonatha" is almost identical with the first passage in the *prima pars* (Ex. 28). With the exception of the resolution, both the harmonic structure and the voice-leading are the same. Only the bass is different. Here, too, the code-note is the E in the soprano; but while in the first passage the chromatic reading calls for disclosure on the basis of style and structure, here it is clearly obligatory, because the E in the soprano occurs at the same time as the signature-indicated E flat in the bass. This, in other words, is an *obligatory* modulation. Worthy of note is the resolution: Clemens leads the harmonies c-f-b♭-C[4323] not toward F major but into the deceptive cadence on D minor. Of haunting beauty is the sound of this modulation, which is daring both for its harmonies and for its notation. How, for example, after all the A flats which just occurred, supply the accidental for the A natural essential to D minor? Through the detailed subsemitone-clausula C[4323] Clemens first provides for a clearly defined *mi* natural. Simultaneously with this *mi* natural of C major the tenor joins in with *la*, which thus is bound to be *la* natural and therefore is explicitly separated, by a rest, from what precedes. The relationship between the modulations in the two sections helps to clarify and to confirm both, each throwing light on the other.

That this work should have been so misjudged by Ambros, who as a rule was so safely guided by his intuition, may be traced to the fact that he failed to recognize its twofold character of tribute and of chromatic experiment. He writes in the famous Volume III of his *Geschichte der Musik*,[31] "Thus we must conclude that the motet *Rex autem David*, whose Part 1 contains a lamentation for Absalom and whose Part 2 a plaint for Jonathan, is a dry work little worthy of a master, that it is without true feeling and in no way to be compared with the analogous older compositions of Josquin." Though we cannot remotely concur with this harsh judgment, which is shared by Bernet-Kempers,[32] one thing is indisputable: the directness and power of expression of Josquin's music is not equaled during this entire epoch. To attain to this height again it took the genius of a Cipriano di Rore or an Orlando di Lasso.

Jesus Nazarenus

The four-voice motet *Jesus Nazarenus rex Judaeorum* belongs to Clemens's ripest creations in the new style of the progressive Antwerp school. It is one of the very few works by Clemens that does not begin with fugal imitation, one in which intricate counterpoint gives place to the sonority of full harmonies and the melismatic style of melody to a prevailingly syllabic declamation of the text (Ex. 29). The three lower voices of the motet have a key signature of two flats; the soprano has one flat. In the first section of Part 1 a beautiful *open* modulation from E flat major to D major surprises us (Ex. 30). The main steps of this modulation are E♭-c-F-d-A[43]-D. Generally, the elevation of the third of a triad in the cadence is not stipulated in the music of the time; Clemens hints at it by the unusual placing of a sharp under the E flat, which would have been self-evident being a *subsemitonium modi*. This sharp points in the direction of the upper circle of fifths, just as we found the flat serving as a pointer in the direction of the lower circle of fifths.

Aside from this stipulated modulation, we find in Part 1 two secret modulations; the first occurs in measures 39–40 (Ex. 31) on the word *malis*, the context being *defendat nos ab omnibus malis* (may He protect us from all‧ evil). The code-note is the E of the soprano, which may be read as E flat because of the two preceding E flats, in the alto and the bass. The E flat produces an A flat in the soprano through the leap of a fourth; at the same time it affects the A in the alto, lowering it to A flat. However, the voice leading of the alto itself, based as it is on the progression of a fifth, favors

---

[31] Page 311.　　　　[32] *Jacobus Clemens non Papa*, p. 77.

the lowering of A to A flat. A comparison with *Rex autem David* provides another reason for the assumption of the chromatic reading. Our passage is almost identical with the first and last secret modulations of that motet (cf. Ex. 25 and 28). The main difference is that the David motet has two flats in the key signature of the bass only, while the Jesus motet carries two flats in three voices.

The second secret modulation occurs in the phrase "agnus dei qui tollis peccata mundi" on the last two words (Ex. 32). The code-note is the A in the bass. It may be read as A flat because (1) it represents a transposition of the motif in the tenor

$$d- e\flat- f- e\flat- d-c-d-c$$
$$g-a(\flat)-b\flat-a(\flat)-g-f-g-f$$

(2) the alto has an E flat expressly demanded by the key signature. In order to avoid *mi contra fa* the A in the bass has to be lowered to A flat. The E flat in the alto may not be read as E natural since there is neither a clausula nor a cadence on F which would justify a *subsemitonium modi*.

The only emotional concepts in the motet text are the two distinguished by a secret modulation: *malis* and *peccata*, "evil," and "sin." Accordingly, we have to do with only small chromatic passages giving a transitory coloring effect to these two words. Certainly the text as a whole is very strange:

Jesus Nazarenus rex Judaeorum titulus triumphalis defendat nos ab omnibus malis. Sancte Deus sancte fortis et immortalis; agnus dei qui tollis peccata mundi miserere nobis.
Jesus autem transiens per medium illorum ibat Jaspar Melchior Balthazar Christus vincit, Christus regnat, Christus imperat.

Jesus of Nazareth, King of the Jews, triumphant title, may protect us from all evil. Holy God, holy, strong, and immortal. Lamb of God who bears the world's sins have mercy upon us.
But Jesus walked through their midst, Jaspar, Melchior, Balthazar, Christ wins, Christ reigns, Christ governs.

Nowhere in the liturgy is such a text to be found, but little fragments of it are scattered about in many unrelated places of the liturgy: [33] (1) the first four words are found in the Lauds of Good Friday (*Liber Usualis*, p. 694); (2) the words *Sancte Deus, sancte, fortis, immortalis* represent the famous Trisagion (but there the case is nominative) and are found in the Improperia of Good Friday (*Liber Usualis*, p. 705); (3) The *Agnus dei . . . miserere nobis* is taken from the Mass or from the Great Litany, which is always sung on Holy Saturday; (4) *Jesus autem . . . ibat* is the conclud-

[33] I wish to thank Mr. Frederic Rutledge Daly for his kind assistance in tracing the liturgical sources of the text.

ing sentence of Luke iv, which describes how the Pharisees wanted to put Jesus to death by throwing him down from a high cliff. We find this text as an Antiphon (*Liber Usualis*, p. 1089); (5) *Jaspar* (for Gaspar), *Melchior, Balthazar* are the names traditionally assigned to the magi. But nowhere in the liturgy of the Epiphany do these names occur. We read only of "the Magi" or of "the kings." (6) The concluding words *Christus vincit . . .* are taken from a set of Acclamations (which may be found in full in A. P. Bragers, *Chant Service Book,* p. 67). It is a chant for the populace at coronations.

Mr. Daly summarizes his impression of the text in these words:

> It is hard to see a clear thread running through these texts. 1 and 2 seem to have to do with Holy Week; 4 is from the Monday of the third week in Lent; 3 may or may not refer to Holy Saturday, while 6 may be appropriate for the triumph of the resurrection, but it is not surely of the liturgy. 5, however, belongs to the Epiphanytide or Christmas, and hardly belongs to the liturgy.

It seems that the most enigmatic part of the text are the names of the three Magi, since their mention does not make any sense in the context. The beginning of a solution was made when I accepted as a working hypothesis the supposition that the motet was composed in honor of three contemporaries of Clemens's who happened to have the names of the three kings. I was fortunate enough to find three such men in Gaspar, Melchior, and Balthasar Schetz. The family Schetz represented one of the most distinguished patrician houses of Antwerp. They were great merchantmen and financiers of the time, doing business with the Fuggers, Tuchers, and Welsers, with the emperor, and with kings.[34] The house was founded by Erasmus Schetz. When he died, in 1550, he left his three sons Gaspar, Melchior, and Balthasar [35] in charge of it. Thereafter the firm transacted its business under the name of Gaspar Schetz and Brothers. In 1556 a medal was struck to commemorate the unanimity in which the brothers lived.

---

[34] To give some idea of the extent of their operations it may suffice to mention some of their transactions with England. In 1547 the English government paid 76,421 Kronen to the house Schetz for deliveries of grain; in 1552 Gaspar Schetz & Brothers advanced more than 100,000 Carolusgulden to the English Crown, in 1554, 120,000 Carolusgulden. In 1555 Gaspar was made "general factor" by Philip II. In 1560 Sir Thomas Gresham, the financial agent of the English Crown, wrote in a confidential report to his government that the house Schetz "rewleth the holl finance and the burse of Antwerp." See Burgon, *The Life and Time of Sir Thomas Gresham, Knt. Founder of the Royal Exchange,* I, 365.

[35] Obviously, Erasmus gave his three sons the names of the Three Kings in allusion to his trading relations with the Orient. His sons would bring the treasures of the Orient, as did the Magi, and they should do it in that spirit of adoration for Jesus which caused the Kings to undertake their long pilgrimage.

One side had the armorial bearings of the family (a crow with wings displayed), encircled by the names of the three brothers "Gaspar, Melchior, Balthasar Schetz." [36] I suggest that the motet was dedicated to the three brothers Schetz on the occasion of their taking over the management of the business. These are the facts in favor of my thesis: (1) the mention of the names of the three Magi, otherwise inexplicable, is fully explained; (2) the date of Erasmus Schetz's death, in 1550, puts the date of the composition in this same year. This agrees perfectly with the "modern" style of the work, which could not have been written long before 1550.[37] The exact date of Erasmus Schetz's death is May 13, 1550. In 1550 Easter Sunday fell on April 6. May 11 was the Sunday *Rogate*, or the fifth Sunday after Easter. In the *Greater and Lesser Litanies* of the Rogation day the text occurs: *Agnus dei, qui tollis peccata mundi, miserere nobis* (*Liber Usualis*, pp. 835 ff.). There we find also a text similar to the words *defendat nos ab omnibus malis*. In the Litany it runs *Ab omni malo libera nos*. The allusions to Easter may be explained by the date of the father's death. *Rogate* is the last Sunday belonging to Eastertime. The following Sunday is Ascension Day. The text now makes sense. Clemens put it together from parts of the liturgy of Easter and Sunday *Rogate*. The motet is a glorification of Jesus, to whom the three brothers are related by their names in a particular way. Part 1 is an invocation of God and a prayer for divine protection and mercy suiting the occasion perfectly. The end of Part 2 celebrates the inauguration of the three brothers, whose names Clemens inserted so as to have them precede the acclamation traditionally sung at coronations. This is not wholly improper in view of the fact that the merchantmen were in reality the uncrowned kings of the time.[38] The beginning of Part 2 is the only section of the text difficult to explain, at least, if connected with the scene of the Gospel from which it is derived. If, however, Clemens wanted to quote the Biblical words without relating them to the original context, they could be used to mean just what they say, Jesus walking through their [the three brothers'] midst.

The facts known of Clemens's life are so meager that any addition is wel-

---

[36] *Ibid.*, p. 79.

[37] In the study of Lasso evidence was given for the emergence of the new style in the last years of the 1540's and its flowering in the early 1550's. Cf. A. Mb., the chapters on "The Modern Trend in the Antwerp Repertoire" and "Relations between the Motet Repertoire of Venice and Antwerp."

[38] To realize this, one has but to read that proud and daring letter of Jacob Fugger's to Charles V in which he tells the monarch that he would not have become Roman emperor but for his, Fugger's, service and financial promotion. See Ehrenberg, *Das Zeitalter der Fugger*, I, 111-112.

come. We see here that Clemens was in contact with a very distinguished patrician family of Antwerp, which represented one of the most powerful commercial enterprises of Flanders. The music may have been commissioned by the brothers just as the rich merchantmen of that day gave commissions for a picture. These "votive pictures" were often dedicated to the Madonna, and the patron was usually included kneeling, with or without family. Clemens's votive motet is dedicated to Jesus, and the three brothers are included—I am tempted to say "kneeling," for (in the best manner of Netherlands musical painting) the attitude of kneeling adoration is vividly expressed in the motif of the soprano, which descends slowly from B flat to A, G, F, and finally, in a pictorial portamento, down a third to D (cf. Ex. 33). Remarkable is the distinct declamation of the three names.

The Schetz family was known not only for its wealth and power but also for its genuine interest in art and culture. The father was a bosom friend of Erasmus of Rotterdam.[39] His son Gaspar was himself a humanist and poet of distinction.[40] Melchior Schetz was headman of the famous chamber of rhetoric, the Painters, of Antwerp,[41] and all three brothers were known for their collections of and passionate interest in numismatics. The youngest brother in the family was Conrad Schetz. He, too, was headman of a Flemish chamber of rhetoric. It is from a dedication of Hubert Waelrant that we know Conrad as a distinguished amateur of music. Waelrant dedicates the first book of his *Jardin musiqual* of 1556 to Conrad and says of him that he is able to judge music without preceding study, by listening only, "de la seule oreille." The Schetz family forms another link between Clemens non Papa and Hubert Waelrant, who are the two main representatives of the secret chromatic art.

Our motet is the only direct document available as to the social background of the circles interested in so sophisticated a technique as the secret chromatic art. It was a highly cultured and exclusive group of people who met in Gaspar Schetz's house. We shall come back to Gaspar [42] and his friends in the discussion of the religious implications of the secret chromatic art.

[39] See Aa, *Biographisch Woordenboek der Nederlanden*, Vol. IX, under *Gaspar Schetz*.
[40] Lodovico Guicciardini in his *Belgicae . . . descriptio*, p. 219, called him "*utriusque linguae doctissimum, magnum poëtam, et . . . non litteris minus quam virtutibus, quam opibus et dignitatibus inclytum.*"
[41] See Burgon, *The Life and Time of Sir Thomas Gresham*, I, 381.
[42] Gaspar's name appears as "Jaspar" in Clemens's motet and also in Sir Thomas Gresham's correspondence.

Vox in rama [43]

Clemens gives us an arresting work in the four-voice plaint of Rachel, "Vox in rama audita est; ploratus et ululatus. Rachel plorans filios suos noluit consolari quia non sunt." (In Rama was there a voice heard, lamentation, and weeping, and great mourning, Rachel weeping for her children, and would not be comforted, because they are not.) With every means of expression both harmonic and melodic, Clemens seeks to give utterance to the anguish of the mother of Israel for her lost children. At the very beginning and throughout the middle part of the work, a whole series of accidentals is to be filled in; the only problematical section is the close, for which a satisfactory solution is reached only after discovery of the secret modulation hidden within. The words "noluit consolari" are sung on the motif *mi-mi-mi-re-ut-fa-mi*, which the alto as upper voice introduces, the soprano remaining silent. When the alto has finished, the soprano takes over the motif and sings it, starting on A (A-A-A-G-F-Bb-A), and finally starting on D (D-D-D-C-B-E-D) (Ex. 34). The transposition-scheme is noteworthy: the motif is intoned on E, then continued first on A and finally on D; it appears first in the *hexachordum naturale*, then in the *hexachordum molle*, with one flat, and, finally, without accidentals—at the very place where logic would demand the transposition with two flats. Here, likewise, the chromatic reading fits in more naturally with the structure of the whole and affords a far more beautiful and expressive sound than the diatonic reading. The chromatic interpretation is in line with the affect-symbolism of the Renaissance, one of whose most widespread characteristics is the use of a specifically indicated *b molle* in order to convey the idea of grief. Thus, it is natural that the final repetition of the grief motif should be emphasized by the use of two flats. Two questions, however, are in order: (1) Why does Clemens leave the modulation unspecified, even though only B flat, E flat, and A flat are involved? (2) Why does he write in the flat for the first transposition at a spot (meas. 59) where the lowering (F-Bb) is self-evident? In answer to the first question it should be pointed out that the motet has no signature, that B flat, E flat, and A flat thus have the same meaning as A flat, D flat, and G flat in a signature of two flats. But the fact that Clemens indicates the flat in a passage where it is self-evident and that he even does so twice, in different voices, recalls the secret modulation in the Lazarus motet. There we were able to establish Clemens's use of the acci-

[43] Cf. Proske, *Musica divina* II.

dental not simply to bring about a transient change in the note directly involved but also as signpost to an intended harmonic development. Here, too, the twice-indicated accidental is used in the sense of a harmonic guide. In this connection the following evidence is significant: Clemens twice starts the motif on D—in the tenor the first time (meas. 59), in the soprano the second (meas. 65), toward the close. In both the preceding instances the motif starts on A, with a stipulated B flat (meas. 59, 66). On the other hand, this B flat is *not* indicated at the very first entrance of the same motif in the bass; in other words, it is not indicated at the one place where it would still have made sense, where its function would have been conclusively to establish the *ut-fa*. And why not? Because a notation of the *ut-fa* is unnecessary and because there is here no need of a harmonic signpost, no transposition on D being involved. It is also significant that on the words "ploratus et ululatus" a similar motif had already appeared (*mi-mi-ut-fa-mi*), likewise with a flat explicitly stationed in front of *fa*, while the same thing is to be observed in the motif of the beginning (A-D-Bb-A). Both times the *fa* is self-evident, in accord with long-established rules of singing. Both times it is written with two-fold intent: to express the idea of lamentation through graphic use of notation; to establish beyond question the *b molle*, with an eye specifically to its effect on the secret modulation at the close.

The code-note for the double modulation at the end is B = B(b) (in the tenor the first time, in the soprano the second). The return is carried out each time without ambiguity: the first time through the voice-leading in the alto, which from D goes a fourth lower to A and in this way restores the diatonic reading (the modulation having gone to A flat); the second time through an explicitly indicated natural, which follows a written-in flat. The admirable way in which the return is carried out is a further argument for the chromatic reading. For example, the above-mentioned A in the alto is reserved for the one place in the first modulation where it can serve to lead the way back. Had it occurred but one *minima* earlier, both a clearly defined A and with it the possibility of a return would have been cut off. For this reason the tenor pauses; the setting is reduced from four voices to three; the harmony retrogresses toward D minor, which is now prepared through the third and the doubled root; the fifth, A, is reserved for the one moment when, through the descent of a fourth from D, the alto can present it without interference and in this way initiate the return. There is but one complication; shortly before the return, the bass intones on E the motif *mi-mi-mi-re-ut-fa-mi*. Since the beginning of the motif falls within the chromatic environment and its end within the diatonic, it reads Eb-Eb-Eb-D-C-F-E. We are thus confronted with the necessity of accepting a change in the motif—either here or in both the tenor and the soprano presentations. Not only do two places stand against one: both, especially the last in the soprano, are far more exposed than the one in the bass. The sound and the expression, moreover, both speak in favor of the chromatic reading; finally, there is this decisive factor, that a diatonic reading of the soprano changes the most vital part of the motif, *ut-fa-mi*, to *mi-la-sol*, whereas a chromatic reading of the bass leaves the heart of the motif untouched, altering only the first note. The strongest evidence for the chromatic reading remains, to be sure, the disagreeable sound and faulty texture of the diatonic interpretation.

How would a Renaissance musician analyze the diatonic version? We are dealing with two passages in Example 34: measures 6–9 and measures 11–15. In both places the musician of that era would take exception to the awkward shift from the *hexachordum molle* to the *hexachordum durum*. In order to demonstrate the disagreeable effect, he would single out, not complete chords, as we do, but individual contrapuntal lines. He would be most likely to point out the soprano and tenor in measures 6–7 and in measures 13–14:

$$bb'\text{-}a'\text{-}g' \qquad d''\text{-}c''\text{-}b' \qquad b'\text{-}a'\text{-}g'$$
$$; \qquad\qquad ;$$
$$d'\text{-}c'\text{-}b \qquad bb\text{-}a\text{-}g \qquad g\text{-}f\text{-}bb$$

In the first two places the diatonic reading imposes the false relation B-B flat, in the third and far worse sounding it necessitates a *mi contra fa*

$$\begin{matrix} b & \nwarrow & a \\ g & \searrow & f \end{matrix}$$, and, after that, a false relation at the octave.

With the chromatic interpretation, on the other hand, the entire passage remains a coherent unit in the *hexachordum molle*, voice-leading and counterpoint flowing along without friction.

A final point in favor of the chromatic version is the use of chromaticism in other portions of the work. I have reference to the chromatic clausula, which has already been discussed.[44]

Job tonso capite

New secret modulations are to be found in the four-voice *Plaint of Job* of Clemens non Papa: [45] "Job tonso capite corruens in terram adoravit et

[44] Cf. the preceding chapter, Ex. 15.   [45] Phalèse 1559, Lib. V, No. 7.

dixit: nudus egressus sum de utero matris mee et nudus revertar illuc. Dominus dedit, dominus abstulit, sicut domino placuit, ita factum est. Sit nomen domini benedictum" (Job shaved his head, and fell down upon the ground, and worshipped, and said: "Naked came I out of my mother's womb, and naked shall I return thither: the Lord gave, and the Lord hath taken away; blessed be the name of the Lord!") The work has a signature of one flat in all four voices (Ex. 35). At first glance it reveals nothing out of the ordinary. But if we follow the score, we come upon an indicated E flat in the bass (measure 15) that has the complement of a simultaneous E (flat) in the superius—necessary because of the leap of a fourth Bb-E (♭). This twice-demanded E flat proves to be the point of departure of a modulation. For the progression of the bass immediately requires an A flat: Eb-F-G-A(♭)-G-C. But in the alto and tenor likewise, A and E have to be flattened. Since beyond dispute we now have in the bass the motif G-G-G-G-E♭-F-G-A(♭)-G-C, and since this sharply defined motif appears note for note in literal transposition to the fourth-above—that is, starting on C, without any accidentals,—the following reading seems to be intended: C-C-C-C-A(♭)-Bb-C-D(♭)-C-F.

Still other grounds speak in favor of this version: (1) The voice-leading in the alto, Bb-A(♭)-G-F-G-G-F-E(♭). The E flat is a necessary consequence of the preceding top note B flat and of the A flat which follows. The A flat is in turn demanded by the three surrounding E flats in the soprano, tenor, and bass and confirmed by the incontestable A flat which follows in the bass. The unity of the melodic phrase in the alto is stressed through the fact of its being sung on a single word. The last tone of the phrase, E flat, is the real code-note. It determines the progression of the voice in the following manner: E(♭)-A(♭)-G-A(♭)-D(♭). The last A(flat) again occurs at the same time as the A(flat) of the bass motif. (2) The voice-leading of the tenor: F-G-A(♭)-Bb-C-D-E(♭)-C. The voice demands a *supra la* lowering of E to E flat. This E flat also occurs at the same time as the A (flat), which in turn is necessitated by the transposition.

The modulation thus resulting is in two parts: from G minor via E flat major to C minor (this part is obligatory); from C minor to A flat major, F minor, B flat minor, and from there again back to C major (this part is susceptible of two readings). Even the return speaks for the chromatic interpretation. Here, too, three voices flow into empty octaves and double-octaves; each time after a pause *la* natural in the alto and *mi* natural in the tenor carry the voices onward diatonically.

In this work, likewise, chromaticism is used to express extreme suffering. Clemens chooses the moment when the messengers have brought Job one report of disaster after another, culminating in the tidings of the death of his ten children; overpowered by grief, Job falls to the ground. On the words "corruens in terram" Clemens writes his modulation in minor. It is strange, however, that the superius should sing the second part of the modulation on the words "adoravit et dixit," in contrast to the other voices, which all repeat the "corruens in terram." Obviously this is a case of inaccurate placing of the text, for which the editor must be held responsible. For the words "corruens in terram" fit the voice-leading far better, and the words following come, as logic would demand, on a new motif, which in expression and movement is directed toward the word "adorare." For this reason our excerpt is quoted with the text distribution just outlined.

We find a second secret modulation on Job's words ("nudus egressus sum de utero matris meae *et nudus revertar illuc*.") The key to this modulation is the note E in the alto (Ex. 36, measure 58). Clemens wants this to be understood as E flat; he shows this through the voice-leading itself. The motif consisting of eight tones brings four times the note B flat, twice the note G, so that the E flat completing the triad at the end of the motif seems logical. But the other voices also point in the same direction. The superius intones the motif g″-c″-c″-d″-c″-bb′-a′. Bass and superius now transpose this motif and thus in turn call forth a lowering of E to E flat: c″-f″-f″-g″-f″-e(b)″-d″, and the bass goes even farther: Bb-bb-bb-c′-bb-a(b)-g. But Clemens is still not at the end of his resources. The voices are put together in so artful a way that wherever bass and superius have an E flat caused by motif-transposition, this E flat is also needed for harmonic and contrapuntal reasons. On the first E flat in the bass (measure 55) Clemens writes a Phrygian cadence, which requires an E flat; [46] in the case of the second E flat in the superius, the flat is needed for harmonic and contrapuntal reasons.[47] This is not all, however; even the two modulations have the same two-part construction, with a cadential caesura in the middle; both times this caesura falls on C; both times the code-note is in the alto; the voice-leading is related:

[46]

	c″	f″
d′⌣d′	c′	d′
bb a	g	a
g f	e(b)	d

[47]

f″	↗e(b)″	d″
bb′↗	g′	↖bb′
d′	↗e(b)′	f′↖
bb↗	c′	↖bb

1. Bb-A(b) -G-   F-G-G-F-E(b)-A(b)-   G-A(b)-   D(b) ...
2. Bb-Bb-Bb-G-Bb-F-   G-   E(b)-A(b)-A (b) -G-A(b)-B-A(b)-D(b) ...

Beyond that, the two passages also have similar voice-leading in the superius. The first modulation uses the motif *ut-re-mi-fa*, while in its second part the second modulation uses the reverse motif *fa-mi-re-ut* (bass and superius). Mention has already been made of the similarity in the structure of the two modulations; the second modulation goes a step farther than the first (to G flat). It goes first from B flat major to C minor, from there via F minor, A flat major, F minor to G flat major and again back to D flat major, F minor, C major, F major. This return Gb^3-Db'^5_{43} -f^3-C^5_{4323} -F^3 is particularly bold and felicitous. The final chord is at the same time the beginning of the new section. The broad F major harmonies come on the words "dominus dedit."

If one reviews with an eye to their interdependence the various arguments in favor of the chromatic reading, one cannot withhold one's admiration for the art which here reigns. Clemens builds an entire structure of pillars and arches which interlock and mutually support each other, dovetailing with another structure in such a way that both in turn secure each other. This phenomenon was already to be observed in both *partes* of the *Lamentation of David;* it will again be found, though in a new form, in the work we are about to examine.

Qui consolabatur me

In turning to the motet *Qui consolabatur me* of Clemens non Papa, we reach the point of departure for a final ascent, which promises us a broader panorama and with it the first compensation for our exertions. We beg the reader, who has followed us thus far, not to give up now. The subject is too significant to warrant relaxed attention at the most decisive moment or to justify presentation along purely general lines. On the contrary, we must call to our aid every kind of analytical device in order to arrive at a true understanding of this the most problematical work of Clemens non Papa.

In a study of chromatic phenomena in Renaissance music, a work with a signature of three flats is bound to arouse the interest of the investigator, all the more when it proves to be a completely isolated case. A signature of three flats is nowhere else to be found in the entire creative output of Clemens, nor is there an analogue either in the Antwerp repertoire or in the Venetian. Willaert, for example, who has often been called the father of the chromatic movement, in his motet *Aspice domine* himself often inserts an A flat into the musical text, but he observes the customary maximum of two flats in the key signature. Thus, we must first recognize that in using this signature Clemens was consciously undertaking something unprecedented. That this is a work in transposed mixolydian mode explains nothing, because the real question is. "Why does Clemens undertake so unusual a transposition?" The case becomes even more enigmatic when one studies the work and realizes that it contains a whole series of false relations and tritone chords.

The difficulties imposed by the interpretation of this motet are plainly to be seen in Commer's edition,[48] which presents an almost tragi-comic picture of the struggle of a modern musicologist with the recalcitrant text of an old Netherlands motet. The result in the end does violence to the original musical text. Apart from the places where as *subsemitonium modi* A flat must be changed to A natural, Commer puts a natural in front of the signature-indicated A flat twice in the bass, six times in the second tenor, and fifteen times in the first tenor, so that one may well ask what is left of the original signature. Why should Clemens have had any A flat at all in the signature of the first tenor, when according to Commer's interpretation it is to be read twenty-five times as A and only six times as A flat? The reason for Commer's strange disposition of accidentals lies in the above-mentioned stylistic anomalies (false relations, tritone chords), which he hoped to conjure away in this manner. It is obvious that he is at the end of his rope in his interpretation of the closing measures. He does what he can. He cancels the A flat and in the plagal ending even a B flat; he twice writes in an F sharp and then betrays his helplessness by setting beside it a question mark. The F sharp in the second tenor, however, is preceded by an E flat, so that the most improbable voice-leading ensues. But the E flat is under no circumstances to be eliminated, since it occurs at the same time as an E flat in the contratenor, which if changed to E would give rise to a tritone and, furthermore, is required both by the signature and by the rule concerning *supra la;* this means that on three different grounds the E flat cannot be avoided. There is no escape from this dilemma.

What was Clemens really trying to do in this unusual composition? In order even to approach this question our first task is to remove Commer's emendations. This requires a study of the sources. The motet *Qui consolabatur me* is available in four different compilations of the period: Phalèse, *Liber primus cantionum sacrarum,* 1554, No. 16; Bosco, *Quintus*

[48] *Collectio operum musicorum Batavorum,* VIII, 112.

liber modulorum . . . ab excellentissimo musico Clemente non Papa, 1556, No. 6; Montanus and Neuber, *Quintus tomus evangeliorum,* 1556, No. 40; Susato, *Liber xiv ecclesiasticarum cantionum fo. xvi,* 1557.

I did not have access to the third source, but judging by other editions of the same publisher [49] it is in all likelihood a German reprint of the Netherlands first edition. According to the superius,[50] the second source is an exact replica of the Phalèse version.[51] This leaves the versions of Phalèse and Susato, which prove to be independent of each other. The two editions show the following differences: (1) Susato has a signature of three flats in all five voices, Phalèse has it only in the three lower voices, and in the two upper voices he contents himself with a signature of two flats (Ex. 37); (2) The endings of the clausulas differ; (3) The notes have different time values (Susato has, for example, ○ ♩ where Phalèse writes ♩ ○ because of the declamation); (4) Susato's reading contains two important printer's errors in the superius (incorrect time values, both of notes and rests, in measures 62–65); (6) Susato's edition has the poorer text distribution and poorer declamation, although in the year 1557 the superior 1554 edition of Phalèse stood at his disposal.[52] Hence we give preference to the Phalèse version.

In studying the work in the Phalèse edition we come upon various places that sound bad, indeed—the very ones in which Commer tried to improve upon the composer by altering the accidentals, though even this could not entirely eliminate the doubtful measures. What are these places? If we work backward, we get these three main passages: (1) the final cadence; (2) measures 60–61, where words are sung on the diminished triad D-F-A flat; (3) measure 48, with the following harmonic sequence:

---

[49] See the discussion of Montanus's reprints in the analysis of Clemens's *Legend of Lazarus* and Josquin's *Absalom* motet.

[50] Koninklijke Bibliotheek, the Hague.

[51] For a critical judgment of texts, the editions of Simon à Bosco do not come into consideration. Investigation reveals that this publisher did not bring out a single work of Clemens non Papa not previously issued by another publisher. The volume mentioned contains eleven works by Clemens, of which nine are reprints from Phalèse collections and two from Susato. (This ratio might be considered symptomatic of the esteem in which these two publishers were held.) What could have been the aim of an edition which did not even display the enterprise to offer to the public *one* work never before published? The format of the publication provides the answer: it was an utterly delightful miniature edition, printed in handsome, clear characters, which the amateur could easily carry in his pocket. If it is obvious that the massive choir books were for churches and for chapels of princes, then the miniature editions of Simon à Bosco are evidence of how deeply the cultivation of motet singing was anchored in the musical life of the *cognoscenti ed amatori;* for it can only have been for the amateur that the edition was issued.

[52] This tallies with the characterization of the two publishers offered in A. Mb. (pp. 48 ff.).

```
        D  -  D
     Ab-Ab-Ab-Bb
     Eb- F - F - D
     C - D  -  G
```

One might argue that the false relations and tritone chords serve to illustrate the text. For the first and second places cited are sung on the words "quia repleta sum amaritudine" (since I am filled with bitterness), the third on the words "fundent oculi mei lacrimas" (mine eyes will pour tears). And, indeed, these harmonies do sound bitter and sharp.

But it is neither Clemens's wont nor that of the Netherlands school to express grief in this fashion. And if Clemens really meant nothing more than these tritone harmonies, why did he put them into a piece in three flats, procedure without precedent in the music of the period? Are not these *diaboli in musica* more likely to be warning voices and signposts in the direction of our new path? We grasp at this as a final possibility. We proceed from the original signature and add accidentals not prescribed by it to the offending measures, in order to replace the tritone chords with normal harmonies; this is the opposite of Commer's procedure. But it soon appears that nothing has been gained. If we start with the most important place, the close of the piece, we arrive at the conclusion that there is no way out: the close remains enigmatic. Whether one cancels the A flat or retains it, whether the F is raised to F sharp or not, whether D flat is introduced or D allowed to remain—in any case whatsoever the passage has an ugly sound and is impossible as a closing cadence. If we examine the second and third places, we find that in each the context forbids the introduction of the D flat needed to remove the diminished triad. In the first passage the soprano would read Bb-A-G-F-Eb-Db, in the second we would get the harmonic sequence

```
         Db
      Bb-Ab-Ab
      F -Eb-F
      D - C - Db.
```

Both are impossible. But it is quite clear that D flat is needed. It can only be that the changes have not been made at the proper places. Let us carefully go back, measure by measure, and systematically examine every possibility. After an arduous hither and yon, we discover that in the entire motet there is but one possibility of introducing the D flat in plausible fashion—in the forty-second measure. Here the harmonic sequence C^{43}-d would have to be changed to C^{43}-Db.

Does the context admit of such a change? Strictly speaking, the interpretation of but one note is involved, the *la* in the contratenor. If we read this as *la* flat, as A flat, the second note can come in on D flat, and the chromatic reading continues in a completely natural manner. The following considerations argue in favor of lowering the *la:*

1. The voice-leading itself (Ex. 38b). The progression of a fifth in the alto is sung on a single word, making a closely knit unit. In order to avoid the diminished fifth, A flat has to be inserted. The B flat which follows in no way contradicts this, since it appears as a mere passing note, emphasized neither rhythmically nor melodically, therefore it cannot cause the *la* to function as *subsemitonium*.

2. This voice-leading is confirmed by the bass, which, note for note, except one passing note,[53] pre-imitates the alto at the fourth below (Ex. 38a).

3. At measure 41 the bass has an A flat, hence the A occurring simultaneously in the soprano must also be read as A flat; measure 42 brings an A flat in the tenor; consequently the A flat in the contratenor (measure 43) follows as a matter of course.

4. Not only melodically but also harmonically the path is prepared by the three A flats already sounded in bass, soprano, and tenor. The harmonic progression consists of $Eb\text{-}f\text{-}C^{43}_{87}\text{-}Db$. The twofold occurrence of F minor in measures 41 and 42 opens the door for the deceptive cadence on D flat in measure 43, which is much more satisfactory harmonically than the diatonic resolution $Eb\text{-}f\text{-}C^{43}_{87}\text{-}d$. The A flat in the contratenor necessitates a simultaneous D flat in the second tenor, this in turn calling for the G flat appearing in the contratenor in measure 44.

5. Professor van den Borren points out that the *la* in the contratenor, on whose meaning everything depends, is the only *la* in the entire voice part. Here again is an unusual feature, which calls for particular attention.

If we consider this passage in relation to the motet as a whole, there come to light several other very important aspects, which support a chromatic interpretation.

a) If a chromatic reading of measure 43 ff. is adopted, all difficulties immediately disappear. At measures 48–49 we get the harmonic sequence $Db^{65}_{43}\text{-}c^{6}b\text{-}Db$; at measures 61–62 the following line in the soprano: $Bb\text{-}Ab\text{-}Gb\text{-}F\text{-}Eb\text{-}Db$, and for an ending we would have, in G flat to be sure, a flawless cadence.

b) Through introduction of the D flat at measure 43 we get two exactly

---

[53] This passing note in the bass—in transposition an A flat—would have necessitated in the alto a premature D flat, and for this reason had to be avoided.

symmetrical sections of forty-two measures each, of which the first is diatonic, the second chromatic.

c) This division corresponds to the text, which, likewise constructed in two sections, enters at measure 43 with what Professor van den Borren so appropriately terms the "épisode lacrimatoire."

d) When we seek to determine whether the musical continuity justifies so marked a division into a chromatic section and a diatonic section, we come to the following conclusions: Insoluble difficulties of structure in the disposition of the voices are offered only by the second section; these are obviated by the chromatic reading. In melodic structure, too, the first section differs considerably from the second. Insight into this is provided by the following tables. They record the number of note repetitions and of melismatic notes in the individual voices.

	NOTE REPETITIONS		MELISMATIC NOTES	
	Section 1	*Section 2*	*Section 1*	*Section 2*
Superius	6	26	27	8
Contratenor	15	30	29	16
Tenor	7	26	21	22
Quinta pars	9	28	21	15
Bassus	5	29	23	15
	42	139	121	76

The following should be appended to the "melismatic notes": The soprano as principal voice has only eight melismatic notes in the second section. That is striking, since the preference for lengthy melismas, especially in the soprano, is a general characteristic of the Netherlands style of this period, particularly of Clemens's own style.[54] The melismas in the second section, furthermore, are distributed between the two words "lachrimae" and "amaritudine."

	LACHRIMAE	AMARITUDINE
Superius	5	3
Contratenor	10 (5 on "fundent")	6
Tenor	11	10
Quinta pars	9	6
Bassus	9	4
	44	29

[54] In my Lasso monograph (p. 93, note 3) I pointed out that the "often interminable lingering on a melisma" is one of the reasons for the length of some of Clemens's compositions.

Seventy-three of the seventy-six notes are set to strongly expressive words, that is, we are dealing in the first section with the customary ornamental melismas; in the second section, with expressive melismas. The first section is of melodic character; the second, as the note repetitions demonstrate, of declamatory character.

The two sections are further differentiated by the disposition of the voices. The first section is constructed of imitations; the second section ("fundent oculi") begins with a scarcely concealed division of the chorus into two groups of three voices, treated in the manner of a free echo and finally joining in a restoration of the five-voice chorus. Only at the end is imitative treatment taken up again.

If we sum up the individual analyses, we get the following picture. The text of this motet is organized in two sections. The first gives the objective reason for the affliction; the second depicts the mental state of the afflicted person. The bipartition of the text finds its echo in the motet's symmetrical organization. The difference in expression is shown most strikingly in the unique transformation of the melodic character of the second section, but its effect is also felt in the disposition of the voices and in the constructive principles applied. A division into diatonic and chromatic sections would add to the formal and melodic contrasts a contrast in harmonic structure and would in no way jeopardize the textual and musical continuity.

The chromatic section of the motet would, to be sure, differ fundamentally from the modulations which we have thus far encountered in Clemens's motets. Until now we have found only small islands of chromaticism rising sporadically out of the mainstream of diatonic polyphony, while here we are confronted with a purely chromatic section. There are two places, it is true, at which a return to the diatonic might be effected: in measure 64 there is a cadence which instead of being resolved toward B flat minor might be resolved toward B flat major, while in measure 72 a resolution toward E flat major would be possible. In emphatic contradiction to this, however, is the close of the motet, for which the chromatic reading alone affords a satisfactory solution; it is the only one, furthermore, which corresponds to the text. Wherever till now it was possible to lead a modulation back to the diatonic, new text regularly appeared. The words "quia repletus sum amaritudine," which would here accompany the diatonic resolution, have already been incorporated into the chromatic section; moreover, their expressive content offers no emotional relaxation which would justify the return to the diatonic. The entire second section is meant to be read chromatically. It fluctuates between B flat minor and E flat minor and finally resolves toward G flat major. The entire second section of the motet is presented in Example 39. We inscribe on the top line the accidentals according to Commer's version (C.), and, underneath, the accidentals provided by our reading (L.).

Around 1550 would it be possible for a Netherlands motet to close in G flat major? Although in its diatonic version the motet is puzzling, would we not in adopting the chromatic reading be replacing a minor enigma with a major one? We shall come closer to a solution of the problem if we submit the text to detailed examination.

It runs: "Qui consolabatur me recessit a me. Quaero quod volui et non invenio. Fundent oculi mei lacrimas, quia repletus sum amaritudine" (He who consoled me has abandoned me. I seek what I wanted and I find it not. Mine eyes will pour forth tears, because I am filled with bitterness). At first glance there is nothing conspicuous about the text; on closer examination, however, one discovers that it has no conclusive feeling of unity, no logical connection of ideas. In the first sentence a person is involved, in the second a thing. In the first we have "*He* who consoled me," in the second, "I seek *what* I want." In the first part "qui" and "quod" do not rhyme, while in the second, the tenses are mixed: "Mine eyes *will* pour forth tears, because I *am* filled with bitterness." More logical, or at least more psychological, would have been the use of the present tense in the principal clause: either "Mine eyes pour forth tears (because I am filled with bitterness") or, at the most, "mine eyes may pour tears." In any event the use of the future tense provides a slightly humorous touch: one who is bowed with grief does not say, "I *shall* weep."

Would, perhaps, the source from which the text is derived give a clew to its meaning? The Old Testament sound of the text impels us to take up the Bible. But like the singer, we seek and find not. According to the sixteenth-century concordances of Hervagius,[55] Stelsius,[56] and Plantin,[57] among others, the text itself nowhere occurs in the Bible, but a number of similar passages do. If we pursue these, we find three principal sources of our text: (1) Lamentations 1:16: "Oculus meus deduxit aquam, quia longe factus est a me qui consoletur me" (Mine eye runneth down with water,

[55] *Concordantiae majores sacrae Bibliae a quodam theologiae studioso Jo. Gast castigatae.*
[56] *Concordantiae Bibliorum utriusque Testamenti . . . quas re vera majores appellare possis.*
[57] *Concordantiae Bibliorum utriusque Testamenti . . . quas re vera majores appellare possis.*

because the comforter that should relieve my soul is far from me).
(2) Song of Solomon 3:1 (also 3:2 and 5:6): ". . . quaesivi, quem dilexit anima: quaesivi eum et non inveni eum" (I sought him whom my soul loveth: I sought him, but I found him not). (3) Jeremiah 15:17: "Solus sedebam, quoniam amaritudine repletus sum" (I sat alone . . . for thou hast filled me with indignation).

If the juxtaposition of quotations from Jeremiah and the Song of Songs is in itself strange, still more remarkable is the obvious distortion of the original text. Since the text nowhere else exists in this form, and since to our knowledge it was never set to music by Clemens's contemporaries, we may assume that he put it together himself. But why did he not choose either an unadulterated Biblical text, as he usually did for his motets, or one of his own invention? He wished to give his text a Biblical camouflage. His contemporaries, well-versed in the Bible, were bound to notice on closer examination that the text was not genuine; the alteration of well-known Biblical passages was designed to arouse their attention.

Of what significance is the text? It is nothing less than the key to the solution of the riddle on which the motet rests. In compiling his text from well-known sources, Clemens changed it in such a way as to provide the background he needed for the musical artifice planned. Indeed, the words express what the performer was bound to experience in his search for the right sound and form. The words "quaero, quod volui et non invenio" coincide with the crucial passage, on whose correct interpretation the fate of the motet depends. "I seek what I wanted, and I find not"; whence "mine eyes will pour forth tears, since I am filled with bitterness." Technically expressed, "I find not," the approach to the secret chromatic section remains hidden, the phrase proceeds diatonically and brings me through the bitterness of false relations and tritone harmonies to the point of weeping; but to him who does find the "lacrimatory episode" is the illustration of the chromatic section in minor.

In this motet the music is not so much illustration of the words as the words are illustration of the music. For the idea behind the work is essentially a musical idea: to confront the old diatonic style with the new chromatic. It was in order to carry out this idea that Clemens in so peculiar a manner compiled the text from familiar Biblical quotations. Thus, the work was on the one hand concealed from the suspicious eyes and ears of musical and religious zealots, while on the other its parodistic intent was conveyed to inquisitive minds by the willful distortion of the original words.

The text in this instance fulfills a role which was by no means unfamiliar to Clemens's contemporaries. From their experience with the mottoes attached to canonic riddles, they were well aquainted with the practice of indicating the solution of musical puzzles by humorous application of Biblical texts. This widespread old Netherlands custom, in which, incidentally, Clemens was adept,[58] is here ingeniously brought to bear upon a new problem. Professor van den Borren's remark, that the code-note *la* in the contratenor is the only *la* in the entire voice part, now takes on added weight. The "quaero, quod volui et non invenio" refers to the code-note; the musician here seeks it out much as the Shulamite sought her beloved in the Song of Songs. Are we going too far if we also put the first phrase of the motet, "who consoled me has abandoned me," within the sphere of the code-note? In any event, the following facts deserve mention: at the words "who consoled me" Clemens constructs his piece in such a way that even the soprano, lacking a signature-indicated A flat, must nonetheless have an A flat, while, contrariwise, at the words "has abandoned me" even in the voices with a three-flat signature the A flat has to be replaced with an A natural.[59] The following table helps make this clear.

		QUI CONSOLABATUR ME		RECESSIT A ME	
		A flat	*A natural*	*A flat*	*A natural*
Superius	(signature 2 flats)	2	0	0	6
Contratenor	(signature 2 flats)	0	0	0	0
Tenor	(signature 3 flats)	1	0	0	0
Quinta pars	(signature 3 flats)	7	2	0	2
Bassus	(signature 3 flats)	2	0	0	2
		12	2	0	10

Clemens effects these alterations partly through the voice-leading—superius: Eb-F-A(b)-G; tenor: F-Bb-D'-C' A(♮)-Bb-A(♮)-Bb—partly through the harmonic structure. If one takes into account how precisely everything in this composition is weighed and calculated, it is difficult to explain away as coincidence a phenomenon which, even in contradiction to the signature, occurs with such consistency.

But there are still more surprises in store for us. Professor van den Borren points out that the imitation in the closing section ("quia amaritudine repletus sum") is composed on the motif of the "Pater noster" and remarks in this connection, "Is there not, in this singular usage, some special in-

[58] See Bernet-Kempers, *Jacobus Clemens non Papa*, pp. 40–41.
[59] One must not, of course, retain Commer's willful alteration of the text-distribution. At this point it must be recalled that Susato has three flats in the signature of all five voices, so that the *la* in the contratenor must of necessity be read as an A flat.

tention in the composer's mind? During the modulatory episode, in any event, this theme undergoes a transformation singularly in accord with the state of mind of one who is *repletus amaritudine* and who, in consequence, momentarily lacks confidence in God." The quotation of the "Pater noster" bears out the parodistic character of the work. This is the musical analogue of the willful alteration of familiar Biblical passages which we observed in the text.

What is the meaning of this work? To all intents and purposes Clemens wanted to symbolize, by contrasting the two sections, the "change in the musical thought of the Netherlanders." [60] In the two sections he places in opposition to each other:

Melodic style	Declamatory style
Melisma as ornament	Melisma as expression
Polyphonic structure	Homophonic structure
Diatonic harmony	Chromatic harmony

In our opinion the work should be classed alongside the series of chromatic experiments carried on by Clemens's Italian and Italianizing contemporaries, which series includes Willaert's *Quid non ebrietas* and Cipriano di Rore's *Calami sonum*. Its form and style are, however, typical of the Netherlanders, in that even this most radical experiment still reveals the Gothic love of secrecy, mathematical speculation, allegoric interpretation of the Bible—and Flemish humor.

The work is constructed with painstaking symmetry: there are twice forty-two bars. The note charged with bringing about the change to chromatic harmony makes a single appearance on the voice-part in question; a series of forbidden and ill-sounding dissonances, laid out like traps at regular intervals, detains the musician in the event he has taken the wrong road. Humor is hidden, however, behind the mathematical strictness of artistic calculation: there are the twisted quotations; the combination of love song and jeremiad; the spectacle of Clemens, at the crossroads between the chromatic and the diatonic sections, making merry over the plight of the hapless musician—"quaero, quod volui, et non invenio." With genuine gratification he lets his victim shed tears of desperation, and at the moment when he asserts that he is filled with bitterness the voices begin to sing a distorted version of the *Pater noster*. This is an incomparable example of old Netherlands musical humor, much like what has become so familiar in the painting of that era, with its allegorical parodistic repre-

[60] See A. Mb., p. 52.

sentations. We find the same spirit in the verses of the Flemish folk poets and in those of the learned poets known as *Rederijkers*. At the same time this work is, however, a true child of the Renaissance: the liberal attitude which it embodies would be unthinkable without humanism and the Reformation.

The fundamental difference between this work and the chromatic riddle duo of Willaert lies in its artistic substance. In this respect, too, Clemens's unique work retains its Janus face. It is one of the strongest manifestations of Flemish humor in music; that is one face. It is at the same time, however, a marvelous piece of old Netherlands expressive music, a work of rare fervor and of profound inner earnestness; that is the other face. Paradoxically enough, its true earnestness and expressiveness are apparent only when one has discovered the humorous secret character which leads to the chromatic reading. One has to hear it at least once or preferably several times, both in chromatic and diatonic interpretations,[61] in order to realize how flat and colorless it sounds in the diatonic reading—quite apart from the insoluble dissonances of the latter—and how rich the sound, how deep the expression it takes on in the chromatic reading. Both in technical construction and in the use of chromaticism this motet is one of the boldest Clemens ever wrote. Elsewhere, true, he also goes as far as D flat major and G flat major (cf. Ex. 20, 22, 26, 36), as does Josquin (Ex. 23), but here he even penetrates to C flat major and A flat minor. Examine especially measures 70 ff. and 79 ff.; also measures 49–50, with the chromatic clausula in the tenor, so effective both harmonically and melodically. In spite of that he succeeds in preserving the tonal balance and in maintaining the connection with the diatonic section. This is evident from the disposition of the cadences. The first section closes in B flat major, but suggests also, through a deceptive cadence, E flat major; the second section elaborates for the most part the like-named minor and its parallels, cadences on B flat minor (measure 59), D flat major (measure 61), B flat minor (measure 78), and, finally, on G flat major. Clemens here shows himself to be every bit as audacious as his boldest Italian contemporaries in any of their works designed for performance.

What shall we say of Clemens by way of summary? He reveals, first of all, a greater measure of inner strength and breadth, of pictorial and expressive power, of spirit and humor, than previously he had been credited with; he is far more receptive to tradition as well as to contemporary in-

---

[61] Indeed, every musicological seminar, every *Collegium musicum* and *a capella* choir would find it rewarding to undertake this dual performance.

fluences than had hitherto been suspected. In the style of his later years, represented by an entire series of masterly creations, he emancipates himself from the Gombert school, which in the Netherlands musical scene was the dominant factor. Making an intensive study of Josquin's later works and following the latter's example, he devotes himself more and more to problems of expression, finding particular interest in the harmonic audacities of the older master, which he tries to carry farther. True creative innovator that he was, he follows with equal interest modern developments in Italy, particularly the Venetian novelties of double choir and chromaticism. Instead of imitating, however, he translates the new style into the spirit and language of Netherlands music, whose horizon he seeks to broaden in an organic way—from the inside out. Without introducing an actual double choir system, which would have upset the old polyphony, he uses the device of choir cleavage with excellent effect.[62] Without instituting an outward revolution in notation, he employs the innovations of the chromatic idiom in order to give to his palette new color and brilliance, above all to achieve greater power of expression. He attains to the position of chief exponent of a typically Netherlands reproduction of chromatic modulations, which, buried within the fabric of the music itself, are not revealed in the notation except in secret fashion, and even then only to an initiated expert. To this end he employs a most original technique, whose foundations have not yet been adequately disclosed. The special feature of this technique is that it admits of two meanings, a diatonic and a chromatic. The present studies show that the diatonic reading is designed as a camouflage for the chromatic reading really intended by the composer.

ADRIAN WILLAERT

Quid non ebrietas

Is there a connection between Clemens's *Qui consolabatur me* and Willaert's chromatic riddle duo *Quid non ebrietas?* Not long ago Joseph S. Levitan published an extraordinarily interesting and penetrating study of this work.[63] We are convinced that the author fully succeeded in working out the correct solution to this puzzle piece, and we seize the opportunity

[62] See A. Mb., pp. 63–69, 83.
[63] *Tijdschrift der Vereeniging voor Nederlandsche Muziekgeschiedenis*, XV, 166 ff. Levitan enumerates the theorists who have mentioned Willaert's Duo in their writings. They are Spataro, Aron, Bottrigari, and Artusi. Dr. Alfred Einstein calls my attention to the following passage in Zacconi's *Prattica di musica*, Vol. II, *cap.* xxx: "Tetracordo, è la Quarta considerata in sua pura, e natural natura. E nota, che perche dalla sudetta Quarta ne nascano non solo la duodenaria quantità de Tuoni armoniali, e Chorali;

to make a comparative study of the two works. The fact that some thirty years earlier Willaert had dared travel through the entire circle of fifths makes Clemens's feat of closing a work in G flat major more comprehensible. If, on the other hand, we apply to Willaert's work the analytical method here developed, some new and interesting aspects come to light. Willaert's duo consists of 40 measures and shows the same mathematical symmetry as Clemens's piece. The decisive spot, on whose interpretation everything depends, occurs in measure 21. Up to that point every new chromatic note from E flat through A flat, D flat, G flat, and C flat was marked with an accidental; from this point on occurs a series of nonspecified notes that are to be flattened or double flattened, a fact which the musician has to discover from the context. The relationship of motifs shows that measure 21 constitutes a turning point. Here the tenor repeats the initial motif in changed and shortened note values, something that happens nowhere else in the entire duo (Ex. 40). This motif relationship has, however, a practical meaning comparable to that of motif transposition in the chromatic secret art of the Netherlanders. If the performer notices the repetition, he will see in it a clew to the solmisation of the tones concerned. Levitan's interpretation confirms the idea that in measures 21–22 the initial motif reappears on another degree, but in exactly the same intervals. Further proof that Willaert attached particular importance to this motif derives from the fact that after the initial announcement of the six-tone motif the tenor presents the same motif in retrograde motion (Ex. 41).[64] It should be noted that the initial motif in Clemens's motet coincides interval for interval with the end of the tenor voice of Willaert's duo—in retrograde order (Ex. 43). Whether this is intentional or accidental we leave undecided. Another question, however, must be answered: is Willaert's duo a forerunner of the Netherlands secret chromatic art? Further: is the technique of nonspecified secret modulation anticipated in his duo? While

---

mà anco la totale vera, e reale distintione del genere Diatonico, Chromato, & Enarmonico, come benissimo si vede in un Duo del S. Adriano, fatto da lui con gran studio, & arte, per mostrare come dalle medeme corde naturali per via di cromatico in virtù di detta Quarta, uno si parte, e realmente si trasporta tanto fuori di dette corde naturali, che in fine si trova esservi lontano un Tuono, da me posto nel trattato de Canoni Musicali." It is evident from this passage that Zacconi not only mentioned and shortly analyzed the Duo in his famous work on music, but that he also published it in another treatise on *Musical Canons* which apparently has been lost.

[64] The connection of the motifs shows, however, that Willaert wanted the fifth tone of the motif to be understood as *subsemitonium modi*, in which role it appears both in the retrograde presentation and in the transposed. This justifies insertion of the accidental (Ex. 42), fitting it better, both melodically and contrapuntally, into the context.

in a general way we can answer the first question in the affirmative, the second merits an emphatic "No," on the following grounds.

Notation.—Willaert specifies the accidentals for chromatic notes as far as C flat. In the Netherlands chromatic secret modulation G flat and C flat do occur, but the signature never goes any farther than an E flat, with the sole exception of the *Qui consolabatur* of Clemens. This means that while the Netherlanders try to veil chromaticism, Willaert intentionally reveals it. Meanwhile, it should be noted that, viewed from the standpoint of voice-leading, all accidentals in the tenor are superfluous. Willaert, too, uses progressions and leaps of a fourth and of a fifth, and every new chromatic note is made necessary by the voice-leading. There are two reasons why Willaert inserts accidentals from E flat to C flat: (1) because of the novelty of his procedure; (2) to give clear instructions for the second or nonstipulated section, whose solution becomes apparent when one logically proceeds along the circle of fifths in the direction that he indicates.

Enigmatic character.—The close of Willaert's duo on the seventh—specified by the notation itself—makes the enigmatic nature of the duo clear. The Netherlands secret art conceals the presence of the enigmatic.

Double interpretation.—While it is characteristic of the Netherlands secret art to permit a diatonic reading alongside the chromatic, this double meaning does not exist in Willaert's music. His duo does not admit of a diatonic solution.

Relationship of the voices.—In the secret art of the Netherlanders all voices are related to each other: an accidental in one voice affects the reading of all the voices. In Willaert's duo, on the other hand, the two voices go their separate ways in medieval isolation. In the secret chromatic art every hexachord shift in a single voice causes harmonic shifts in the ensemble. Quite the contrary in Willaert's duo, where the tenor's amazing voyage through the circle of fifths has no harmonic consequences, since the cantus takes no part in the modulation, clinging stubbornly to its initial hypodorian mode from beginning to end. Much as I admire Levitan's comment, of one thing his study has not convinced me—that Willaert's duo is "a very beautiful composition." [65] Measures 14–21, with their false relations and whole-tone progressions, are anything but beautiful even in his interpretation. This is a case, furthermore, of interval connections that were never sanctioned by theorists of that day or likely to be found elsewhere in Willaert's works. According to the rules of counterpoint the passage would have to stand as in Ex. 44. This reading should be com-

[65] *Ibid.*, p. 180.

pared with the actual sound of the passage when all accidentals are omitted from the upper voice. But Willaert was not so much concerned with a pleasing sound in his duo as with the realization of a certain idea. The following considerations would lead us to believe that he intended this work, not as a composition, but as an ingenious experiment.[66] (1) The duo was published, not in editions intended for performance, but in editions of theoretical works. Willaert left to posterity a considerable number of outstanding publications; had he considered this work a very beautiful composition, he certainly would have found ample opportunity to publish it. Further proof that he did not desire its publication resides in the fact that it did not appear in theoretical publications till long after his death and is nowhere to be found among the numerous tracts of his pupils—as, for instance, the great Zarlino, or even the ultraprogressive N. Vicentino. (2) In all Willaert's extensive creative output there is nowhere any evidence that he was disposed to follow through the implications of his experiment. In my Lasso monograph [67] I pointed out that with respect to harmonic structure Willaert displays a continence and a moderation which are typical of his style; this opinion is borne out by examination of the first volume of his complete works, of which publication is now in progress.[68]

In conclusion it should be pointed out that the title "Father of Modulation" [69] still belongs to Josquin, who was the first to employ, in a sacred work, modulation through the circle of fifths from B flat major to G flat major; [70] this was in his *David's Lament for Absalom*.[71] Nobody will deny Willaert the distinction, however, of having been the first to undertake a complete circumnavigation of the circle of fifths.[72]

---

[66] Levitan is of the opinion (*ibid.*, p. 180) that the title *Quid non ebrietas* must have been added later, since no mention of it is made in the correspondence between Spataro and Aron. Such allusions to antiquity were very much in vogue at that time, however, and the verse of Horace here involved fits the riddle duo so perfectly that it is more than likely Willaert chose the title himself. We have in mind especially the following: "Quid non ebrietas dissignat? Operta recludit . . . addocet artes" (What a miracle cannot the wine cup work! It unlocks secrets . . . teaches new arts).

[67] Pages 54, 58–59, 74, 81–82.

[68] Gesammelte Werke, Vol. I, ed. by H. Zenck, *Publikationen älterer Musik, Jahrg. 9.*, 1937.

[69] See Levitan, *op. cit.*, pp. 197, 231.

[70] Studies undertaken by the author after completion of the present work (see p. 25n) have definitely settled in favor of Josquin the question of priority in the use of chromatic modulation.

[71] See pp. 24 ff. and Ex. 24.

[72] An attempt at an interpretation of this event in the history of music has been made in the author's paper on "The Renaissance Concept of Physical and Musical Space," read at the annual meeting of the American Musicological Society, in December, 1941.

Returning to Clemens, we encounter a second question: Is the art of chromatic artifices limited to the work of this master? That would not only be contrary to the group spirit which is so convincingly manifested in the motet writing of this period: it is just as unlikely that this technique would have found devotees in a circle of initiated amateurs and professionals, had it been the purely individual method of a single composer. On the other hand, it was of such subtlety, and the chromatic movement was so much in its infancy, that one can scarcely expect this species of the new chromaticism to have flourished very abundantly in the conservative climate of the Netherlands. The very fact of its secrecy reveals how difficult it must have been for a Netherlands musician to acknowledge his allegiance to modern concepts.

THOMAS CRECQUILLON

Domine Deus exercituum

Among the motets of Thomas Crecquillon we have found only one which shows that the secret technique of modulation was not unknown to this master (Ex. 45). This example—the close of Part 2 of the four-voice motet *Domine Deus exercituum*—has already been quoted in the monograph on Lasso.[73] Crecquillon does not go so far afield as Clemens. He modulates no farther than to A flat major; he leaves the A unstipulated, but through the leap from E flat to the fourth-above he calls for it so unquestionably that no other solution is possible.

This obligatory secret modulation at the end of Part 2 does, however, have a counterpart in an ambiguous passage at the end of Part 1. Here Crecquillon addresses the musician in humorous fashion, saying "Aperi oculos et vide!" (Open your eyes and see!). And if the musician opens his eyes, he will notice that Crecquillon takes the *ut-fa* motif which he is here using and starts it first on G and C, then on F, and finally, at the equivocal spot, on B flat. The E flat arrived at in this way is likewise stipulated. At this point the progression of the individual voice as well as the harmonic context call for the accidental on the unstipulated A flat (Ex. 46). The voice-leading Eb-D-C-A(b) proves to be a typical device for securing a b *molle;* subsequent examination will bear this out. There are two other reasons, however, for the chromatic reading: (1) The preparation of the cadence. In order to conform to the rule for the subsemitonium, the clausula in the upper voice would have to be read diatonically;

[73] A. Mb., Ex. 11; cf. p. 63.

A-G-G-F♯-F♯-G. That would lead to a less satisfactory contrapuntal disposition F♯-G; in the chromatic reading, however, we get a normal Phrygian
C -D
cadence:

$$
\begin{array}{ccc}
f' & g' & g' \\
c' & d' & c' \\
c' & c' \; b & c' \\
a\flat \; g & & c
\end{array}
$$

(2) The close of the cadence. In the chromatic reading the latter is thoroughly satisfactory and confirms our general observation that the cadences
of chromatic passages frequently flow into an empty fifth or octave [74] in
order to set up a no-man's land between chromatic minor and diatonic
major sections. The diatonic reading, which calls for F sharp in the upper
voice, would suggest a close on the full triad:

$$
\begin{array}{ccc}
f\sharp' \; g' & & g' \\
c' & d' & e' \\
c' & c' \; b & c' \\
a \; g & & c
\end{array}
$$

That this triad is avoided provides one more reason for adopting the chromatic reading. A final argument is provided by the connection between the
two modulations: both use the *ut-fa* motif. If we put them side by side we
discover the use of a systematic transposition: G-C, C-F, F-B♭, B♭-E♭,
E♭-A♭. In the light of our previous findings we can scarcely take this
transposition structure to be mere coincidence.

NICOLAS GOMBERT

Suscipe verbum Virgo Maria

Although it stands as an isolated example,[75] we must include in this
discussion the chromatic final section of a motet by the Netherlands master
in whose work chromaticism was least to be expected—the end of Part 2
of the motet *Suscipe verbum Virgo Maria*, by Nicolas Gombert.[76] It is

[74] While in Josquin's time the use of an empty fifth or octave as cadence-ending was
still common, around 1550 this practice had become rare, indeed.
[75] Gombert's chromatic passage stands between *musica ficta* and secret chromaticism.
It belongs to *musica ficta* in that it implies the flattening of but one tone left unspecified by an accidental without, however, leading up to a modulation. It borders upon
secret chromaticism because it is of such a puzzling character that it can be interpreted
with certainty only by the methods developed here. Particularly, the use of motif
transposition in the service of chromaticism relates this passage to the technique of
secret chromaticism. Incidentally, the use of A flat seems to represent the greatest
departure from the diatonic system indulged in by both Gombert and Crecquillon.
[76] Strangely enough this passage, to my knowledge the only chromatic one in Gom-

at once obvious that the transposition here involved is obligatory, going as far as A flat (Ex. 47). This is, indeed, a new use of chromaticism. There is no actual modulation; the phrase does not go into the domain of another key, as one five-voice entity, but is divided into two half choirs—discant-alto and tenor-bass—while the fifth voice takes part in both choirs. Each half choir has its own tone color, determined by the intervals used (lower choir, parallel thirds; upper choir, parallel sixths) and by the hexachords to which it belongs. The sound of this passage, in which A flat is immediately followed by A natural and A flat major by F major, is to our ears at first very strange, but, considered from the vocal standpoint, not devoid of charm. The same motif is carried out in all the voices: first, as *sol-mi-ut-fa*, then as *la-fa-re-sol;* first in major, then in minor. In the lower half choir the hexachords on C and B flat are coupled, in the upper one the hexachords on F and E flat. The lower half choir enters on F, the higher one closes on A flat. The meeting of these two keys causes a peculiar effect: while the upper half choir is still sounding in A flat major, the lower one comes in with a repetition of its motif in F major, so that for the duration of a minima A flat major and F major are heard simultaneously. But on no account is the A of the tenor to be changed to A flat. Against this change are the following considerations: (1) the triad-motif; (2) the previous reading of the motif and the disposition of the several voices in triads; (3) the analogy to the unusual sound contrast provided by the separation of a five-voice entity into two half choirs (this is a rare procedure in Gombert's writing) and the transposition and repetition of a short plastic motif.[77] While the repetitions of the motif in the four voices of the two half choirs remain the same, note for note, the first alto alone changes its motif; its *sol-mi* (G-E) have to be read as *la-fa* (G-Eb) in the two following repetitions. But even this inconstancy finds its counterpart in the disposition of

---

bert's motets, is mentioned neither in Eppstein, *Nicolas Gombert als Motetten-komponist,* nor in Schmidt-Görg, *Nicolas Gombert.* We quote the passage according to the edition in the second volume of Montanus and Neuber, *Magnum et insigne opus musicum* . . .

[77] Nor can the A flat in the soprano be replaced by A. In this connection Professor van den Borren remarks: "For a moment I was of the opinion that in an impulse of supreme audacity Gombert had conceded the possibility of using the tritone *mib-la♮.* But aside from the fact that the result is antimusical and utterly dreadful, the flat expressly placed in front of the *mi* in the bass (meas. 64), at a point where it might have been omitted, is in itself certain evidence that Gombert did not wish to use the tritone farther on." Concerning the simultaneous use of A flat and A for the duration of a minim, Professor van den Borren is of the opinion: "I am quite ready to accept the dissonance Ab-A, provided the A flat in the superius is no longer than a *minim,* or that it is well sung, with so marked a diminuendo that it is barely audible at the moment when the A♮ of the other voice enters."

the voices. The first alto is the only voice to change its half choir affiliations. The first time, it definitely keeps company with the first half choir; the second time and the third time, the first two notes of its motif come in with the last two notes of the motif in the first half choir. Corresponding to this allegiance to both half choirs and to their differing tonalities is the change in the tonality of the first alto itself.

While thus far we have always found a convincing parallelism between chromaticism and text, the link between chromaticism and the praise of the Virgin Mary remains a riddle.[78] The discovery that Gombert here uses the same motif as Clemens in the first modulation of the Lazarus motet, the same as Josquin in his *Lament for Absalom*, does not make the case any clearer. For, logical as seems the connection between the plaints of Jesus and of David, what is the ideological link between a lament for the dead and a eulogy of the Virgin? In the Absalom motet Josquin quotes himself: the tones *sol-mi-ut-fa* not only appear as initial motif in his other lament of David for Jonathan, *Planxit autem David*, but also are the beginning of his *Stabat Mater*. That would seem to offer a key to the understanding of this remarkable passage in the Gombert *Annunciation*. The closing words of this motet run "ut benedicta dicaris inter omnes mulieres" (in order that Thy name may be blessed among all women). By the division of the chorus into two half choruses; by the stark contrast of sound between parallel thirds and parallel sixths; by the surprising sequence of two totally different tonalities and the motif transposition as far as A flat Gombert strongly emphasizes the quotation of a famous passage from Josquin's *Stabat Mater*,[79] which, even in changed rhythm, must easily have been

[78] The reader might argue that a similar connection between chromaticism and praise of the Lord were encountered in Crecquillon's motet *Domine Deus exercituum*, in which the words "quia tu es deus solus" are set to a modulation from F major to A flat major. The objection is justified and provides occasion for pointing out the connection between the use of flat keys and that of chromaticism and modulation. In the vocal music of this era the flat keys and their harmonies were often used to express awe and veneration. In motet settings of the Adoration of the Magi the words "adoraverunt eum" occur often on E flat major harmonies; these are presented on long-drawn-out chords, to express the solemn mood of adoration. Crecquillon, too, composes his modulation toward A flat major on solemnly sustained harmonies. On the other hand, Gombert resorts to every device to create an impression of the strange, so that instead of being rested and satisfied by the closing strains of the motet, the performer and the listener are on the contrary disturbed, and are left, as it were, with a question. Professor van den Borren says apropos of this: "These alterations . . . produce above all an impression of the strange, of the abnormal, accounted for by the composer's desire to recall symbolically the motif previously used by Josquin—making it stand out in a manner conspicuous because of its very strangeness."
[79] The connection with the *Stabat Mater* is verified by a whole series of further motif references to Josquin's composition.

recognized by his contemporaries. In so doing Gombert combines the scene of the Annunciation of the Angel with the scene at Golgotha, using, as it were, a leitmotif to weave present and future into one. Similarly, contemporary painters—for instance, Hieronymus Bosch—point to the passion of Christ in an *Adoration of the Magi* by means of crowns of thorns and of other symbols of the passion. This same intention on the part of Gombert may have been responsible for the weird sound and the strange dissonances of the passage in question.

The only chromatic passage thus far known to exist in Gombert's motets, these measures display an entirely personal use of chromaticism, both musically and in symbolic content. This is readily understood if the period of origin be taken into account. The motet appears for the first time in a publication of Jacques Moderne, of Lyons, around the year 1532.[80] We are dealing with an early effort of the great singer of the Virgin, which precedes the flowering of secret modulation, thus throwing new light on his reverence for Josquin; of this we had already learned from other sources.[81] The poor declamation likewise points to an early date of origin.

HUBERT WAELRANT

A richer harvest awaits us in the works of Hubert Waelrant. In my Lasso monograph he is shown to be a progressive spirit; he took also an active interest in the chromatic secret technique. As with Clemens, we shall take as point of departure a work of which the chromatic reading is incontestable and then proceed to analyze the more difficult cases.

Afflictus sum

In this motet of mourning, which has already caught our attention because of its chromatic style,[82] we find a marvelously euphonious and resourcefully elaborated secret modulation composed on the words "rugiebam a gemitu, a gemitu, a gemitu cordis mei" (I groaned in the deep affliction of my heart). It links F major with E minor and B minor. Its exact itinerary is F-C-e-b-G-C-G-A[43]-D. The return to D major, which makes as flawless a connection backward, toward B minor, G major, A major, as it does forward, toward G minor, is made possible through a clearly stipulated F sharp (Ex. 48). In comparison with previous material, even the route of the modulation reveals a new element: Waelrant modulates toward

---

[80] Eitner 1532c; cf. the bibliography in Schmidt-Görg, *Nicolas Gombert*, p. 367.
[81] Cf. his motet of lamentation on Josquin's Death, "Musae Jovis," in Josquin des Prez, *Werken*. Ed. by A. Smijers, 1. Aflevering.
[82] Cf. A. Mb., p. 76.

the sharp keys. Quite apart from the fact that in the sixteenth century the use of a sharp key was something out of the ordinary, in the previous technique of modulation we have found it neither in Josquin nor in Clemens and Crecquillon. The modulation toward sharp keys enables Waelrant, again in contradistinction to the practice thus far observed, to choose a nonchromatic tone as code-note. In all five voices there is a signature-indicated B flat. The code-note is the E in the first tenor. The ensuing fourth-below—B flat—has to be changed to B natural so as to conform to the rule for "*mi-contra-fa*." In order to stipulate even more definitely the change from B *rotundum* to B *quadratum*, Waelrant worked with motif transposition, as did Clemens. We find the transpositions B♭-D-A, C-E-B, G-B-F♯, and the germ of a further transposition: D-F♯-D. The secret modulation is constructed and integrated with admirable finesse. The code-note is assured in three ways: (1) by the choice of a nonchromatic note; (2) by the motif transposition; (3) by the simultaneous E in the discant, which is indisputable. In similar fashion the following notes of the modulation are established beyond doubt: The B natural of the first tenor (1) by the skip of a fourth E-B; (2) by the motif transposition B♭-D-A, C-E-B; (3) by the E in discant and bass; the F sharp of the first tenor (1) by the motif transposition B♭-D, C-E, D-F♯; (2) by the B natural in discant, alto, second tenor, and bass; (3) by the F sharps in the second tenor and the alto, which in any event are unavoidable because of the leap of a fourth from B natural. The way in which the voices are joined is of interest: the discant follows the first tenor at the smallest possible distance, that of a minim; the bass likewise follows the discant in stretto imitation at the same distance, and again this stretto technique is used to link together second tenor and alto. We see that Waelrant works with imitation and transposition of motifs made mutually interdependent in the most artistic manner imaginable, so that each voice supports the other and the entire structure stands firm and unshakable. The technique of unstipulated modulation here attains its climax. While till now a chromatic interpretation was possible only by altering the pitch of the code-note, here it is the reverse: a diatonic reading is possible only when the code-note E is changed to E flat, although occasion for the latter change does not arise. By choosing a nonchromatic tone as code-note Waelrant assures the point of departure which, once established, brings the modulation inevitably in its wake. Nonetheless there remains to the hard-bitten diatonicist the possibility of reading the E as E flat. Had Waelrant himself wanted the E flat, however, he would have provided a different voice-leading and a different notation. This he demonstrates in exemplary fashion in his motet *Et veniat super me misericordia tua*.[83] In this composition, which has the same signature and combination of voices, Waelrant brings a similar motif (of a fourth) and a transposition of this motif. But in this instance he inserts the flat for E not only in the soprano but also, superfluously, in the bass and in the first tenor (Ex. 49). This exaggeratedly careful insertion of accidentals can perhaps be explained by the chronological proximity of the two works. Waelrant published them one directly after the other, the motet *Et veniat super me* in the fourth book of his motets, the other one in the fifth book.[84] Did he wish to give a commentary on the analogous place in the *Afflictus sum* by thus conspicuously inserting accidentals? The pains taken by Waelrant in constructing this secret modulation, the relation of the two motets of mourning,[85] and their chronological proximity no less lead one to suppose that this may have been his intention.

Et veniat super me misericordia tua

This motet contains another genuinely ambiguous passage (Ex. 50) on the words "et respondebo *exprobrantibus mihi verbum*" (I shall give answer *to them that mock me*). The code-note is the E in the contratenor. Evidence in favor of the change to E flat is provided by the accented semibreve E flat, which precedes in the discant, and by the harmonic structure, which in diatonic reading results in a particularly harsh and exposed false relation (C minor-A minor) on the word "respondebo." In the chromatic reading, however, we get a frictionless progression from C minor via A flat major to F minor, where it lingers for two measures; it then starts a cadence toward B flat minor, but evades it in favor of E flat minor, finally leading back to the diatonic by way of the neutral fifth on F. The voice-leading of the discant is especially expressive in the chromatic reading, whereas in the diatonic reading it sounds badly and—dubious. For the progression of the melody would in itself demand an E flat; the diatonic reading opposes this by not lowering the preceding code-note E.

There is still another consideration: the initial motif of the motet runs in the four upper voices A-Bb-G-G (D-Eb-C-C in the answer) and in the

---

[83] *Ibid.*   [84] *Ibid.*

[85] It is worthy of note that both works have the same signature and clef combination and that the bass of both motets makes its entrance on the same motif, while the other voices vary it freely. In the *Afflictus sum* even the soprano takes over the motif of the bass. Common to both works is also the beautiful plagal cadence (D minor-A major) at the close.

bass D-E♭-E♭-D. In the entire motet this motif does not occur again except in the secret modulation. Provided, for textual reasons, with an upbeat, it first appears in the bass: D-A-A-B♭-G′; next in the alto: D′-A′-A′-B♭′-A′; then in the soprano: G′-D″-D″-E♭″-C″; and, finally, again in the bass, where it most closely approximates its initial form and occurs on a transposition degree which requires a G flat: F-F-F-G(♭)-F. This G flat is further demanded by anticipatory imitation in the bass, the alto, and the soprano, where the halftone step is obligatory because of the written-in accidentals. Purely for reasons of sonority, however, it is required: the cadence toward B flat minor requires as its subdominant E flat minor, which has G flat.

The initial motif appears again in the soprano, starting on C and hence requiring a D flat. This place corresponds to the return to the diatonic in Josquin's modulation (cf. Ex. 23). The latter also tarries on a suspension, G flat-F, to be resolved into the fifth-and-octave chord on B flat. It is characteristic of the technique of the return that each resolution of a chromatic note occurs after a rest: in the second tenor after a rest of a breve and a dotted semibreve, in the first tenor after the rest of a breve, in the alto after a cadential caesura. The use of the initial motif—at the place where the secret modulation begins—recalls Willaert's procedure in his riddle duo "Quid non ebrietas." This passage occurs, furthermore, at midpoint (measures 36–43) of a composition in 84 measures.

One might ask why Waelrant utilizes the secret technique when in both the works we have examined [86] he does not in the least hesitate to apply chromaticism openly. Quite apart from the charm which it must have had for a progressive composer, the secret technique enabled Waelrant to introduce modulatory audacities such as he would scarcely have dared resort to openly. In the modulation just discussed, for example, he actually uses the notes A flat, D flat, and G flat, but his signature never reveals anything beyond an E flat.

The Motet-Cycle on the Life of Jesus

Scattered among the two books of four-part motets which Waelrant himself published, apparently in 1556, we find four pieces of his own composition. They appear to be closely related, both in style and in content, and they form a cycle dedicated to the life of Jesus. *Videntes autem stellam* [87] pictures the Adoration of the Magi; *Venit fortior post me*,[88] the

[86] Cf. A. Mb., p. 76.
[87] *Liber primus sacrarum cantionum . . . quatuor vocum. . . .* No. 3.
[88] *Liber secundus*, No. 9.

prophecy of John the Baptist and the baptism of Jesus by John; *Si pec-caverit in te frater tuus*,[89] the kernel of Jesus's teaching, the exhortation to love and forgiveness; *Recumbentibus undecim discipulis apparuit illis Jesus*,[90] the appearance of the risen Christ before the disciples and the investiture of the Apostles.

At first glance one is struck by the abundance of accidentals,[91] by that characteristic glimmering major-minor tonality which marks the end of the church modes, and by the vivid musical realization of the textual content, as well as by the admirable declamation. The intimate relation between the four pieces is further demonstrated by the common use of the same *chiavette:* all four motets have a combination of treble, mezzo-soprano, alto, and baritone. Only the third motet, *Si peccaverit*, has a tenor clef instead of the baritone.[92] The presence of secret modulations in the second and fourth pieces of the tetralogy cannot be regarded as coincidence. For these are the mystic sections: the prophecy of John and the appearance of the risen Christ. The connection between the two pieces manifests itself also by the unity of the textual sources: both are taken from the Gospel according to St. Mark, the one text from the first chapter (verses 7–11) and the other from the last chapter (verses 14–18). The text of the motet *Videntes autem stellam* derives from the Gospel according to St. Matthew (2:10–11), the text of *Si peccaverit frater tuus* from the Gospel according to St. Luke (17:3–4).

Venit fortior post me

In the prophecy of St. John there is a double secret modulation on the words "ille vero baptizabit vos spiritu sancto" (but He will baptize you with the Holy Ghost) (Ex. 51, measures 17–28). The preceding words "ego baptizavi vos aqua" (I have baptized you with water) are set entirely in F major; Jesus's baptism through the Holy Ghost is symbolized by Waelrant by the use of an initial secret modulation toward F minor, which leads back to F major and is followed, after the repetition of the prophecy, by a secret modulation toward D major. The code-note for the first modulation is the E in the alto. Its change to E flat is motivated by the preceding E flat in the discant. The E flat in the alto, however, changes the A in the

[89] *Ibid.*, No. 2.   [90] *Liber primus*, No. 5.
[91] Cf. the table of accidentals in the preceding chapter.
[92] Throughout the entire work we give the harmonies as written, without transposing the chiavette, since we are here concerned with definitive confirmation of the composer's mode of notation. The original clefs are indicated in the examples which gives the reader the opportunity to make the possible clef transpositions himself.

discant to an A flat. The progression of a fifth in the voice part in itself calls for the lowering of A to A flat: E♭-D-C-A(♭)-A(♭). We have already found a number of such progressions of a fifth in other modulations. In Clemens's *Qui consolabatur me* we have E♭-C-C-B♭-A♭; in his Job motet, B♭-A♭-G-F-G-G-F-E♭; in his *Rex autem David*, E♭-D-C-A♭; in Crecquillon the same idea: E♭-D-C-A(♭). But there seems to be weighty evidence against the adoption of the modulation. If one takes E flat as code-note, the voice-leading of the alto brings about a tritone: A-A-G-G-G-E♭. Since it was customary, however, to use the tritone in such a way that its evasion induced a modulation, it would be strange, indeed, to find it here used with reverse implication. Light on the problem is furnished by the text itself. The preceding words, "ego baptizavi vos aqua," end on the notes A-A-G-G-G and the new "ille vero" begins on E flat. This is not simply a logical caesura, rather is it an antithesis, which in the more modern music of that era was likely to find expression in a plastic musical antithesis. Of the tritone A-E♭ little is now perceptible, anyway, since it is bridged over melodically by the thrice-presented G, harmonically by the E flat, sounding one semibreve earlier, in the discant. The return is here likewise effected by a suspension on the dominant—C_{43}^5—which makes the resolution toward F major obvious. The modulation consists of F-c-A♭-f-b♭-f-C⁴³-F³.

The code-note for the second modulation is F(sharp) in the soprano. Favoring the sharpened reading are the preceding twice-presented F sharp in the tenor and the explicitly demanded C sharp and F sharp in the cadence terminating on D major. The question here is not whether this is a modulation or not—inasmuch as the cadence in D major is specified through the use of accidentals—but whether or not the modulation is consistently carried through. "Why," one might ask, "does Waelrant insert so obvious a sign as the *subsemitonium modi* at the exit of this passage, while leaving unindicated the decisive sharp for the code-note?" The answer is, "Because the secret character of the modulation would in this way be lost." If we take the idea of *secret* art as the point of departure, however, then the question would be: "What accidentals must the composer insert in order to erect a signpost for a modulation and at the same time to preserve its secrecy and its double meaning?" We soon realize that Waelrant's notation is the only one possible if the modulation is to be hinted at, but not written out. The unusual interval of the major sixth,[93]

[93] Had Waelrant inserted the sharp before F, he would openly have been demanding the use of an interval which for melodic purposes was virtually barred (see note 95).

which Waelrant here presents in a particularly effective form, is drawn into the picture in order to represent the extraordinary. The last shred of doubt disappears when the passage is compared with the first secret modulation in the cycle's Resurrection motet, which we are about to examine. We discover that the two modulations so closely conform that they can be considered variations of the same theme. We have already pointed out the close connection between the two motets. Unity such as that which exists between the two almost identical secret modulations is no mere coincidence. The inner relationship is made clear by the text: in the first motet John prophesies baptism by the Holy Ghost, in the last, the risen Christ imbues the disciples with His spirit. What the first motet prophesies, the last fulfills.

The novel feature of this double modulation is the use of chromatic readings toward both flat and sharp keys. The first modulation leads to F minor, the second to D major; this means a chromaticization of the tonic (F major) and of its parallel key (D minor). The linking together of minor and major, of flat keys and sharps, becomes fully comprehensible only when we recognize that this association is used by Waelrant in order to portray the power of transmutation of baptism by the Holy Ghost. Minor becomes major, and major becomes minor, or, in the language of the time, a minor third becomes a major third, a minor sixth even becomes a major sixth. In order to emphasize this, the a'-f#''-e''-d'' in the soprano is preceded by a'-f''-e''-d''.

How well this double modulation fits into Waelrant's harmonic style is illustrated by the measures preceding and following the secret modulation. The measures 29–36 following it lead from D major, the end of the double modulation, through G major, C major, F major, E flat major, to B flat major (Ex. 51). Noteworthy is the long-drawn-out chord of E flat major on the name "Jesus." [94] The measures 9–14 preceding the passage end in a little secret, but obligatory, modulation touching upon C minor and F minor and occurring on the word *eius* (His), referring to Jesus.

Recumbentibus undecim discipulis apparuit illis Jesus

The Resurrection motet contains several secret modulations toward sharp keys. Each one occurs at a particularly appropriate spot: the first, to celebrate the apparition of the risen Christ ("apparuit illis Jesus"); the second on Jesus's words, "praedicate evangelium *omni creaturae*" (preach the gospel to *every creature*); the third on the words "in nomine meo" (in

[94] Cf. note 78 above.

my name). All three modulations are introduced in the same manner, through a sharp on the signature-indicated B flat and on F, in other words through B natural and F sharp; all three cadence in D major. The code-note for the first modulation is the F in the tenor (Ex. 52). In favor of raising it to F sharp we have (1) the voice-leading itself: B-D-F(♯) (however, it should be noted that the text calls for a caesura after the B); (2) the signature-indicated F sharp in the contratenor, which sounds but a minim earlier; (3) the voice-leading in the contratenor, which subsequently requires F sharp and B; it is written G-F♯-A-B♭-B♭-F-A-A-A-F♯; read chromatically it sounds G-F♯-A-B-B-F♯-A-A-A-F♯; only in this reading do the discrepancies of the voice part disappear; (4) the harmonic structure, which in diatonic interpretation calls for a chord of the augmented fifth (F-C♯), which Waelrant always avoids in a clausula, as in the motet *Et veniat*, analyzed in the preceding chapter. Measure 6 of the present motet does have an F above a stipulated C sharp:

$$a' \quad g' \quad f'$$
$$f' \quad e' \quad d'$$
$$c♯' \; - \; d'$$
$$a \quad - \quad b♭$$

But here it is first of all a case of the far less harsh sounding interval of the diminished fourth; secondly, the dissonance is mitigated by the contrapuntal associations, while in the passage we are analyzing the augmented fifth is followed by an augmented fourth; thirdly, measure 6 has the dissonance in the middle voices, while in our example the most exposed outer voice, the soprano, is involved (Ex. 52). Here, too, Waelrant joins to the unusual modulation the seldom-used interval of the major sixth, this time in the bass.[95] While all three modulations are introduced through sharps on F and B flat, their endings are accompanied by sharps on C and F; only the third modulation has no F sharp, because it cadences on the empty fifth-and-octave chord on D and consequently requires only the leading tone C sharp. The secret modulations are so girded with accidentals at both beginning and end of the enigmatic passage that a diatonic reading is almost impossible. The first modulation consists of

$$c\text{-}G\text{-}D\text{-}b\text{-}A^{11\text{-}10\text{-}9\text{-}10}_{6\text{ —— }5}\text{-}D.$$

The continuation—toward the fundamental tones F-C-B♭—occurs in all

---

[95] The case under discussion is no isolated one. The major sixth appears as a dead interval, for example, in Clemens's motet *Vox in rama audita est*, on the repetition of the words "ploratus et ululatus" in the bass (G-e; meas. 35–36). Waelrant uses it as an actual interval in the first tenor of the motet *Veniat super me*, on the word "exprobrantibus" (cf. Ex. 44, meas. 34).

the voices after a pause has ensued. The voices enter slowly: d-d'-D minor triad.

The code-note of the second secret modulation at the end of the first part of the motet ("praedicate evangelium omni creaturae") is the note B flat in the alto (Ex. 53). In favor of raising it to B natural we have (1) the voice-leading itself; the preceding F sharp calls for B natural: F#-G-Bb-Bb-A = F#-G-B-B-A; (2) the B(natural), which sounds a minim beforehand in the discant; (3) the bad final cadence resulting from the diatonic reading:

$$
\begin{array}{ccc}
e'' & d'' & d'' \\
c'' & - & a' \\
f' & - & f' \\
f & - & f
\end{array}
$$

The major seventh is not only harsh but also very unusual in a final cadence; its change in the chromatic reading to the euphonious minor seventh

$$
\begin{array}{c}
e'' \\
c\sharp'' \\
f\sharp' \\
f\sharp
\end{array}
$$

is fully justified by the cadential character which here predominates; (4) the sound of the alto part, likewise calling for chromatic reading, the last note being an explicitly indicated F sharp. In diatonic reading it would lead to the progression of a diminished fifth, which is most unlikely, since it appears on the strong beat of a final cadence. We place side by side the chromatic and diatonic versions of the part:

Diatonic: F#-G-Bb-Bb-A-A-A-C -C -A-A-F#

Chromatic: F#-G-B -B -A-A-A-C#-C#-A-A-F#

The modulation consists of the following:

$$
\text{g-D-G-b-f\sharp-D-e}^{6\sharp}_{3}\text{-f\sharp}^{7}_{5 \atop 3}\text{-f\sharp}^{6}_{3}\text{-A}^{43}\text{-D} \quad (\text{Ex. } 47)
$$

We find the third secret modulation on the words "in nomine meo." Here, too, the code-note is the B flat = B natural in the contratenor. The B natural is made likely by the F sharp which precedes by two notes and has an accidental, even though it is implied as *subsemitonium modi*; it is *obligatory* because of the preceding B natural in the tenor, which comes in while the B flat (= B natural) of the contratenor is still sounding, giving us $\text{D}^{43}\text{-G-b-A}^{65}_{43}\text{-D}$ (Ex. 54).

The three secret modulations display a striking similarity of pattern. There are not only the resemblances revealed in the accompanying accidentals but harmonic and even melodic ones as well. This may be seen at a glance:

Harmonic structure of the three modulations:

1. c-G-D - b — $A^{11-10-9-10}_{6 \underline{\quad} 5}$-D

2. $\quad$ g-D -G-b-f♯-D-$e^{6♯}_{3}$-$f♯^{7}_{5}$-$f♯^{6}_{3}$-A^{43} - $\qquad$ D
$\qquad\qquad\qquad\qquad\qquad\qquad_{3}$

3. $\qquad$ D^{43}-G-b $\qquad$ - $\qquad$ A^{65}_{43} - $\qquad$ D

Individual voice-leading:

Bass	Tenor	Alto
1. g - d-b-a	1. d'-f♯'-d' -f♯' - e'-d'	
2. d-g-a - b-b	2. d'-f♯'-c♯'-f♯'-g'-f♯'-e'-d'	2. f♯'-g'-b'-b'-a'
3. d-g - b-a	3. d'-f♯' - e'-d'	3. g'-f♯'-g'-b' - a'-g'

The voice-leading of the alto, which in this passage is the top voice, since the discant pauses, corresponds to the discant of 1: d″-c♯″-d″-f♯″-e″-d″, of which the discant of 2. appears to be a figuration: d″-f♯″-c♯″-f♯″-e″-d″-c♯″-d″.

How do the modulations fit into the harmonic structure as a whole? There is a signature of one flat in all four voices; strictly speaking, this is transposed Dorian. But the score of the two parts together contains no less than sixty-three specified accidentals,[96] so that the individuality of the Dorian mode is completely obscured. We showed briefly, in the preceding chapter, how this affects the melodic structure; naturally it affects the harmonic structure as well. The plagal cadence C minor-G major is used several times with admirable effect; we frequently find D major stipulated; and on the words "linguis loquentur novis" (they will converse with new tongues) Waelrant lets the harmonies B flat and A major succeed each other without interposition of another chord. In a word, the chromatic interpretation in no way contradicts the spirit of the whole; although the modulations fit into the general style of the piece, they are climactic moments of harmonic brilliance. We give the first modulation in its context, (Ex. 52) in order to show how marvelously its sonority and its expressive power depict the apparition of the Risen Christ, in a way comparable to the bright glow with which painters of that era represented the Resurrection.

With the analysis of the two Jesus motets of Waelrant we have exhausted our repertoire. It is clear that in this field as in others, Waelrant goes his own way. In the entire Netherlands group he is the only composer

[96] Compare the statistics of accidentals in the preceding chapter.

to modulate to sharp keys; he is the only one to use secret modulations in order to symbolize Jesus's mystic personality. In his tetralogy devoted to the life of Jesus he creates a new type of evangelical motet, which in its tenderness and pathos as in the novelty of its musical language points the way two generations ahead to the style of a Heinrich Schütz. It also becomes clear that Waelrant's alteration of the old solmization system was but the theoretical side of his practical innovations as composer, replacing as it did the six old solmization steps with seven new ones and bringing under the name of "bocedization" the octave in place of the hexachord.[97] All the evidence tends to picture Waelrant as radical innovator: [98] as editor, as theorist, as composer, and it was as composer that he was most gifted. He has thus far not been recognized in his full significance.[99]

It cannot be mere coincidence that with the exception of Gombert, who is a special case, we were able to find examples only among the works of Crecquillon, Clemens, and Waelrant. Examination of the Antwerp motet repertoire of 1556 clearly reveals that these three masters were leading spirits of the modern movement; equally in accord with conclusions based on our previous investigations is the fact that the lion's share of chromatic composition was done by Clemens and Waelrant.[100] It is not impossible that only a small proportion of the works dedicated to the secret chromatic art was actually published. That would be in keeping with its *secret* character as well as with the fact that "modern" chromaticism met with stiff opposition. Enough of this work was published, in any event, to enable us to form a clear picture of its character and technique.

[97] The system of "bocedisation" derives its name from the first three syllables bo, ce, di of the new solmization. Waelrant evidently follows Bartholomeo Ramis, who was the first to use the octave system in place of the hexachord system, introduced a new type of solmization, and in his general musical philosophy may be regarded as a forerunner of Hubert Waelrant and of kindred spirits toward the middle of the *cinquecento*. It has been pointed out in the Lasso monograph that Waelrant occupied a special place in the Netherlands, both as composer and as editor, and that there is little doubt of his having been in Italy, even as tradition would have it. His concurrence with Ramis's theories provides further confirmation of his having been there. Waelrant was born in 1517, was active in Antwerp from 1544 on; his stay in Italy must have occurred toward the end of the third decade or at the beginning of the fourth decade of that century. Ramis's revolutionary theories were at that time still the subject of the most animated controversies, and it is more than likely that the youthful Waelrant took an active part in them.
[98] He is called "novorum appetens" by Franciscus Sweertius in *Athenae Belgicae*.
[99] Professor van den Borren, in the latest issues of the *Biographie nationale belgique*, offers a judgment of Waelrant which takes into account the more recent research.
[100] See A. Mb., p. 87: "it is . . . clear that Clemens and Crecquillon approach the modern style from different vantage-points. Clemens's preoccupation is with the sound and harmony, Crecquillon's with the word and declamation . . ." Waelrant creates the synthesis of the two.

ADRIANUS PETIT COCLICO

Crevel (*Adrianus Petit Coclico*, p. 281) discusses a chromatic modulation from the 33d motet of the "Consolationes piae ex psalmis Davidicis" of Adrianus Petit Coclico, 1552, which bear the collective title *Musica reservata*. Let us examine the passage to ascertain whether or not it represents a "secret modulation" in the Netherlands sense of the word (Ex. 55). In measures 5–7 there are six accidentals: four instances of a flat preceding E and two of a flat preceding A; they determine the fate of the modulation. Even without these six accidentals, however, there could be no question of a secret modulation, since the code-note (the E flat in the tenor in measure 5) does not admit of a double interpretation. Even if this E flat were not explicitly stipulated, it would have to be regarded as obligatory, since the note at the fourth below, B flat, which has just sounded, allows of an E flat only. All of Coclico's six accidentals are, strictly speaking, for this reason superfluous.

The contrast with the Netherlands practice is even more obvious in the return. In a literal sense there is no return. Neither does Coclico modulate back in artistic fashion nor does he lead his modulation into a cadence, which would be its natural termination and which would provide natural resumption of the diatonic. He is even guilty of a serious error of style and structure. In the manner so often adopted by his Netherlands contemporaries he introduces the modulation through the motif of a fifth, which, with progressive transposition, of necessity leads into the circle of fifths, since to replace the perfect fifth with the diminished is forbidden. Thus the very thing which at the outset the musician is supposed to avoid, in order to make the modulation possible, Coclico himself in the end perpetrates: he shortens the pentachord "to the compass of a diminished fifth" (Van Crevel, *Adrianus Petit Coclico*, p. 287). We here see Coclico trapped in the labyrinth of his own modulation, from which he knows no escape save through violence and at the cost of transgression of the musical rules at that time under observance (Ex. 55, meas. 11–12).

In a purely artistic sense, too, Coclico lags far behind his Netherlands compatriots. Through the stereotype five-times-repeated sequence and through the monotonous rhythm, the modulation, which in the music of the Netherlanders is a climax of expression, becomes in Coclico's motet a climax of boredom.

Van Crevel adds to an analysis of Coclico's modulation the following general observation: "From the foregoing it is evident—the same being true, *mutatis mutandis*, of all such modulations through the circle of fifths by the at that time "modern" composers of the Josquin-Willaert school—that this is no modulation in our present-day sense; in other words, that although the end result of such a modulation may be harmonic in its implications, it is the result, not of harmonic media, but of purely melodic media. This is confirmed by the fact that we were able fully to probe such a modulation only through melodic analysis. For the most part the harmonic realm was still unexplored virgin territory, one not yet to be mastered from the vantage point of an organized harmonic system, but to be ventured—sporadically and still through melodic media, in certain cases through systematic transposition of a pentachord."

Here we must take issue with Van Crevel. An entire series of "modulations through the circle of fifths by members of the Josquin-Willaert school" is to be understood only from the harmonic viewpoint, not from the melodic. We allude to the innumerable modulations in works of Italian composers of that time, all of which are indicated by accidentals and are the result of purely harmonic media. Many instances are analyzed in the Lasso monograph. How does it come about, then, that almost all our secret modulations are to be grasped only through the melodic approach? The Italians and the Netherlanders living in Italy openly indicate chromaticism; the musicians living in the Netherlands, who use no written-in chromatic indications, are obliged to find other ways of bringing about the chromatic tonal phenomenon: they discover that harmonic changes without written stipulation are to be attained through melodic means, such as motif transposition. The facts are consequently the reverse: the composer is motivated by harmonic considerations; the melodic media he utilizes stand exclusively at the service of the harmonic concept and were invented in its behalf.

Chromatic progressions in secret modulations.—We found instances of chromatic progressions openly indicated by accidentals in motets by Waelrant and Clemens non Papa (Ex. 1–7); we encountered, furthermore, chromatic progressions in the chromatic clausula (Ex. 14–19). The reader may have discovered that the progression of two half tone steps occurs also in a number of motets as a by-product of the secret modulation. In Example 20, measure 69–71, the soprano proceeds from B natural via a thrice-repeated C to D flat; in Example 26, measures 44–45, the soprano goes directly from G flat via F to E natural; in Example 35, measure 20, the soprano has the progression D flat-C-B natural; in Example 36, measures 61–62, the contratenor moves from G flat via F to E natural; in Example

39, measures 50–51, the tenor goes from C flat via B flat to A natural. In all instances, except Example 20, we have to do with a chromatic cadence. There are, moreover, a number of examples containing indirect chromatic progressions, for instance: G-F-G flat (Ex. 22, meas. 9, tenor); A flat-G-A natural (Ex. 36, meas. 62–63, soprano); C flat-B flat-C natural-D flat (Ex. 39, meas. 54–55, tenor); G-A flat-G flat (Ex. 50, meas. 38–39, contratenor); A flat-G-A natural (Ex. 51, meas. 21–22, soprano).

Conclusion

Of all the valuable results of the chromatic movement, the secret chromatic art may be regarded as one of the most outstanding, a unique phenomenon appearing in the interval between two tone-systems, even between two musical philosophies. This phenomenon is also of interest in a geographical and cultural-historical sense, for the secret chromatic art defines the precise limits of the Netherlanders' approach to the new musical language of the Italians.

III: TECHNIQUE AND SYMBOLISM OF THE SECRET CHROMATIC ART

SINCE the motet literature of this period only has been systematically examined by the author and even in this field not all the sources were at his disposal, it is fully conceivable that there are further discoveries to be expected in the field of the secret chromatic art. For this reason it seemed of particular importance to develop a method which might serve as guide for further investigation.

The individual analysis of secret modulations has shown that a consistent technique is the basis and foundation stone of the secret chromatic art. At the same time the intention to express meaning by the use of chromaticism became clearer with each example. Our present task is to define the essential elements of both the technique and the symbolism of the secret chromatic art.

TECHNIQUE OF THE SECRET MODULATION

The unstipulated modulation imposes upon the composer two principal problems: *approach* and *return*.

Approach

Since the modulation is not indicated by the notation, it has to be announced through the voice-leading, motif structure, harmonic and contrapuntal texture. Most difficult to achieve is a clear indication of the place at which the modulation is to begin. For, once the modulation has been set in motion, its continuation is almost automatic. The composer devotes his greatest attention to the preparation of the point of departure. In order to work out the opening phase of a modulation, he concentrates on bringing a single note in such melodic and harmonic context that—according to *musica ficta*—it suggests chromatic reading, thus constituting the starting point for a modulation. This note, which indicates the tonal code for the modulation, we call "code-note." We have seen how much depends upon the code-note; its role is particularly clear in the riddle motet of Clemens non Papa, *Qui consolabatur me.*

Insertion of accidentals.—Although the modulation is not stipulated, the key signature, or accidentals at the opening of a modulation, are used in the function of messengers of the coming harmonic change. In Examples

22, 25, 26, 28, 31, 32, and 39 the key signature is the factor of influence, while in Examples 20, 34, 35, 45, 47, 50–54 accidentals are used as signposts at the beginning of the modulation.

Voice-leading.—One of the principal means of indicating the code-note is to set it at the end of a motif built on a triad, a fourth, or a fifth in such a way as to cause its being given chromatic reading, lest there be a diminished triad, diminished fifth,[1] or an augmented fourth. (Cf. Ex. 20, 22, 26, 35–36, 39, 46, 48, 52–53.)

False relation.—The false relation is used in the same way. (Cf. Ex. 20, 22, 31, 50–54.)

Motif-transposition.—The chief means of getting a modulation started is to transpose a motif to a degree which calls for the insertion of accidentals. In Example 22 the triad motif F-D-Bb is repeated on E flat and hence requires insertion of A flat. In Example 20 the ostinato motif C-A-Bb-G-F is started on B flat and calls for chromatic reading of E and A. Clemens also uses the device of motif transposition in Ex. 25–27, 32, 34–36. Crecquillon transposes in Ex. 45 not a single motif but an entire four-voice phrase, with but slight variation; in Ex. 46 Gombert transposes the final motif of his motet from one degree to another. In Ex. 48 Waelrant also works with motif transposition, and in the middle of his motet *Et venit misericordia* (Ex. 50) restates the initial motif in transposition. The same procedure is followed in Willaert's riddle duo (Ex. 40–41).

Transposition-structure.—The same modulatory scheme underlies all these motif transpositions; they all modulate in the direction of the fourth above. The only variable factors are the number of transposed motif repetitions and the distance covered in the upper circle of fourths. In Examples 32 and 35 the motif is transposed to the first fifth below, respectively fourth above; in Examples 34 and 36 to the first and second fourths; in Examples 26 and 27, through the sequence of overlapping voices, either

---

[1] Van Crevel (*op. cit.*, p. 286) is of the opinion that I am wrong in classifying the diminished triad among the "forbidden sounds" of Lasso's day, since the use of the diminished fifth had been approved by such theorists as Aron and Zarlino. In support of his opinion he quotes Levitan, who in his essay, "Adrian Willaert's Famous Duo," writes: "Aron (*Lucidario in musica*, 1545, Lib. 2) and Zarlino (Istitutioni Harmoniche, 1558, pp. 180 ff.) . . . allow the use of the false fifth." Levitan does not pursue the question further. If we study the appropriate theoretical writings, however, we find that the deep-rooted aversion to the *mi-contra-fa* still existed even in Aron and Zarlino and that they conceded the use of the diminished fifth only under quite special conditions. What further escapes van Crevel is the evidence implicit in Levitan's quotation even of so late a theorist as Praetorius, who specifically forbids the use both of the tritone and of the diminished fifth. Furthermore, Praetorius's opinion is particularly pertinent, since he repeatedly refers to Orlando di Lasso and his age.

to the first, second, and third, or to the first, second, third, fourth, and fifth fourth above. In Crecquillon's motet *Domine Deus exercituum* (Ex. 45–46) we found in the interrelated closing measures of the two parts a fourfold transposition to the upper circle of fourths: G-C-F-Bb-Eb. Where there are repeated transpositions a single step in the circle of fourths is often omitted. Gombert follows this procedure in Ex. 47, transposing first to the second, then to the third, and finally to the fourth step in the upper circle of fourths, presenting only at the end of the modulation the omitted first fourth above. In the two modulations of the Lazarus motet, Examples 20 and 22, Clemens goes in the first instance directly to the second fourth above, in the latter example onward to the fourth step in the upper circle.

We find in the secret modulations the same transposition scheme as in the category of total transpositions discussed in Chapter 1, paragraph 2. Here, too, the Netherlanders carry their transpositions only to the flat keys. The one exception to this rule is Waelrant, who in the motet *Afflictus sum* (Ex. 48) transposes his motif to the second and the third fifth above, with an indication for a transposition to the fourth step in the upper circle of fifths. In other words, Waelrant is the only composer of the school to transpose to sharp keys, just as he is the only Netherlander to make systematic use of sharps as accidentals.

Return

The secret modulation causes a temporary excursion into the chromatic. Since the return to the diatonic is not stipulated through the use of naturals, it has to be brought about through the inherent musical development.

Cadence.—The transition from chromatic to diatonic is in every instance effected through the intercession of a cadence. In most cases it is a question of going from the minor key to the like-named major. The cadence is the natural transfer point in such a process. Suppose we take the case of a return from F minor to F major: through the cadence f-C[43], E flat is changed to E natural, in accord with the rule for the *subsemitonium*, and the door to F major is opened (Ex. 22, 27, 28 (D minor), 31, 32, 36, 51 (first modulation)). The chromatic reading can be followed only as long as it is called for by the voice-leading, harmonic structure, and general musical and expressive content.[2] The musical phrase, and with it the effi-

[2] Padre Fra Giovanni d'Avella, in his *Regole di musica*, Rome, 1657, expresses this same opinion, when he writes that the efficacy of an accidental lasts as long as does the

cacy of the stipulated or unstipulated accidentals, are both terminated in the cadence. In the two extensive modulations of the Lazarus motet the effect of the cadence is supported by the entrance of the diatonic ostinato.

Neutral sounds.—In order to facilitate the transition from major to like-named minor, the chromatic episode is often brought to an empty fifth or octave. Thus, between minor and major a neutral zone is set up (Ex. 25–26, 35, 46, 50).

Structural pauses.—Aside from the unwritten rests resulting from cadences, an actual pause is often inserted between the chromatic and diatonic zones, which likewise serves to cancel the effect of the accidental (Ex. 25, 28, 35, 46).

Text structure.—Closely allied to the musical phrasing is the text. The segment of the text bearing the chromatic episode always constitutes the close and climax of a series of repetitions of the same words. As though determined by natural law, a new portion of the text appears after each return to the diatonic. The only exceptions to this rule are the rare instances where the chromatic episode occurs at the end of the motet or at the end of Part 1 of the motet; in this case no new portion of the text is available. Since, however, the composer must effect a return to the diatonic, he is compelled to repeat once more the words of the chromatic episode. He tries to help himself in this situation by repeating only a part of the words (Ex. 34), by avoiding all repetitions in the soprano part, leaving the approach to the diatonic to other voices (Ex. 46–47), or by closing in the tonality toward which the modulation is moving (Ex. 53).

Symmetry

A peculiarity of the secret modulation is that it hardly ever occurs in isolation, but accompanied by several analogous passages within the same motet. Thus, we find in the Lazarus motet (Ex. 20–21) two extensive modulations, one at the beginning, the other toward the end of Part 1; Parts 1 and 2 of the work are intentionally contrasted by confronting the chromatic style in the one with the diatonic in the other. The two secret modulations in *Jesus Nazarenus* also occur in the first part of the motet (Ex. 31–32). The *Lamentation of David* (Ex. 25–28) contains four modulations; the first is parallel with the third, and the second with the fourth. The two modulations in the *Plaint of Job* (Ex. 35–36) are likewise paired, while the

---

affect: *tanto canterà per quel modo o segno accidentale, quanto durerà quel senso et affetto.* (Schwartz, "Zur Akzidentienfrage im 16. Jahrhundert," *Wiener Kongress-bericht,* 1909, p. 109.)

modulation at the end of the *Plaint of Rachel* (Ex. 34) appears twice in different versions. In the motet *Qui consolabatur me* (Ex. 39) we find a mathematically exact balance between the diatonic first section and the chromatic second section, which recalls the symmetrical bipartition in Willaert's chromatic riddle duo. In Crecquillon's *Domine Deus exercituum* (Ex. 45–46) the chromatic closing measures of Parts 1 and 2 are built along identical lines. In Waelrant's *Venit fortior post me* (Ex. 51) we find the interesting case of a double modulation, first toward flat and subsequently toward sharp keys, while in his *Recumbentibus undecim discipulis* (Ex. 52–54) all three secret modulations are interrelated. The secret modulation in Waelrant's *Et veniat* (Ex. 50) has no analogue within the motet; equilibrium is maintained, however, through its position at midpoint of the work and through its relationship to the beginning of the motet. Waelrant's *Afflictus sum* (Ex. 48) likewise presents only one secret modulation, but this finds its tonal analogue in the chromatic style of the entire motet,[3] while the modulation's close on D major finds its counterweight in other cadences: on D major (measure 31) and on A major in the motet's plagal close. The musical analogues display a noteworthy sense of tonal balance. The repeated symmetrical excursions to distant tonal centers establish a feeling of balance which the isolated modulation would jeopardize.

Double Meaning

Double meaning is an inherent characteristic of the secret art. When in addition to its obvious literal meaning the text must also embody a secret significance, it must needs be susceptible of two interpretations. To the world at large it offers its outward form, reserving for the circle of the initiated its secret meaning. We found only a few exceptions to this ambivalence—e. g., the end of Part 2 of the motets of Crecquillon and Gombert (Ex. 46–47); in both cases the code-note is explicitly chromaticized through the use of an accidental, the ensuing modulation, in consequence, becoming necessary instead of optional. Although a diatonic reading is almost always possible, it is compromised time and again by the insufficiencies likely to put the initiated on the lookout for the secret meaning. By virtue of its musical flow and of its incomparably more expressive and more beautiful sound, the secret reading reveals itself as the one actually intended.

[3] See p. 60.

SYMBOLISM OF THE SECRET MODULATION

The secret chromatic art is no musical game; therefore it is not an end in itself, but an attempt to create a new musical symbolism and new media of expression. Chromaticism always represents the extraordinary. With Crecquillon it is a device to symbolize the oneness of God; with Gombert, the oneness of the Passion and the Annunciation; with Waelrant the supernatural personality of Jesus, the baptism through the Holy Ghost, the Resurrection, and the exhortation to preach the Gospel. Chromaticism is, however, above all the symbol of deepest suffering; this is its implication in Waelrant's psalm motets and in Clemens's *Plaints of Jesus, David, Rachel,* and *Job.* Again and again we find chromatic treatment given to such highly emotional concepts as crying, lamenting, mourning, moaning, inconsolability, shrouding one's head, breaking down, and so forth.

In the Italian madrigal the same concepts find expression through the medium of chromaticism. There they represent man as entangled in his earthly passions, while in the music of the Netherlands they symbolize the devout believer struggling with the burden of sorrow which God has laid upon him to test his faith. Thus, the Netherlanders transform not only the chromatic technique of the Italians, but likewise their chromatic symbolism.

Secret Symbolic Connections

We have just pointed out the connection between the modulations of a given work. These connections are of a spiritual as well as tonal and formal nature.

There are also symbolic connections both between various works of the same master and between works of various masters. Thus, Waelrant interrelates through the use of the same motif: in his two mystic Jesus motets, the Baptism by the Holy Ghost and the Resurrection; in the two Psalm motets, human desperation and divine mercy. Likewise, between Josquin's *Stabat Mater, Planxit autem David,* and *Absalon fili mi* we find motif connections, through which Mary's sorrow and David's are brought into inner relation with each other. Most astonishing of all is the secret link between Josquin's Absalom motet on the one hand, and, on the other, Clemens non Papa's Lazarus motet and Gombert's motet of the Virgin. The connection is revealed both in the use of Josquin's motif *sol-mi-ut-fa* and in the chromatic modulation associated with it. The symbolic meaning has already been discussed; it is a phenomenon which can perhaps be considered a harbinger of the leitmotif.

IV: COMPOSERS, PUBLISHERS, AND TEXTS IN RELATION TO INSERTION OF ACCIDENTALS AND TO CHROMATICISM

IN ORDER to obtain a clear idea of the relation between insertion of accidentals, chromaticism, texts, composers, and publishers, we draw up in the following table a comparison of the works considered in the present study, on the basis of their original sources. Many works listed in one group of the table 1 likewise occur in another group; this is shown by the totals at the end of the table, which also indicate that there are all in all forty works under consideration, of which twenty-four are by Clemens non Papa, seven by Waelrant, four by Crecquillon, three by Benedictus (Appenzeller), one by Gombert, and one by Josquin Baston. Twenty-six works are composed on texts of lamentation and supplication, the rest on texts devoted to scenic representation, religious mysticism, or verses from the Song of Songs. Twenty-four works were published by Phalèse, ten by Waelrant, and eight by Susato. In this connection it should be noted that Susato's name occurs only once under the heading "frequent stipulated accidentals," and under "stipulated chromaticism" likewise only once, and that he published in the first edition not a single work containing secret modulations. His only publication of this nature was a reprint, in 1558, of the chromatic motet of Clemens non Papa, *Qui consolabatur me*. This table is based on Netherlands publications, except when a work was available only in a foreign edition.

COMPARISON OF THE MOTETS ON THE BASIS OF THEIR ORIGINAL SOURCES

I. Key Signature of Two Flats	II. Frequent Stipulated Accidentals	III. Stipulated Chromaticism	IV. Unstipulated Chromaticism	V. Secret Modulations

COMPOSERS

I. Key Signature of Two Flats	II. Frequent Stipulated Accidentals	III. Stipulated Chromaticism	IV. Unstipulated Chromaticism	V. Secret Modulations
Clemens non Papa 14	Clemens non Papa 6	Clemens non Papa 2	Clemens non Papa 7	Clemens non Papa 6
Crecquillon 3	Waelrant 7	Waelrant 1	Waelrant 1	Waelrant 4
B. Appenzeller 3	Crecquillon 1	B. Appenzeller 1	Crecquillon 1	Crecquillon 1
	J. Baston 1		B. Appenzeller 1	

PUBLISHERS

I. Key Signature of Two Flats	II. Frequent Stipulated Accidentals	III. Stipulated Chromaticism	IV. Unstipulated Chromaticism	V. Secret Modulations
Phalèse 16	Phalèse 5	Phalèse 2	Phalèse 5	Phalèse 6
Susato *a* 7	Waelrant 10	Waelrant 2	Waelrant 2	Waelrant 5
		Susato 1	Susato 4	Susato 1

TEXTS

I. Key Signature of Two Flats	II. Frequent Stipulated Accidentals	III. Stipulated Chromaticism	IV. Unstipulated Chromaticism	V. Secret Modulations
Lamentation 11	Lamentation 5	Lamentation 3	Lamentation 3	Lamentation 7
Supplication 6	Supplication 2	Song of Songs 1	Supplication 3	Supplication 2
Song of Songs 1	Scenic Representation 4		Forgiveness 1	Prophecy 1
Sayings of Jesus 1	Sayings of Jesus 1		Fear 2	Resurrection 1
Consolation 1	Prophecy 1		Wonder 1	
	Song of Songs 1			
	Prayer of Thanks 1			

TOTALS

I. Key Signature of Two Flats	II. Frequent Stipulated Accidentals	III. Stipulated Chromaticism	IV. Unstipulated Chromaticism	V. Secret Modulations
20 works	15 works: 1 in Group I	4 works: 3 in Group II, 1 in Group I	10 works: 5 in Group I; 2 in Group II; 1 in Groups I and III	11 works: 5 in Group II; 4 in Group I; 1 in Groups II and III; 1 in Group IV

a The same work was often printed by various publishers.

V: SECRET CHROMATIC ART AND ITS RELATION TO THE "NETHERLANDS ARTIFICES"

IT HAS LONG been taken for established fact that the generation of Clemens non Papa had lost interest in the "Netherlands artifices." The present inquiry demonstrates, however, that the old love of riddles, which some time earlier had brought into being the famous "artifices" of the early Netherlands school, toward the close of the Netherlands epoch again burst forth in a flame which, however quickly spent, was of surprising intensity.

Common to both is an enigmatic character, a spirit of speculation, an admirable technique, and a strong tendency toward symbolism. Even the idea of tonal ambiguity, which plays so important a role in the chromatic art, already existed in the old artifices. Ockeghem wrote a *Missa cuiusvis toni* to be sung in any church mode. Together with his riddle canon this work was recently the subject of a most interesting analytical inquiry,[1] in which the author refers to Glareanus's classification of tonally ambiguous compositions: "Καθολικὰ in cantu, hoc est Cantiones instituere, quae multis cantarentur modis ad cantorum propemodum arbitrium, ita tamen, ut Harmoniae ac consonantiarum ratio nihil secius observaretur." Levitan remarks in this connection: "According to Glareanus, the works belong to the class of catholica, which means that they can be sung in various ecclesiastical modes at the discretion of the singers, provided the ratio or the relation of the harmony and the consonances be observed." Even Nicolas Gombert wrote a Magnificat *Tertii et octavi toni* and another *Sexti et primi toni*.[2]

The contrast between the old and the new "artifices" is as marked as their resemblance. The old artifices proclaim their enigmatic character in the title, in a motto, or in added instructions; the new conceal it. The old artifices reached a high degree of abstraction and of spirituality, but they stood in the way of beauty of sound and musical expression, which are the very source and substance of the new. The old arts embody a mathematical *jeu d'esprit*; the relationship between the mottoes (*canones*) of the old artifices and music itself is arbitrary, not organic. Their purpose is allegorical-practical. By referring to an arbitrarily introduced Biblical

---

[1] Levitan, *Ockeghem's Clefless Compositions, The Musical Quarterly*, XXIII (1937), 4.
[2] Schmidt-Görg, *Nicolas Gombert*, p. 216.

quotation the singer is supposed to find the clew to practical execution of the musical text, many details of which are left unspecified. Ingenious as these allegorical-artistic games are, they remain extraneous, something *added to* the music. In the secret chromatic art a long-restrained passion breaks forth from the apparent frigidity of Netherlands counterpoint, a religious fervor seeks new paths to living expression. The old "artifices" are of an allegorical nature, that is, they seek to represent an idea in an intellectual way, by means of arbitrary or conventional associations; the chromatic art creates new sound symbols, which through sound itself and without recourse to rational explanation express what the composer wishes to say. Objectively, both allegorical and symbolic representation are excellent in their own right.

A similar distinction holds for the tonally ambiguous compositions of the Netherlanders, the "catholica," whose pattern comes closest to that of the secret chromatic art. By including in the title the words "cuiusvis toni" they, too, intimate to the performer that he is dealing with a riddle to be solved. In their case, likewise, the enigmatic character has no inner relationship to the text. Above all, they know no distinction between an exoteric and an esoteric solution, inasmuch as all solutions are equally possible and equally admissible, and since no fundamental difference between them exists. The secret chromatic art, on the other hand, shatters the old tonal system; instead of the coördination of the various ecclesiastical modes, two entirely different tonal concepts are contrasted.

In reviewing the evolution of enigmatic art in Netherlands music, one is tempted to apply the Hegelian historical perspective. The Netherlands artifices undergo the dialectic process of thesis, antithesis, and synthesis. Their ingenious, subtle, technical-mathematical, and allegorical-theological constructivism is confronted with two new and opposing concepts: the concept of the organic work of art (the motet constructed from beginning to end on the principle of contrapuntal imitation); the concept of music as expression (*musica reservata*). The new art constitutes a synthesis of expression and technique of construction, of old counterpoint and new harmony. Out of love of riddles is born a secret art; out of sly theology, newly awakening fervor of belief; out of allegory, symbol.

VI: A GERMAN SOURCE ON THE SECRET CHROMATIC ART

THE TREATISE *Musica* of the German theorist Nicolaus Listenius [1] offers what amounts to clear and irrefutable evidence of the technique of secret modulation. As could be expected, the passage in question occurs in a chapter on *musica ficta*. Here is the quotation in full.

De Cantu Ficto.

Superest cantus Fictus, seu ficta Musica, de qua ut potero, brevissime dicam. Nihil enim attinet multis ac magnis uti ambagibus, in re non admodum obscura, cuiusque non sit permagnus usus. Est igitur Musica Ficta, cantus contra Scalae situm aeditus, hoc est talis in quo voces, debitos suos locos non sortiuntur, veluti cum Vt in E, Re in F, Mi in G etc. aut secus canitur. Fingit enim haec in quacunque clave quamcunque vult peregrinam vocem, contra clavis naturam et proprietatem. Cuius mutatio et evitatio, in plerisque cantilenis est transpositio. In quibusdam sine discrepantia omnino mutari nequit. Exempla sunt ubique obvia, quare tantum hic exemplum unius vocis, pro eius declaratione ac immutatione ponam.

On *musica ficta*.

There remains the *cantus fictus*, or *musica ficta*, of which I shall speak as briefly as possible. For it is of no avail to indulge in much circumlocution in a matter that is not very obscure and of which not very much use is made. *Musica ficta* designates a composition constructed counter to the position of the scale, i.e., a composition in which the tones do not choose their due places, as, for example, when *ut* is sung in E, *re* in F, *mi* in G, etc. For *musica ficta* feigns on each tone of the scale any chromatic tone it wants, counter to the nature and propriety of the tone. To change and eliminate this, most compositions make use of transposition. In certain works it is impossible to change everything without discrepancy. Examples are extant everywhere; therefore, I give for explanation and as a substitute only this one-voice example.

(Ex. 56.)

The important thing is the example. Here we find a tenor voice without a key signature; the melody starts on C, the first accidental occurs on B flat, the second on E flat, the third on A flat, and the fourth on D flat. Since Listenius wants to explain the use of *musica ficta*, he has to stipulate what otherwise remains unstipulated. This example may be compared with

[1] The *Musica Nicolai Listenii* is available in a facsimile edition by G. Schünemann, Berlin, 1927, Vol. VIII of the "Veröffentlichungen der Musik-Bibliothek Paul Hirsch."

the preceding examples of Netherlands secret chromaticism. It will be found that it employs exactly the same technique: modulation consistently carried through the circle of fifths by means of melodic progressions of fourths and fifths. The similarity seems to indicate almost an identity of motives. Let us compare, for example, the beginning of Listenius's example with the motif which Clemens uses in his *Qui consolabatur me* to lead toward the code-note. We transpose Clemens's motif for convenience.

Clemens: d-a-bb-g-g-f-eb

Listenius: c-a-bb-g -f-eb

(Ex. 39, measures 41–43.)

But all motives used by Listeninus to establish a new chromatic tone are familiar to us from the Netherlands sources examined.

Very strange, however, is Listenius's comment: "It is of no avail," he says, "to indulge in much circumlocution in a matter that is not very obscure and of which not very much use is made." It may be worthwhile to examine this terse statement more closely. So far as I know Listenius is the first theorist to offer a concrete example of secret chromaticism. In any event, the procedure was novel enough to warrant detailed comment. Instead, Listenius denies the necessity of using what he calls "ambages," that is, circumlocution, evasion, obscurity, ambiguity, "ambages" may mean all this. He does not declare the matter to be clear, but to be "not very obscure." And as a further reason for his failure to explain the technique he uses in the example, he maintains that "not very much use is made" of it, whereas in the last sentence he states that "examples are extant everywhere." Perhaps one may explain his vague and contradictory utterances by assuming that they are the result of two opposite tendencies in his mind: on the one hand he may wish to record the strange technique; on the other hand he may not be inclined to give away too much of it. Again, it seems that the expert only is addressed. Certainly the schoolboys, for whom the book was written, could not understand the implications of this example.

One thing is certain: Listenius succeeded by his evasive comment in eluding the modern music historian. For it seems hard to explain why this example, which is simply revolutionary in the history of *musica ficta*, remained unnoticed by modern scholars, though it has been available in a facsimile edition for many years. Not even the editor himself seems to have noted it.[2] In another passage of a contemporary theorist about secret chro-

---

[2] Schünemann says only: "Ganz kurz wird von der Musica ficta gesprochen." Introduction, p. xxiii.

maticism (to be taken up in the next chapter) we shall find a similarly evasive manner of expression, and in the discussion of the religious background of the secret chromatic art we shall come back to Listenius's comment and its possible meaning. The importance of Listenius's example rests in the fact that it constitutes an unmistakable confirmation on the part of a contemporary theorist of the existence of modulations that go as far as four steps in the circle of fifths beyond the key signature and of the technique used to establish a chromatic tone by melodic progressions of fourths and fifths. It represents documentary evidence as to the correctness of our method in basing the decipherment of the secret modulations on the principles of *musica ficta*. Our analysis of practical examples, however, adds to the melodic element singled out by Listenius the elements of harmony, counterpoint, motif transposition, and text relation strengthening its foundation so much the more. On the other hand, Listenius's comment on *musica ficta* poses the question as to where those examples of the modulatory technique are which he maintains "are extant everywhere." The secret chromatic art furnishes the answer, presenting as it does the only evidence of contemporary music that uses the technique illustrated in Listenius's example. It has already been pointed out that many of the works containing secret chromaticism may never have been published at all, while others may not yet have been found. Striking is the fact that Listenius's treatise appeared for the first time in 1537. This early date may serve as an indication for future research in this field.

VII: A NEW APPROACH TO MUSICA RESERVATA

IT IS A STRANGE coincidence that at the same time as secret modulations make their appearance in the Netherlands, a new musical concept arises, which from the very beginning is shrouded in mystery and over which musicologists have been breaking their heads for decades. This concept is known as *musica reservata*. The first works published with secret modulations bear the date 1549; first mention of the concept of *musica reservata* occurs in the year 1552, in the *Compendium musices descriptum ab Adriano Coclico* and in the same author's *Consolationes Piae ex Psalmis Davidicis*, which bear the generic title of *Musica Reservata*.

Ever since in his dissertation on *Ivo de Vento* [1] Kurt Huber raised for discussion the question of *musica reservata*, on the basis of Sandberger's references to it,[2] the concept has become a veritable crux in Renaissance music research. Year after year books appear in which a new solution or a new definition of this concept is offered. That to this very day new solutions are being offered is in itself evidence that no convincing interpretation has been found. It is not only the solutions proposed, but above all the methods employed, which are inadequate. This was discussed in an unpublished essay on *The Problem of Musica Reservata*, which I wrote a decade ago.[3] At that time I had come to the conclusion that "one can do no more than acknowledge the enigmatic aspect of this concept. . . The *musica reservata* can legitimately be the subject only of historical research, not of aesthetic interpretation.[4] History, theory, style, and change of style in Renaissance music must be investigated in a much more exhaustive fashion before a new and fruitful discussion of the concept of *musica reservata* can be arrived at." I am of the same opinion today. The

---

[1] Chap. iii.
[2] *Beiträge zur Geschichte der bayerischen Hofkapelle unter Orlando di Lasso*, Vol. I.
[3] In van Crevel, *Adrianus Petit Coclico* (pp. 305 ff.), the reader will find a condensation of this study, which, incidentally, should be dated as of 1933.
[4] Van Crevel is of the opinion that the antithesis here used is likely to lead to misunderstanding, "that musicological research and aesthetic interpretation should be mutually exclusive." I should think that the context would make my meaning clear. What I reject is the premature, the historically unfounded interpretation. Our first task is not to interpret the concept of *musica reservata*, but to find out in what way it was interpreted by its contemporaries. Did it mean the same thing to all of them? Did they know its origin? These questions and others shall be answered if possible.

solution of the *reservata* problem can at best be but the by-product of
a general investigation of Renaissance music. Exploration of the known
is the safest way to an approach of the unknown.

Secret Chromatic Art and Musica Reservata

Thus the discovery of the secret chromatic art, which a decade ago
was unknown to me, offers as by-product what seems a provocative opportunity to make a fresh approach to the problem of interpreting this
hotly discussed concept. One shortcoming of existing interpretations is
that they either leave the linguistic origin of the term unexplained or are
able to provide for it only a far-fetched derivation at best. We have already
seen that in the secret chromatic art we have before us a music with two
different faces: the face presented by the notes, which is turned to the
outer world, and the hidden face of the inner relation and secret associations, which is available only to a circle of informed and initiated—the
face, in other words, of a true *musica reservata*. Our previous investigation has also demonstrated that the secret chromatic art has its very being
in the new relationship between word and tone, which is also the core of
musica reservata.

A New Document on Musica Reservata

The only theorist known to have mentioned the concept of *musica reservata*, without, however, having offered any explanation for it, is Coclico.
But there is another theorist who not only mentions the concept, but even
defines it in musical terms—Nicola Vicentino, in his *L'antica musica ridotta
alla moderna prattica*. It is strange that the passage in question has until
now remained undiscovered, although Vicentino has been widely read
and quoted in more recent years and his writings have been drawn into
discussions of the *musica reservata*. Jeppesen refers to Vicentino in his
remarks concerning the *reservata;* in his splendid work *Die mehrstimmige
italienische Laude um 1500,*[5] he writes as follows: "The 'musica reservata,'
as Josquin's pupil Adrian Petit Coclico terms it and as it is commonly
referred to, bears as its motto 'dare spirito alle parole,' its aim being, first
of all, interpretation of the text and representation of emotion. Its stylistic
antithesis is the second great musical current of the cinquecento, the
'musica comuna,' which term I borrow from Vicentino; this is the customary tradition-bound and perhaps even 'academic' music, which derives

[5] Page lii.

more from a purely musical impulse." Jeppesen then quotes Vicentino: "Edition of 1557, p. 48 v.," where the ecclesiastical modes are discussed. After the observation that in the event of Italian texts which are uncommonly expressive and variable as to mood "il Compositore potrà uscire fuore dell'ordine del Modo & intrerà in un'altro, perchè non haurà obligo di rispondere al tono, di nissun Choro, ma sarà solamente obligato à dar l'anima, à quelle parole, & con l'Armonia dimostrare le sue passioni" (that is, after Vicentino has characterized the typical *reservata* viewpoint), he remarks further that he will now discuss the treatment of the first mode, how the composer is to use it: "nella Musica communa, cioè in quella che tutti professori di Musica compongano in questo tempo."

In this connection van Crevel remarks (*Adrianus Petit Coclico*, p. 321):

Used to characterize the music of the entire sixteenth century, the antithetical concept *comuna reservata* could lead to a mistaken impression—that it is established fact that this antithesis had for musicians of the sixteenth century the same implication as for Jeppesen. His use of the term *musica comuna* as opposed to *musica reservata* is founded, however, only on one passage of Vicentino's *L'antica musica ridotta alla moderna prattica* (1557), where the latter, in his discussion of the ecclesiastical modes, points out that the composer "in the event of Italian texts which are uncommonly expressive and variable as to mood *potrà uscire fuore dell'ordine del Modo & intrerà in un'altro*," i. e., that he does not have to remain within the prescribed limits of the ecclesiastical mode, but that this is not the case in the *musica comuna*. Jeppesen forthwith assumes that Vicentino, in his mention of freedom of treatment in connection with ecclesiastical modes, "characterized a typical *reservata* viewpoint," although this term does not occur in Vicentino's writings.

In this connection there are two points to be stressed:

(1) Jeppesen sees the *reservata* viewpoint in its connection not only with ecclesiastical modes but also mainly with Vicentino's demand that in the case of a certain type of text calling for expressive treatment the composer watch out for one thing above all: to endow the words with soul, to "show" their passions through the harmonies. To whom does this not recall the "ante oculos ponere" in Quickelberg's definition of *musica reservata*? Only on the basis of this positive demand is a negative stipulation voiced—that the composer may disregard certain purely musical laws, such as, for instance, the purity of the modes. There is no doubt that Jeppesen is justified in seeing in this demand of Vicentino's a "typical *reservata* viewpoint," "although this term does not occur in Vicentino's writings."

(2) But the term actually does occur in Vicentino's treatise. On page 10ᵛ [6] Vicentino says the following:

... comprendono che (come li scrittori antichi dimostrano) era meritamente ad altro uso la Cromatica & Enarmonica *Musica riserbata* [7] che la Diatonica, perche questa in feste publiche in luoghi communi à uso delle vulgari orecchie si cantava: quelle fra li privati sollazzi de Signori e Principi, ad uso delle purgate orecchie in lode di gran personaggi et Heroi s'adoperavano.

... they understand that (as the ancient writers demonstrate) the chromatic and enharmonic *musica reservata* deservedly had a different application from that of the diatonic, since the latter was sung in public festivals and in common places, being designed for ordinary ears: whereas the former was used in private entertainments of the nobility and of princes, for refined ears and to sing the praise of great personalities and heroes.

In its bearing on *reservata* research the importance of Vicentino's statement cannot be overestimated. So far as we know today, he is the only Italian theorist ever to have used the term; he is also the only one to give not only a definition of the concept but also an explanation of its origin and its etymological significance. The passage quoted shows that Jeppesen's differentiation between *reservata* and *comuna* has foundation in fact, defining as it does on four separate counts this distinction:

	Musica Comuna	Musica Riserbata
Music	Diatonica	Cromatica Enarmonica
Place	Luoghi comuni	Privati sollazi de Signori e Principi
Purpose	Feste publiche	In lode di gran personaggi et Heroi
Audience	Vulgari orecchie	Purgate orecchie

Vicentino gives us a series of musical and sociological characteristics of *musica reservata*. It is music for the few—for people with cultivated taste, not for the common folk; [8] it is, furthermore, music reserved for the

---

[6] Edition of 1555. It is a strange fact that Hermann Zenck, who evidently read the above passage since he quoted from it in another context, did not discover its bearing on *musica reservata*. In his essay on *Nicola Vicentino's "L'antica musica"* (1555) (*Festschrift für Theodor Kroyer*, p. 88) he writes: "Vicentino has explored this musical science in Ferrara; before princes and noblemen he demonstrated his chromatic and enharmonic art that was destined only for 'cultivated ears' (*purgate orecchie;* diatonic music is sung *in feste publiche in luoghi communi à uso delle vulgari orecchie*)."

[7] Italics not in the original.

[8] In this context Baldesar Castiglione's demands on court music deserve consideration, since they prove the ideal of exclusiveness to be a rather old one (Castiglione's *Il Cortegiano* appeared in 1528, but was written between the years 1508 and 1516): "Therefore let the Courtier resort to music as a pastime and almost unwillingly, *and not before vulgar people nor very many* ..." (author's italics).
"Then, as to the time for enjoying these various kinds of music, I think it is when-

nobility and princes and designed for the praise of heroes and eminent personalities, not for popular festivals; music, finally, whose sociological character comes to the surface in its choice of particular genera, in its preference for the chromatic and the enharmonic. In addition to these sociological and musical characteristics of *reservata* we are given still another, which has to do with performance. In Book II, chapter 23, Vicentino makes the following distinction: "nella Musica che sarà cantata à piena voce; ma nella musica da camera, cioè, quando si canterà piano." Here it is apparent that Vicentino identifies chamber music with music sung softly.[9] Since he defines *musica reservata* as chamber music, we must add to its characteristics that of soft and discreet performance.

The Sociological Character of Musica Reservata

How does Vicentino's definition of *musica reservata* compare with the evidence thus far available? It is worthy of note that our first record of the existence of *reservata* is in connection with a court, that of Albert V, Duke of Bavaria. Both Dr. Seld and Samuel Quickelberg belonged to it; the well-known passage from a letter of Vice-Chancellor Seld likewise points to the character of *musica reservata* as something designed for private performance, in contradistinction to church music. Dr. Seld writes to his prince in the above-mentioned letter of April 28, 1555,[10] as follows:

---

ever a man finds himself in familiar and beloved companionship and there are not other occupations. But above all it is fitting where ladies are present, because their aspect fills the listener's heart with sweetness, renders it more sensitive to the tenderness of the music, and quickens the musician's soul."

"As I have already said, it pleases me well that *we should avoid the crowd and especially the ignoble crowd*" (Italics not in the original). Quoted from B. Castiglione, *The Book of the Courtier*, trans. by L. Eckstein Opdycke, pp. 86–87.

[9] Elsner, *Untersuchung der instrumentalen Besetzungspraxis der weltlichen Musik im 16. Jahrhundert in Italien*, p. 63: "Softness and mildness are specifically demanded of the musician performing chamber music. The theorists make a great distinction between the loud sounds suited to large halls and that suitable to the drawingroom, which had to be tender and soft. This differentiation is maintained throughout the entire sixteenth century, not only in Italy but elsewhere likewise." It is interesting, indeed, that at the court of Italian princes chamber music was often called *musica secreta*. In this connection we find in the same work (p. 61) the following: "Music is often performed by small groups for the private pleasure of the prince. This music is of so private a character—indeed, it is often called 'secret'—that little information concerning it is available. . . . From Fiorino we learn that he conducted all concerts in Ferrara—'capo di tutte le musiche dell' Altezza sua, cosi publiche, come private, domestiche é secrete'" (Bottrigari, *Il desiderio*). Could there be some connection between the *musica secreta* and what Vicentino called *riserbata*?

[10] Sandberger, *Beiträge zur Geschichte der bayerischen Hofkapelle unter Orlando di Lasso*, III, 300.

Gefelt mir vast wol, hatt ain gerade guette Stimm, sonderlich In der kirchen. So habe ich Ine volgends mitt mir haimb gefuert vnd zu gast gehapt, auch andere vnsere gesellen mit Ime. Da wir allerlay Reseruatam vnd Ime vnbekhante Musick gesungen, befind, das er der aller gewiss genug. . . .

It is clear from this letter, as van Crevel also points out,[11] that the "*reservata*" which Seld placed before the singer was sung in his home after he and his guest had returned from church.

There is a whole series of other documents, however, which bear witness to the private nature of *musica reservata*. There are the famous Penitential Psalms of Orlando di Lasso, which Albert V left to posterity in a luxurious manuscript lavishly decorated with miniatures, and for which the explanatory notes were written by Samuel Quickelberg, humanist and physician of the court of Munich. In this volume of commentaries, which was bound in smaller format than that of the massive choir book, Quickelberg gives his well-known and often-quoted definition of *musica reservata*, according to which this style of musical composition consists in

. . . ad res et verba accommodando, singulorum affectuum vim exprimendo, rem quasi actam ante oculos ponendo . . .	adjusting [the music] to the text and its subject matter, in expressing the power of the different human emotions and in suggesting the textual content as vividly as if you saw it represented before your very eyes . . .

Although completed in 1560, the Penitential Psalms were not made available to the general public until printed in 1584; up to that point they had been "reserved" for the prince. This exclusive character was in extraordinary fashion accentuated, furthermore, by the handsome artistic garb with which this work was endowed, at Albert's behest, by the court painter Hans Mielich. Albert V singled out for similar distinction other works of Lasso. Sandberger tells [12] about an autograph of Lasso's bound in parchment, with decorations painted by Hans Mielich. This was not in choirbook format, but consisted of four small, elegantly bound part books in oblong quarto, whence it is safe to assume that the setting was for a small choir. This manuscript bears no date, but the portrait of the composer accompanying each part book specifies his age as twenty-eight, whence Sandberger's conclusion that 1558 was the year of their composition. Since,

---

[11] *Adrianus Petit Coclico*, p. 307.
[12] "Mitteilungen über eine Handschrift und ein neues Bildnis Orlando di Lassos," in *Ausgewählte Aufsätze zur Musikgeschichte*, pp. 34 ff.

in accord with van den Borren,[13] we assume the year 1532 to be Lasso's birthdate, the completion of the manuscript would occur in the year 1560. This manuscript contains two cycles: (1) the nine *Sacrae lectiones ex propheta Job;* (2) the *Prophetiae Sibyllarum.* The first collection was published in 1565—"ex ejusdem Principis immensa ac incomparabili munificentia in communem omnium usum." The second cycle was published, not during the composer's lifetime, but posthumously, by Lasso's son Rudolf (1600).[14] With respect to style, both works may be considered typical of *musica reservata.* The *Prophetiae Sibyllarum* are written in the extremely chromatic idiom described by Vicentino. Both in general plan and in minute detail they are inspired by their text. Still awaiting publication in a modern edition, the *Sacrae lectiones novem ex Propheta Job quatuor vocum in officiis defunctorum cantari solitae* not only preserve with painstaking exactitude the rhythm of the spoken word but likewise reproduce the tone and the manner of speech and of lamentation, bringing Job's words to stirring musical expression. Although not composed in the chromatic style of the *Sibyllae,* they do not hesitate "to depart from the accustomed order of the ecclesiastical modes" and are endowed with a wealth of bold modulations, which arise out of one consideration only—"à dar l'anima à quelle parole & con l'Armonia dimostrare le sue passioni." Both cycles were reserved, during a certain period at least, for the exclusive use and pleasure of a prince.

[13] A. Mb., p. 3, note 1.
[14] It is strange that H. J. Therstappen, who recently published a new edition of the *Prophetiae Sibyllarum,* should in his effort to assign a date of composition to the series of sibylline works have taken no notice of this manuscript. He does not accept Sandberger's assumption that the *Prophetiae* are a work of Lasso's youth. Possibly influenced by Helmut Osthoff, who gives no reasons for his opinion (see his "Einwirkungen der Gegenreformation auf die Musik des 16. Jahrhunderts" in *Jahrbuch Peters* 1934, pp. 40–41), Therstappen maintains that the sibylline cycle belongs to Lasso's late works. Had Therstappen never seen the Paris publisher Adrian le Roy's well-known letter to Lasso (Sandberger, *Beiträge,* III, 309)? In this letter the publisher tells Lasso, among other things, about his having shown the sibylline series to the King (Charles IX) and about the latter's enthusiasm over the chromatic works. The letter is dated "le 14ieme Jour de Januyer 1574," and the publisher speaks of the compositions, not as something which he had just received, but as something which he happened to have with him on his visit to St. Germain: "Je luy ay outreplus presente quelque petite cromatique et de Cibiles que Javoys par deca." This date automatically puts the *terminus post quem non* back as far as 1573. There remains the above-mentioned manuscript containing the *Sibyllae* and a picture of Lasso at the age of twenty-eight, which brings the date back still farther, to 1560. Both these documents, so important where the *Prophetiae* are concerned, are in this connection not even mentioned, let alone discussed, by the editor. Instead of that he works with stylistic arguments, to which there is no withholding the reproach of vagueness and superficiality.

We know of two other works which are explicitly specified as belonging to *musica reservata:*

1. One was Adrianus Petit Coclico's settings of the psalms, to which he gave the title *Musica reservata.* Published in Nuremberg by Montanus and Neuber, this collection can under no condition be considered court music. But from Dr. Seld's letter alone we can see how Vicentino's typically southern antithesis of open-air music and chamber music was transformed in northern cities to a like antithesis: church music and chamber music. From the Dedication and the Preface of Coclico it is obvious that he intended these psalms, not for use in the church, but as home music. He dedicates his collection to the Nuremberg senate and says:

. . . collegi consolationes ex Psalmis et scriptis Propheticis his temporibus calamitosis apprime utiles, quas Melodiis concinnavi, et eas potissimum vestrae prudentiae dedicare conatus sum, ut θελκτήριον [15] habeatis aliquod, quo animos vestros presertim hoc turbulento tempore, in regenda republica, curis et solicitudine gravatos reficiam, atque recreem. . . .

Coclico explicitly dedicates his *Musica reservata* to the relaxation and edification of the elders of Nuremberg, and in so doing he defines them as music for the home.

2. The other work belonging to *musica reservata* is the madrigal collection, 1556, of Vincenzo Ruffo. Its title's allusion to *reservata* was first pointed out by Helmut Osthoff. Van Crevel (p. 299) quotes this title from Eitner: *Opera nuova di musica intitolata armonia celeste nella quale si contengono 25 madrigali, pieni d'ogni dolcezza, et soavità musicale; composti con dotta arte et reservato ordine dallo Eccellente Vincenzo Ruffo.*[46] Since it consists of madrigals, the work obviously belongs to the domain of chamber music.

In the light of the foregoing, what shall we say of the Netherlands motets dedicated to secret chromaticism, which we classify among the *musica reservata?* The motet *Jesus Nazarenus* dedicated to the brothers Schetz furnished direct evidence that these sacred works were likewise intended, not for the church, but for the home, for a circle of initiated performers and amateurs. There is indirect evidence to that same effect. (1) In Leyden are preserved the massive choir books which in the years 1549–1565 were written for St. Peter's Church in that city. The motet repertoire of these choir books, which likewise contain masses, Magnificats, hymns, and so

[15] Magic pacifier.
[16] Vogel, *Bibliothek der gedruckten weltlichen Vocalmusik Italiens.*

forth, affords a very dependable survey of the motet-output of the Netherlanders of that period. Here we find a series of works already known to us
from the published repertoire of Susato, Phalèse, and Waelrant. It may be
considered symptomatic that these choir books contain no works with
secret modulations, though many of them are composed on texts used in
the liturgy of the Church.[17] But we likewise find not one of the works
associated with "the modern trend in the Antwerp motet repertoire" com-
manding attention because of particularly careful treatment of the text
and affect.[18]

The one exception is the Lazarus motet of Clemens non Papa in the
Codex conservatoire Bruxelles MS 27.088. The choir book under discussion
is from the year 1563.[19] The exception is, perhaps, accounted for by the
comparatively late date of origin of the manuscript and by the great
favor in which this motet was held.[20] The ambiguity of the secret modulations was, indeed, the cap of invisibility of the more "modern" works. We
have seen, however, that these motets were to such an extent dedicated to
the solution of problems of expression that the reason for their omission
from a definitely ecclesiastical repertoire is obvious.

2. We have reliable evidence of the fact that, particularly in the first
half of the sixteenth century, the Netherlands motet developed from a
predominantly ecclesiastical form to one more and more appropriate to
the uses of private gatherings and of performance in the home. With manifest emphasis Susato discusses this change in the Preface to his first publication of five-voice motets, in the year 1546: [21]

Nunc vero foelicissimo hoc nostro aevo, caeteris liberalioribus artibus (ceu exlongae hyemis situ) rursum reflorescentibus, cum hanc artem non tantum in principum aulis Divorum templis (ut pridem) sed in domibus, sed in conclavibus, sed in honestis bonorum coetibus, undique ab eruditis, nobilibus, a probissimis quibusque, summo in precio haberi, mire exercitari ac magna cum gloria, in italia, in gallia, in germania typis excusam. . . .

Today, however, in this our most fortunate age, while the other liberal arts, as out of long hibernation, again come to flower, this art likewise is held in highest honor not only in the courts of princes, or in shrines (as formerly), but in dwellings, in private houses, in all honorable gatherings of good citizens. The cultivated, the distinguished, the high-minded everywhere join in its praise and practice, and the printed page spreads its glory throughout Italy, France, and Germany. . . .

[17] Chapter VIII, *The Religious Background.*
[18] A. Mb., pp. 53–78.
[19] v. d. Borren, *Inventaire des manuscrits*, p. 181.
[20] A. Mb., p. 94, note 2.
[21] *Ibid.*, p. 47.

Waelrant, the second Antwerp publisher of importance and the most emphatic exponent of modern tendencies, provides his motet publications with the following title: *Sacrarum cantionum (vulgo hodie moteta vocant) quinque et sex vocum ad veram harmoniam concentumque ab optimis quibusque musicis in philomusorum gratiam compositarum; liber. . . .*[22] In this title the composer-publisher states that his publications are for lovers of music, or, more precisely, "for friends of the muse." Since a publishing house is first and foremost a business enterprise, it is easy enough to perceive who were the buyers of these musical publications.[23] In the words *ad veram harmoniam concentumque*, furthermore, it is by no means farfetched to see an allusion to the new musical style, of which Waelrant was a stanch advocate. This is confirmed, moreover, by his dedicatory preface to the "Inclyto Augustae Vindelicorum Patricio, Marco Welsero" in the third book of his motets for five or six voices (1555), which reads as follows: "Nos in communem omnium gratiam, novos quosdam . . . congessimus sacrarum cantionum modulos, qui nova Harmoniae suavitate, & audientium aures, & attendentium mentes sunt oblectaturi. Eos autem perelegantibus his formis quam castigatissime descriptos, tibi inclyte Marce, dicatos volumus." With gratifying clarity, Waelrant's dedication to the famous merchant confirms the motet's transformation from an ecclesiastical art form, closely bound to liturgy, to a free and untrammeled medium of expression, whose chief aim is to arouse the aesthetic feelings of a music-loving audience. He appeals characteristically enough both to the mind and to the ear of the listener, since *musica reservata* based completely on the text asks for both aural and mental understanding; he speaks of elegance of form and of a new sweetness in the harmony. This, as well as all the other documents, confirms Vicentino's sociological definition of the *reservata* as music for private circles.

Concerning Performance of the Musica Reservata

At this point mention should be made of Kurt Huber, for it was he who called attention to two attributes of *reservata:* chamber music style and intimate manner of performance.[24] From the scholarly standpoint, however, we cannot accept his conclusions as being valid, for they are

[22] *Ibid.*, p. 48.
[23] In general, one is justified in concluding that the publication of musical works in printed copies was designed first and foremost for the music-loving public; of this there is further evidence in the fact that for ecclesiastical purposes handwritten choir books with their particular part arrangements were kept in use and even newly written out.
[24] *Ivo de Vento*, pp. 109 ff.

based on false premises; indeed, that is the reason why in his analysis the true and the false are so closely intermingled. Until recently his viewpoint has held sway: that the basic issue in the *reservata* was a new style of performance, whose uniqueness lay in the practice of embellishments, of improvised ornamented song. In the essay on behalf of a critical evaluation of *reservata* research, mentioned above, I wrote: "In speaking of the *reservata*, Coclico says nothing about coloratura; in speaking about coloratura, he says nothing about *reservata*. The same condition obtains in the letters of Chancellor Seld." [25] Huber built his thesis on the writings of Coclico and of Dr. Seld, both of whom make use of the concept of *musica reservata* without in any way defining it. Since both speak of the practice of coloratura, though, indeed, never in connection with *reservata*, he links *reservata* and coloratura singing together.

At present writing we know of two authorities who give a definition of *musica reservata:* Samuel Quickelberg and Nicola Vicentino; the latter was unknown to Huber. Neither of these men ever mentioned *musica reservata* and coloratura singing, even remotely, in association with each other. Ludovico Zacconi, however, published in the year 1592 a treatise entitled *Prattica di Musica,* which takes up in considerable detail the *gorgia,* or, as we know it, coloratura.

Although Zacconi never mentions the concept *musica reservata,* and although he lived a generation later, his textbook on coloratura singing is considered by Huber to apply to *musica reservata;* indeed, Huber even calls this text an "organon of the practice of reservata." [26] According to Huber, Zacconi defines the goal of the vocal art as "the soft, distinguished 'singing of gentlefolk,'" whence Huber arrives at his definition of *reservata* as discreetly performed chamber music designed for the pleasure of princes. The basis of this chamber music style is "the completely one-sided solistic training, treatment, and conception of the singing voice." Thus does Huber mingle truth with error, having built both on erroneous premises.[27] Yet it remains Huber's indisputable merit to have drawn at-

---

[25] In a thorough analysis of Seld's letters (*Adrianus Petit Coclico,* pp. 239 ff.), van Crevel has taken up the latter question in greater detail.

[26] I pointed this out in my first study of *reservata.*

[27] Sandberger protested not long ago (*Orlando di Lasso und die geistigen Strömungen seiner Zeit,* p. 31, note 6) against the concept of *musica reservata* as solo music. He identifies chamber music with music for soloists, whence he concludes that *reservata* cannot have been chamber music. I see no compelling reasons for the identification of chamber music with music for soloists. Sandberger also gives no reasons. In most cases, however, one is justified in assuming a setting for a small group—small, that is, by comparison with the common usage of church music.

tention to the *musica reservata* in his dissertation which in many aspects is a brilliant piece of research.[28]

But to return to the subject: improvised coloratura was a common practice of the singers of that day. Coclico and Zacconi were both singers and teachers of singing, and as such they taught coloratura singing. Our inquiry has made it clear that *musica reservata* had to do primarily with a style of composition, at whose center stood the intimate union of word and music and with it the transition from a purely melodic-melismatic style to a syllabic-declamatory. This in itself contradicts any likelihood of a fusion of *reservata* with coloratura solo singing, while a study of contemporaneous theorists shows that the composers of the day were by no means edified by the singers' "embellishment" of their works. In this matter Zacconi himself may certainly be considered a trustworthy witness. He tells of composers who renounced performance rather than deliver their compositions to the mercies of coloratura singers. They preferred to hear their works in simple and straightforward execution, so that the listener might perceive with what art the music had been contrived and constructed.[29]

Zarlino's judgment carries more weight than any, but so far as I know his recorded opinion has not yet been consulted. In a chapter addressed to singers [30] he takes up the cudgels against the practice of improvised diminution in choral singing as follows:

Quelle cose che appartengono al Cantore sono queste: Primieramente dee con ogni diligenza provedere nel suo cantare, di proferire la modulatione in quel modo, che è stata composta dal Compositore; non fare come fanno

The singer must watch out for the following things: in the first place he must take particular care, in the act of singing, to deliver his part as composed by the composer. He must not do as do certain persons of scant un-

[28] From an article by Walter H. Rubsamen, "Kurt Huber of Munich," *The Musical Quarterly*, XXX (April, 1944), 2, I learned that Kurt Huber was recently executed by the German government "as one of the instigators of a student demonstration against the regime." Huber's death is one of the few precious signs that have reached us here to prove that there are some men left at German universities who dare defy the rule of brute force and who oppose the systematic substitution of falsehood for truth in every field of scholarship as practiced by the Nazi regime. Kurt Huber will be remembered as long as scholarship is understood to be an eternal search for truth, however elusive and remote, and an uncompromising fight against untruth, however firmly entrenched.

[29] ". . . io ho trovato alle volte i compositori haver fuggito l'occasione di far cantar alcune cose loro: per non farle cantare, et darle in mano de simili cantori: non per altro solo perchè haveano a piacere di sentirle con li accenti schietti, et semplici: acciochè s'udissero gli artificii con che le haveano tessute et fatte" (F. Chrysander, *Ludovico Zacconi als Lehrer des Kunstgesanges, Vierteljahrsschrift für Musikwissenschaft*, VII, 368).

[30] *Istitutioni harmoniche*, ed. of 1558, Lib. III, pp. 239-40.

alcuni poco aveduti, i quali per farsi tenere più valenti più savij de gli altri, fanno alle volte di suo capo alcune diminutioni tanto salvatiche . . . tanto fuori di ogni proposito, che non solo fanno fastidio a chi loro ascolta; ma commettono etiandio nel cantare mille errori: conciosia che alle volte vengono a fare insieme con molte Discordanze due, o più Unisoni, o due Ottave, overamente due Quinte & altre cose simili, che nelle Compositioni senza alcun dubio non si sopportano.

derstanding, who, because they consider themselves more efficient and more clever than the others, from time to time insert extempore such wild . . . and utterly inappropriate embellishments that they not only annoy the listener, but likewise commit a thousand errors in singing. Not seldom do they produce, quite apart from many dissonances, two or more unisons, or parallel fifths and octaves, or other things of this nature, which in compositions simply cannot be tolerated.

These are the words of a composer and a theorist to whom in all choral music clear projection of the words was a prime consideration: it is significant that precisely such an authority should have put himself on record as being against free diminution in choral singing. The same insistence upon clear diction and against the practice of diminution was voted by the elders of the Council of Trent.[31] Decades later we find the same viewpoint in the writings of the dramatic theorist Ingegneri. According to Ingegneri's *Della poesia rappresentativa 1598,* "great importance must be attached to clarity of diction; for this reason it would be wise, for example, in tragedies, where only the chorus enters, to choose only a few, but particularly good, voices. The words must not get lost in coloratura—*'nè se ne perda sillaba nelle fughe e nelle tante diminuzioni che s'usano al giorno d'oggi.'* " [32] Is there any reason to assume *musica reservata,* the first great movement in the history of polyphony to make the word the focus of attention, to reduce the melismatic principle to a bare minimum in order to arrive at as syllabic a setting as possible, its constant aim being the clearest possible projection of the text—is it reasonable to assume that such a movement at the same time was meant to give new impetus to the singers' taste for improvised coloratura? We have seen that all pertinent considerations argue against such an interpretation.

Even in purely instrumental music the practice of embellishments by no means won the unanimous approval of musicians of the day. Otto Kinkeldey makes this clear in the discussion of the Spanish theorist Juan Bermudo contained in his rewarding book *Orgel und Klavier in der Musik des 16 Jahrhunderts.* He quotes the following passage from Chapter xliii of Bermudo's

[31] Cametti, *Palestrina,* pp. 82–83.
[32] Elsner, *Untersuchung der instrumentalen Besetzungspraxis,* p. 48. Italics not in the original.

Declaración de instrumentos musicales, 1555: "But there is one counsel in particular which the performer must follow, and that is not to make any melodic ornamentations, but to play the music as it was set down by the composer. If, perhaps, music in the older style needs such embellishments because of its clumsiness, the music of our day does not need them. I do not see how the accusation of being ill-bred, ill-informed, and impertinent can help but be leveled at the player who in performing the works of outstanding artists adds embellishments. The performer who embellishes does nothing less than revise, or, more precisely, he blurs all the parts. . . In robbing good music of good melody and lovely imitation, he ruins it. . . The music of our day is so complex, so complete in its melodic line, that it is at one and the same time foundation and embellishment." What particularly interests us in Bermudo's declaration is its new line of reasoning: that precisely the music of around 1550 (he cites Morales, for example), unlike the older music, is so carefully elaborated and so precisely provided with ornaments by the composer himself that for this reason alone it no longer tolerates any additions on the part of the singer. If one compares for example the *Fuga quatuor vocum ex una*, which Coclico publishes both in its original and with embellishments,[33] the programmatic intention is clear. A theme as primitive as this—especially in the foursquare rhythm typical of Coclico ♩♪♪│♩♩, imitated at the unison and at equal time intervals—would, indeed, need some sort of ornamentation in order not to become deadly in its monotony. But one would search in vain in the motet repertoire of around 1550 for an example of such a theme handled in such a way.

The Chromatic Style of Musica Reservata

Greater difficulties are encountered in investigating the chromatic character ascribed by Vicentino to *musica reservata*. The chief difficulty is the scarcity of sources, which makes it impossible to examine all the compositions referred to as *musica reservata*. Such examination is indispensable; we must leave it, however, for future research. For the time being it can certainly be established that Lasso, the composer *par excellence* of *musica reservata*, was likewise one of the most significant chromaticists;[34] that

[33] Newly printed in Haas, *Aufführungspraxis der Musik*, "Handbuch der Musikwissenschaft," p. 114.

[34] It is in his comment to the Penitential Psalms that Quickelberg speaks of Lasso as a *reservata* composer. The chromaticism of the Penitential Psalms, therefore, will be of interest. It has not been observed yet that all seven Psalms work with exactly the same tone material. Each Psalm uses eleven tones. If we examine these eleven tones, we find that each time they fit into the pattern of a scale comprising two chromatic tetrachords. The only chromatic tone missing is the one between the tetrachords, or in

Coclico busied himself with chromatic problems, at the very least; that Ruffo may be counted among the adherents to the chromatic movement. I have in my possession no madrigals from the above-cited Ruffo collection of 1556, but I do have scores of a number of his madrigals from the year 1555.[35] Full of modulatory ideas, they display a great harmonic freedom, employing frequent chromatic alteration of fundamental tones.[36] In any one of these instances chromaticism is an important medium of expression standing at the service of the central idea of *musica reservata:* to represent in music the text and its pictorial and emotional content.

If at this point we return to the Netherlands motets with secret chromatic modulations, we can make the following pronouncements concerning them: (1) They are strikingly preoccupied with the narrative and expressive elements of the text. (2) One of their media of expression is chromaticism. (3) Their chromaticism is always devoted to the expression of the strange, the solemn, and the extraordinary. (4) They are composed, not for the church, but for a circle of initiated amateurs and professionals. They are intended for performance in the home.

If we compare these pronouncements with Quickelberg's definition on the one hand and with Vicentino's on the other, it is obvious that the works analyzed in the present inquiry belong to *musica reservata* and that they were so reckoned by their contemporaries.

We must not, however, lose sight of the differences between the Netherlands concept of *reservata* and that of the Italians as typified by Vicentino. The Netherlands *reservata* is by preference dedicated to religious ideas, the Italian preëminently to the secular sphere. The favorite subject matter of the Netherlands *reservata* consists of episodes from the life and sorrows of Jesus Christ and other figures of the Old and New Testament, the Italian *reservata* sings the praises "of great personalities and heroes." Vicentino stresses the "reserved" tonalities of the chromatic and the enharmonic—of which the latter embodies even quarter tones. In the Netherlands *reservata* chromaticism is not in the foreground: it is but the ultimate result of the

other words the tritone. To give one example: Psalms 1 and 3 have no key signature and employ the tones of this scale: A-G♯-G♮-F♯-F♮-E — D-C♯-C♮-B-B♭-A. Lasso uses the chromatic tones in the Penitential Psalms, not in the direct way of the sibylline compositions; he wants to secure freedom of harmonic modulation mainly. The compass of harmonies used may go from G major to D flat major and B flat minor implying the most amazing modulations as, for example, in Psalm 4.

[35] *Di Vicentio Ruffo il secondo libro di madrigali.*

[36] I hold to von Ficker's view that the impulse behind the chromaticism of the epoch is toward a freer harmonic structure, not, as Kroyer believes, toward a more precise notation of accidentals, which is but a by-product (von Ficker: *Beiträge zur Chromatik des 14.–16. Jahrhunderts*).

effort to use music as an expressive and pictorial medium. Finally, the Netherlanders develop, by composing without stipulated accidentals, a true secret art, a *musica reservata* which is typically northern and as such not practiced by the Italians.

A Netherlands Source on the Secret Chromatic Art

In the *Compendium Musices* of Adrianus Petit Coclico there is a passage which I can interpret in no other way than as a protest against the secret chromatic art. In the chapter "De compositionis regula et notarum sincopis et ligaturis," Coclico enumerates the demands to be made of the composer, of which the fourth is described as follows:

Quartum quod in componista requiritur est ut . . . attendat, cuiusnam toni compositurus sit cantum, quia dedecori & ignorantiae datur Musico, si tonos regulares aut irregulares ignoret. Summe itaque curabit, ne in Tenore tonus excedat limites suae naturae, nec faciat cantum divagantem incantabilem, modestia & dulcedine carentem, sed magis quaerat Symphoniam, quam profundam, extraneam, & inusitatam Musicam, & ut magis placeat audientibus, quam rixandi occasionem praebeat.

The fourth requirement to be made of a composer is that he take heed of the mode in which he intends to compose his song, since it is likely to bring him into discredit and to betray his ignorance if he shows no knowledge of the regular and irregular modes. Hence he will be at particular pains to see that the mode of the tenor does not overstep its natural boundaries, that the song is neither vacillating nor unvocal, but fashioned with an eye to simplicity and sweetness. He should be concerned more with good concord (*symphonia*) than with writing a profound, strange, and unaccustomed music, and animated more by a desire to please the listener than to find an occasion for controversy.

Van Crevel's quotation from this passage [37] starts with the second sentence; he interprets it as follows: "In the passage quoted, the word 'symphonia' expresses the demand of the ear; by 'profunda et inusitata Musica,' however, is meant music which satisfies the constructive need of the intellect. In other words, the ear inclines toward homophony, the constructive intellect toward polyphony. In terms of the history of musical styles, Coclico is here the exponent of a change from the constructivism of the older Netherlands school to the harmonic principle of the Italians, which terminates in the adoption of monody around 1600."

Neither from the text nor from the context is this interpretation justified;

[37] *Adrianus Petit Coclico*, p. 43.

it implies, moreover, that around 1550 a fundamental opposition had arisen between homophony and polyphony, as though at this time there had been a group which repudiated polyphony. This was not the case. The new form just then evolved by polyphony was that of an organic contrapuntal composition renouncing the *cantus firmus* and using through-imitation instead; as such, it was still young and the delight of its contemporaries. In the *Practica musica*, published in 1556 by Rhau of Wittenberg, Hermann Finck writes:

Porrò inventis jam concinnis & textui accommodatis clausulis, illis quoque non in una tantum voce uti oportet, ita ut illi voci aliae qualescunque concordantiae in reliquis vocibus affingantur: Sed eaedem clausulae per plures, & si fieri posset, per reliquas omnes voces, apte ducendae variandaeque sunt, quae res mirifice cantilenam ornat commendatque. (Liber quartus.)

Furthermore: if the themes go well together and are well suited to the text, they should be used not just in one voice, adding other consonances at random; on the contrary, the same themes should in several and, if possible, in all voices be artfully applied and varied. This technique adorns and commends the song in a most extraordinary way. (Book IV.)

Zarlino, in his *Istituzioni harmoniche* (Book III, chap. liv, "Delle fughe, o consequenze") expresses himself as follows on the beauties of the fugued style:

Et quantunque . . . non si ritrovasse nelle compositioni alcuna cosa, che fusse degna di riprensione . . . ne si udisse in esse, se non buona & soave Harmonia; li mancherebbe nondimeno un non so che di bello, di leggiadro & elegante, quando in esse non si udisse alle fiate (poiche impossibile è di poterlo far sempre) alcune Repliche, o Reditte di una particella, & tallora di tutta la Modulatione di una parte contenuta nella cantilena; fatte da un altra, overo da più delle altre parti; quando tra loro vanno cantando insieme; dopo un certo spacio di tempo l'una all'altra quasi à guisa di uno riflesso di voce, il quale è detto Echo, rispondendosi: intorno alle quali arteficiosamente si affatica ogni buon compositore.

And even if the compositions were without flaws and one found in them nothing but good and suave harmony, still a certain beauty, charm, and elegance would be missing if they did not from time to time—for they cannot always do so—present a few repetitions of part of or even all the melody of one of the voices in one or more of the others; when they begin to sing, one follows the other after a certain time, as though the voices were thrown back when they answer each other in the manner of an echo: this is the acme of artistic endeavor in every good composer.

We need not, however, go any farther; it suffices to quote a few phrases more of the above-mentioned chapter of Coclico's treatise.

Septimum et ultimum est, ut prospiciat, si possibile fuerit, quod una vox aliam sequatur per fugam in inchoatione cantus. Haec ferme fiunt per Quintam, Sextam, & Octavam & Dezimam in ligaturis et Syncopis. . . . Nam huiusmodi Syncopis et ligaturis utuntur nunc in Italia, Gallia, & Flandria eruditissimi Musici. Et qui se illis socium in canendo adiungit, nisi fuerit practicus tenens haec firmiter, cito succumbet, atque cum rubore discedet, ac ridebitur.

Seventh and last, the composer must take care that at the beginning of the song one voice follow another in fugued style. This happens at the fifth, sixth, octave, and tenth in ligatures and syncopes. For ligatures and syncopes of this type are used nowadays by the most cultivated musicians of Italy, France, and Flanders. Whoever joins them in the art of music without having attained practical mastery of their technique will soon be vanquished and will have no choice but to withdraw from the field in shame and derision.

It is inconceivable that in the mid-sixteenth century it could have occurred to a theorist to characterize the polyphonic style as "extranea et inusitata Musica." One might imagine that what Coclico intended was simply to take a stand against the canonic *tours de force* of the older Netherlands school. There are, however, two considerations against such a conclusion.

1. At that time the canonic arts of the older Netherlands school had, it is true, lost their former significance, but they still had a place, however modest, in the technique of composition. The music of the older Netherlands school, furthermore, was still a living thing. Consequently, it is out of the question to believe that a Netherlands theorist would have called this typical Netherlands practice "inusitata musica."

2. There is no connection whatsoever between the canonic arts and the violation of the natural boundaries of the ecclesiastical modes. Such a connection does, however, exist between the modes and the secret chromatic art. I know of no other technique to which this passage could refer without being far-fetched and meaningless. If we analyze the second sentence of Coclico's fourth requirement, which for us is of particular import, we find the following points stressed: (*a*) The tenor [38] must not overstep the nat-

[38] In the motet technique of the older Netherlands school the tenor was the bearer of the *cantus firmus* and occupied the place of importance. Tinctoris called it "fundamentum relationis." In the motets employing free imitation throughout, the tenor lost this special function. Instead of the "fundamentum relationis," there gradually arose a "fundamentum harmoniae" represented by the bass. Thus, Coclico writes in the chapter "De eleganta, et ornatu, aut pronunttiatione in canendo" of his treatise: "Bassus est

ural limits of the mode. This can mean either one of two things: either the tenor must not overstep the spatial boundaries—upward or downward—or else he must not violate the tonal boundaries through the introduction of chromatic notes. For our interpretation only the second possibility enters into consideration; in connection with the canonic arts the first has, furthermore, no meaning. (*b*) Overstepping the bounds of the church mode makes the melody vacillating, unvocal, and complicated, robbing it of its "sweetness." (*c*) The composer must guard against a profound, strange, or unaccustomed kind of music. (*d*) He must be concerned more with giving pleasure to the listener than with offering a pretext for dispute.

Let us compare these stipulations with four characteristics of the secret chromatic art: (1) All the voices, tenor included, overstep the natural bounds of the mode by adding chromatic notes. (2) Through this procedure the composition undoubtedly becomes more complicated and more difficult to sing; it also loses its "modesty" and—for the ear attuned to diatonic music—its "sweetness." [39] (3) There arises a new kind of music: profound, strange, and unaccustomed. (4) The ambiguity of the secret chromatic art offers to partisans of diatonic and chromatic music alike an object for discussion and strife.

This interpretation is supported by the passage from Vicentino's treatise, which is quoted by Jeppesen and presented at the beginning of this inquiry. This passage constitutes the affirmative analogue of Coclico's prohibition: ". . . il *Compositore potrà uscire del Modo & intrerà in un' altro, perche non haurà obligo di rispondere al tono, di nissun Choro, ma sarà solamente obligato à dar l'anima, à quelle parole . . .*"

Ottmar Luscinius, the Strassburg organist and theorist, expresses much the same viewpoint in his *Musurgia* as Coclico. It is obvious that he had in mind, not a spatial, but a tonal violation of the boundaries of tonality when in Chapter VI of the "Commentarius secundus" to the *Musurgia* of 1536 he says:

---

fundamentum omnium aliarum partium." Even though Renaissance theory produced no terminology adequate to harmonic procedure in its individual aspects, this observation of Coclico, made also by other theorists, must be counted among the evidence that during the Renaissance there was a general consciousness of the change from a contrapuntal whole to an organic harmonic entity as basis of composition. It is interesting to note that in the treatises of theorists the tenor, despite the loss of its former function, still retains its nominal importance: with Coclico as with other theorists, the tenor is the voice which determines the mode.

[39] We must try to realize that for the ear of the conservative listener in the sixteenth century the transition from the diatonic to the chromatic represented fully as radical a change as the music of a Schönberg for the majority of our present-day concert-goers.

Sunt enim, qui maiore licentia, quam artificio, extra praescriptam tonorum melodiam exspacientur: quasi vero artis alicuius esse videatur, ea quae ars ipsa expostulet, corrumpere. . . Adimitur autem amoenitas compositioni primo, per usurpationem impertinentium clavium. Veluti si in tertio tono, aut quarto, quae in E frequentius exeunt, praeter solitum in b *fa* composueris: aut eo loci sedem carminis quaeras in ipso progressu, ubi omnis ratio toni reluctetur: ut si in memoratis in F clausulam facias.

There are musicians who, with more license than art, overstep the prescribed bounds of the modes—as though it were an art to corrupt the very laws of art itself. The beauty of a composition suffers most of all through the use of inappropriate tones. By way of example: if while in Phrygian or Hypophrygian mode, which frequently close on E, you suddenly composed in b *fa;* if you allocated the point of repose of the song to the very spot where it contradicts every law of the mode: for instance, if in the above-mentioned modes you constructed the clausulas on F.

By way of comparison, let us look at a few of Glareanus's comments, to which Levitan [40] has referred and which are quoted and discussed in detail by van Crevel.[41] In his *Dodekachordon* Glareanus says:

Atqui pro dolor in tantam lasciviam nunc devenit haec ars, ut doctis propemodum sit taedio: Idque multas ob causas, maxime vero, quod cum majorum vestigia, qui Modorum rationem exacte observaverunt, sequi pudet, incidimus in alium quendam tortum cantum, qui nulla ratione, nisi quia novus est, placet.

Unfortunately this art has now degenerated to such an extent that to connoisseurs it is almost a source of disgust. And this for many reasons, but most of all because composers are ashamed to follow in the footsteps of their elders, who scrupulously observed the rules of ecclesiastical modes. Thus we have arrived at an eccentric sort of writing, which pleases for no reason other than that it is new.

Van Crevel quotes still another passage (p. 289); there, too, the author refers to *tortis cantibus.* Van Crevel brings Riemann into the discussion, who translates these words as follows: "in pieces with chromatic passages." Glareanus's objections to tonal innovations are mentioned by van Crevel himself in connection with passages such as the modulation in Josquin's Absalom motet. Glareanus's reference to "*tortus cantus*" and "*novus*" and his criticism of the nonobservance of the modes do, indeed, hint at violation of the modes and possible "chromatic turns"; there is no indication, however, that they have any connection with secret modulation. The passage from

[40] Adrian Willaert's Famous Duo, p. 226.   [41] *Adrianus Petit Coclico,* p. 288.

Coclico is particularly relevant, because it offers many more concrete points of comparison than the corresponding opinions of Glareanus and constitutes an authentic expression concerning the secret chromatic art by one of its contemporaries. That is, indeed, the impression it made upon the uninitiated: "profunda, extranea, & inusitata musica."

In his study of Willaert,[42] Levitan called attention to the medieval tradition according to which *musica falsa* or *musica ficta* was also called *musica inusitata*. Levitan quotes the following passage from Nicolaus de Capua's *Compendium musicale:* "Item possumus habere per fictam musicam, videlicet ubicumque possumus per ordinem dare *ut re mi fa so la:* VOCATUR ENIM FICTA SEU FALSA MUSICA NON TAMEN EST FALSA, SED INUSITATA." [43] Levitan then points out [44] that the expression *musica inusitata* is used synonymously with *musica ficta* in Anonymous II, Coussemaker, Scriptores I, p. 310 b; Pseudo-de Vitry, Ars Nova, Coussemaker, Scriptores III, p. 18 a; Nicolaus de Capua, ed. Lafage (Lutetiae, Paris, 1853) p. 33. This was already referred to by Karl Dèzes in his thesis, *Prinzipielle Fragen auf dem Gebiet der fingierten Musik*. Karl Dèzes not only establishes the synonymous use of *musica falsa* and *musica ficta* but also the gradual replacement of the first concept by the second and the evolutionary series *musica falsa—inusitata—colorata—ficta*. He also quotes a passage from Walter Odington's *Speculatio musicae* (Coussemaker, Scriptores I, 216), which for a more accurate description of *musica falsa* not only anticipates Coclico's concept *musica inusitata* but also the *extranea et inusitata*. The quotation runs as follows:

"Duae voces mobiles (sc. b acuta et $\frac{b}{b}$ superacuta) sunt propriae voces monocordi; reliquas vero vocant falsas musici, non quod dissonae sint, sed extraneae et apud antiquos inusitatae."

The evidence brought forward by Coclico jeopardizes our identification of secret chromatic art with *musica reservata*. Coclico is the first known authority on *musica reservata*, whence one ought to assume that he knew what the concept involves. Since he expressed disapproval of the secret chromatic art, we have to assume that chromaticism has nothing to do with the *musica reservata*, which he tries to promote. On the other hand, Coclico himself, in his *musica reservata*, makes use of chromaticism and of unstipulated modulation, though not in the strictly Netherlands sense of secret chromatic art. It cannot be a question of a change in Coclico's viewpoint, either, inasmuch as both works—treatise and motet collection—were

---

[42] Adrian Willaert's Famous Duo, p. 189; see also p. 185, note 90.
[43] Capitals not in the original.   [44] *Ibid.*, p. 190, note 117.

written and published at about the same time.[45] We find ourselves confronted by a whole series of contradictions. Are they to be explained? If so, how?

1. What is Coclico's concept of *musica reservata?* According to Quickelberg the core of the *reservata* theory resides in the new intimate union between word and tone, subject matter and music. That Coclico was keenly aware of this fundamental change in the orientation of music is evident from a number of passages in his treatise—from none more clearly than from the following:

Sextum, quod in componista requiritur, est, ut bene ruminet textum, qualem tonum, aut Harmoniam exigat, eundemque textum ornate suo loco applicet, quia sunt plus quam caeci palpantes in tenebris, qui verbis consolatoriis, et gaudij plenis addunt tristes numeros, ac vicissim moestis verbis laetas melodias applicant. Maxime etiam Musico vitio datur, si brevem syllabam addat longae notae. Quia Musica multum commertij cum poësi habet.

The sixth requirement to be made of a composer is that he ruminate the text well as to which mode or harmony it asks for, and that he apply that text with taste to its proper place; for those who set words full of consolation and joy to a sad music, and who vice versa compose gay melodies to sad words are in a plight worse than the blind groping in the dark. It is a matter of serious reproach if a musician sets a long note to a short syllable. For music has an intimate relation with poetry.

Coclico grasps fully the fundamental significance of the *musica reservata* which removes music from its traditional place in the *quadrivium*, from its union with mathematical order and the harmony of the spheres, and associates it with the *trivium* consisting of grammar, dialectics, and rhetoric, or, in other words, with the human world and its main vehicle of communication, human speech.

2. Has Coclico a clear concept of the secret chromatic art? The analysis of Coclico's secret modulation has revealed that he has no mastery of the technique of secret modulation. He does not know how to bring about an effortless approach to the modulation or a like return from it; he makes no use of the Netherlanders' device of ambiguity; his modulation is no musical climax, but, on the contrary, almost a caricature of chromaticism. The connection between text and chromaticism is revealing: Coclico employs chromaticism in order to express an abnormal, paradoxical state of affairs ("virga peccatorum super sortem justorum"). It is obvious that his

[45] Van Crevel, *Adrianus Petit Coclico*, pp. 289 ff.

practice of the secret chromatic art fully conforms to his theoretical evaluation of it: both are negative.

Summary

What are the conclusions to be drawn from our identification of secret chromatic art with *musica reservata?*

1. Since Coclico does not define the term *musica reservata*, there is no strictly reliable way of knowing what he means by it. We see, however, that he is thoroughly familiar with the concept of music as defined by Quickelberg, but unfamiliar with Vicentino's chromatic and enharmonic music as well as with the secret chromatic art. Thus the conclusion seems justified that he identified himself with Quickelberg's concept of *musica reservata.*

2. One can safely assume that there was a concept of *reservata* which had no connection with the secret chromatic art. This conclusion is confirmed by Quickelberg's definition, which specifies no musical or technical conditions, and by that of Vicentino, which simply speaks of stipulated chromaticism and of enharmonic writing.

3. The unshakable foundation of the *reservata* concept is the dominating role played by the text in the music itself. This gives us the right to bring the secret chromatic art into the sphere of *reservata*, since it constitutes an ultimate intensification of the effort toward musical expression. Vicentino's comment in every way supports this thesis. The secret character of the new technique at the same time lends depth to the concept of *musica reservata*, raising it to the rank of a true secret art reserved for a select circle of initiated listeners.

This much is certain: the concept *musica reservata* is no unified one. While Quickelberg speaks only of its pictorial and expressive tendency, presenting no etymological explanation, Vicentino adds to this definition sociological and musical facets and describes the conditions of its performance, thus for the first time throwing light upon the literal meaning of the concept. We know at present of three centers of *musica reservata*: the Netherlands, Germany, and Italy. In each of these centers *musica reservata* took on a different aspect, both musically and sociologically. It has by no means been established, however, that even in each of the several countries the concept *musica reservata* was a unified one. It seems to me on the contrary that *musica reservata* might be compared to a terrain consisting of several layers, which the historian must slowly and carefully cleave asunder and examine separately in order to find answers to the several questions which arise. In what country did *musica reservata* originate? At what epoch? Whence the unusual concept? What metamorphoses did it undergo, both as to time and as to place?

For the time being these and other questions remain open. We trust that in the present inquiry we have at least succeeded in indicating the direction which must be taken by future research in *reservata*. The first requirement is to return to the strictly historical approach, with its various musical, textual, theoretical, and sociological aspects, as well as the avoidance of any kind of vague generalization. The second requirement is the systematic extension of the documentary foundations and the critical examination, comparison, and interpretation of the documents assembled.

The Attitude of the Church toward Chromaticism

IN THE *Index of Chosen Authors from Whom a Genuine Catholic Library May Rightly Be Constituted* drawn up for the use of monasteries in Bavaria in 1569 we find these memorable sentences on new and old medicine.

Medicinae autem cognitionem tutissime patefacient Galenus, Hyppocrates et qui Galenicam rationem sequuti sunt. Novis cum si nemo libenter credat, absque periculo vix erit in monasteriis locus, praesertim cum magna illorum pars, qui veterum medicinam nunc oppugnat, etiam in religione peregrinas alat opiniones.[1]	The knowledge of medicine will most safely be disclosed by Galen, Hippocrates, and Galen's disciples. New theories which no one likes to trust shall not without danger find a place in monasteries, particularly since a great part of those who nowadays fight the old medicine foster heterodox opinions in religion too.

The Church watched with a wary eye all attempts to reverse old ideas and old techniques. The man who started to revise traditional opinions in one field of human thought might easily apply his critical attitude to religious problems as well.

The new chromaticism in the music of the Renaissance met with a similarly hostile attitude on the part of the Church. The defense of the diatonic system of the Ecclesiastical modes against the rising wave of chromaticism presents one of the most fascinating chapters of Renaissance theory. A study of the material available reveals with the utmost clarity that the Church took a most lively and serious interest in the matter of preserving the old diatonic system of modes. In his polemical pamphlet against Bartolomeo Ramis's novel theories Nicolaus Burtius [2] speaks of the diatonic, chromatic, and enharmonic genera. He states unmistakably that "mater ecclesia ex his

---

[1] *Index selectissimorum auctorum ex quibus integra bibliotheca catholica institui recte possit.* See Fr. Heinrich Reusch, *Die Indices librorum prohibitorum des 16. Jahrhunderts,* p. 331. A very amusing confirmation of the identification of innovation and heresy in the view of the sixteenth-century conservative is to be found in Giordano Bruno, *Del infinito universo e mondi.* In the third dialogue Burchio, the follower of Aristotle's physics, pours a flood of invective on Fracastorio, the disciple of Copernicus and of Bruno. Among other things he calls him—and in this order—"a friend of innovations, an arch foe of the truth, and suspect of heresy."

[2] Cf. *Nicolai Burtii . . . musices opusculum . . . Bononie . . . 1487.*

tribus dyatonicum delegit . . ." ("the Mother Church chose from these three the diatonic genus"). And this is the tenor of medieval [3] as well as of Renaissance tracts that pleaded for the purity of the modes.

Chromaticism arose in Italy. But there the composers limited its use mainly to secular music, at least in the first half of the sixteenth century. The Netherlands composers, however, committed the most daring violations of the diatonic system and of the modes in spiritual works, in church music.

There are a number of works containing hidden chromaticism whose texts would invite liturgical use. The story of Lazarus raised from the dead (*Fremuit spiritu Jesu*) belongs to the liturgy of the fourth Sunday in Lent,[4] the appearance of Jesus to his disciples (*Recumbentibus undecim discipulis*) to the liturgy of Ascension day,[5] Christ's baptism (*Venit fortior post me*) belongs to the service for Sunday after the New Year,[6] the motet *Vox in Rama* would be sung *In die Innocentium*,[7] *Suscipe verbum* on Annunciation day,[8] *Absalon fili mi* and *Rex autem David* on Saturday before the seventh Sunday after Pentecost.[9]

The Attitude of the Chromaticist toward the Church

While there is no doubt about the hostile attitude of the Church toward chromaticism, we wonder what was the attitude toward the Church on the part of the composers who favored chromaticism.

The relation of the man of the sixteenth century to the Church showed all possible varieties from strict loyalty to open hostility. Aside from those who were unequivocally for or against the Church there was the great mass of thinking people who were not able to make a clear-cut decision one way or the other. Theirs was a hard lot. Attracted by the courage, sincerity, and the idealism of the Reformers, repelled by their use of violence, possessed of a deep loyalty toward the Church, but painfully aware of the utter imperfection of her servants, they suffered in a sense more than the martyrs of the new gospel. Erasmus was the personification of this large group of men with divided loyalties.

There were also secret heretics who dared not confess their convictions or those who, suddenly confronted with certain death by burning at the

---

[3] Several centuries earlier a similar situation had developed in the Gregorian chant. The chromatic alterations occurring in the chant, though never going farther than E flat or C sharp, were nevertheless either eliminated or hidden by means of transposition, because the Church rejected chromaticism. See G. Jacobsthal, *Die chromatische Alteration im liturgischen Gesang der abendlaendischen Kirche.*
[4] Moser, *Die mehrstimmige Vertonung des Evangeliums*, p. 43.
[5] *Ibid.*, p. 44.   [6] *Ibid.*, p. 40.   [7] *Ibid.*   [8] *Ibid.*, p. 43.   [9] *Ibid.*, p. 14.

stake, retracted their previous utterances, as did Jacobus Praepositus, head of the Augustine monastery in Antwerp,[10] and Cornelius Grapheus,[11] secretary of the same city. And who would dare throw stones at these men who were struggling in utter sincerity, but were not of the stuff that makes a martyr? It seems that the story of many of these men may never be known because evidence is lacking, which is understandable enough, since they did everything to hide their real feelings and convictions.

Particularly difficult is the situation for the music historian who has nothing at hand but the musical documents. Whether we consider Clemens non Papa or Hubert Waelrant—the two main representatives of the secret chromatic art—we know little more than the vague outlines of their lives, partly veiled in deep obscurity. How can we disclose their struggles and their innermost thoughts?

The Choice of Texts in the Light of Reformed Plays, Songs, and Tracts

A very great part of the music of the time is vocal music. It seems reasonable to suppose that a composer who fostered heterodox opinions might express them, albeit in a veiled manner, through the choice of his texts. As long as he wanted to avoid an open break with the Church, he could choose his texts from the text sources officially acknowledged by the Church, but he could do it in such a way as to hint at contemporary events, situations, or ideas contrary to the orthodox faith.

Our method, then, seems clearly delineated. In studying the religious movements of the time, we must find out which are the new ideas and which symbols and similes, which Biblical persons and events are used to illustrate the new ideas. Obviously, in many cases it will be difficult to draw a clear line of demarcation between the old and the new. The new faith may choose texts and symbols used earlier and may give them a new meaning. At times both may use similar symbols. Only a series of pieces obviously supplementing each other may be accepted as a basis for a hypothesis.

A religious movement finds its most genuine expression, not so much in the learned writings of the theologians, as in the simple songs and verses, the plays and tales of the plain people. It was in the famous and numerous Netherlands chambers of rhetoric, whose members were known as *Rederijkers*, that the spirit of anticlerical revolt began to stir. Therefore they were persecuted with increasing bitterness by Charles V, Philip II,

---

[10] There exists a very rare autobiography by Jacobus Praepositus, *Ein schone und clegliche history bruder Jacobs probst Augustiner ordens.*
[11] Reitsma, *Geschiedenis van de Hervorming en de Hervormde Kerk der Nederlanden.*

and the duke of Alba, to be finally suppressed by Alexander Farnese, the duke of Parma. The chambers of rhetoric on many occasions associated themselves with the guilds of musicians and singers. We know of many plays which were given with the assistance of a chorus, which either performed incidental music for the occasion or sang simple folksongs or even motets by famous contemporary composers.[12] A composer who intended to transmit some of the new ideas living in the hearts and minds of the people would most naturally allude to scenes and thoughts of these popular plays, which spread so fast throughout the country.

If we examine the *Indices librorum prohibitorum* of the sixteenth century, we find among the forbidden writings a substantial number of comedies and of plays of the *Rederijkers*. One series of plays in particular appears on almost every Index throughout the second half of the sixteenth century. Its title is: *What Is the Greatest Consolation of a Dying Christian?* [13] Nineteen chambers of rhetoric gathered in Ghent in the year 1539, and each chamber performed one play to answer the question.

The representations of the chambers of rhetoric in Flanders were a great affair, in which the population of the whole town and the communities near and far participated. In 1539 the plays were given in the open air. They lasted from June 23 to July 12. They were attended by an enormous crowd. It is noteworthy that almost immediately after this performance the memorable insurrection of Ghent broke out, which compelled Charles V to leave Spain in all haste for Flanders.[14]

In one of these plays Dying Man appears. He is consoled by Hypocrisy and Vain Purpose, dressed as monks; they advise him to put on their cas-

[12] Liliencron, "Die Chorgesänge des lateinisch-deutschen Schuldramas im XVI. Jahrhundert," in *Vierteljahrsschrift für Musikwissenschaft*, Vol. VI, 1890; J. A. Worp, *Geschiedenis van het Drama en van het Toneel in Nederland*.

[13] Reusch, *Die Indices librorum prohibitorum*, p. 49: Index of the University of Louvain ". . . les esbâtemens en Flamen, composez en rytme, lesquels ont estez jouez et exhibez en la ville de Gand, sur ceste question: Quelle chose soit le plus grand soulas du chrestien mourant."

[14] How distinctly the events in Ghent had impressed themselves on the contemporaries' minds may be gathered from a report made twenty-two years later. In a letter to Sir Thomas Gresham in London written from Antwerp in 1561 at the occasion of the magnificent gathering of Flemish chambers of rhetoric in that city Richard Clough recalls the events in Ghent in 1539 in these words: "But ther was at thatt tyme syche plays played that hath cost many a thousantt man's lyves; for in those plays was the worde of God fyrst openyd in thys contrey. Weche plays were, and ar forbeden, moche more strettly than any of the boks of Martyn Luter: as allso those plays was one of the prynsypall occasyons of the destrouccyon of the towne of Gantt." Quoted by Burgon, *The Life and Time of Sir Thomas Gresham*, I, 379. It was one year later, in 1540, that an edict was issued forbidding any allusions to Scripture or the sacraments in the plays of the *Rederijkers*. Pirenne, *Histoire de Belgique*, 1922–1932, III, 365.

socks so that he can die in peace. Since they are dressed in two different cassocks, they start an acrimonious fight over the merits of their respective orders, and Dying Man chases them out of his house. Then Scriptural Sense and Figured Demonstration enter, presenting Lutheran preachers. They advise him to take refuge in the arms of Eternal Mercy, which forgave David, the inhabitants of Nineveh, the prince of the apostles, and other sinners.[15]

In another play of Ghent, Man says: "Where shall I find a comforter? It seems that I am alone. I am simple, no cloister books or libraries will help me. I find myself full of misdeeds and bottomless. I invoke God's mercy. Deeper is his mercy than the depth of human misery." [16]

It was one of the main contentions of the Reformation that forgiveness is not to be had from the Church by confession and absolution, by praying and fasting, to say nothing of observance of ceremonies and paying for indulgence; forgiveness is to be achieved only by genuine and deep repentance and by faith in God's unending mercy and can come from Him alone. The twelfth article of the *Confessio Augustana*, of 1530, treats of the true repentance, which is defined as a coincidence of two things seemingly opposite: terror, caused by insight into man's sinfulness, and faith in forgiveness, guaranteed by Christ's sacrifice.[17] Melanchthon emphasizes time and again the interdependence of fear and faith. "Where there is no fear . . . there is no faith . . . Therefore Isaiah says God wishes to dwell in fearful hearts." [18] Melanchthon's concept of faith undergoes changes in the development of his theological thinking; but belief in God's mercy and in the forgiveness of sins continues to be the very essence of faith to him. He actually defines *fides* as *fiducia misericordiae divinae*.[19]

Clemens non Papa's Choice of Texts

This twofold message of fear and hope was spread throughout the Netherlands by the plays of the chambers of rhetoric, and we find it pronounced with all desirable clarity in the works of Clemens non Papa.[20]

---

[15] Altmeyer, *Les Précurseurs de la réforme aux Pays-Bas*, II, 160.

[16] Kalff, *Geschiedenis der Nederlandsche Letterkunde in de 16de eeuw*, I, 275.

[17] "Nu is ware rechte busse eigentlich nichts anders, denn rew vnd leid, odder schrecken haben uber die sund, vnd doch darneben gleuben an das Evangelium vnd Absolution, das die sunde vergeben, vnd durch Christum gnad erworben sey, welcher glaub widderimb das hertz tröst, vnd zufrieden macht." See Melanthonis, *Opera*, ed. C. G. Bretschneider. XXVI, 561.

[18] "Denn wo nicht schrecken ist fur Gottes Zorn . . . da ist nicht glauben . . . Darümb auch Esaias spricht, Gott wolle sein wonung haben jm erschrockenen hertzen . . ." *Ibid.*, p. 576.

[19] Roemer, *Die Entwicklung des Glaubensbegriffes bei Melanchthon*, pp. 9–11, 13, 24.

[20] In this analysis we draw from texts of all motets of Clemens non Papa including those belonging to the secret chromatic art.

In a series of motets the mood of Dying Man, despairing because of his burden of sins, is truly portrayed:

Domine, quando veneris iudicare terram, ubi me abscondam a vultu ire tue, quia peccavi nimis in vita mea. Commissa mea pavesco et ante te erubesco dum veneris iudicare noli me condemnare, quia peccavi nimis in vita mea.[21]

Tristitia et anxietas occupaverunt interiora mea, moestum factum est cor meum in dolore et contenebrati sunt oculi mei. Ve mihi, quia peccavi. Sed tu, domine, qui non derelinquis sperantes in te consolare et adiuva me propter nomen sanctum tuum. . .[22]

Cogitatio peccatorum me premit. Infelix ego qui celum terramque offendi. Quid igitur faciam? desperabo? absit! Misericors est deus, pius est salvator meus, ad te igitur, piissime deus, tristis ac merens venio en quaeso miserere mei, deus, secundum magnam misericordiam tuam.[23]

These texts convey both the desperation of man when he becomes aware of his imperfection in the face of God and the deep faith in God's unending mercy, which the plays of Ghent held out as the greatest consolation for a dying Christian.

Dying Man is approached by Hypocrisy and Vain Purpose. In the songs of the Reformers the term "hypocrite" is used in the same sense as in the plays of Ghent, namely, to designate the clergy.[24]

The plays of Ghent contain very sharp stanzas against the hypocrites who claim to be pure, but buy women; who pretend humility, but seek honors and sumptuous meals and pray to God with mummeries.

This idea is reflected in Clemens non Papa's text (Luke 6:37) *Nolite iudi-*

[21] Phalèse, 1559, Lib. VI, No. 3. A number of these texts, for example, the present one, have been set to music by Orlando di Lasso. Lasso was a Catholic and director of the chapel at the Catholic court of Bavaria. As such, he enjoyed much more freedom than did a church composer in a Netherlands town. He, as well as the Bavarian court, could not quite escape the influence of a Germany which, to a large part, was Lutheran. The stipulations of the Indexes of Munich, printed by Adam Berg in the years from 1566 until 1582, are a case in point (F. H. Reusch, *Die Indices librorum prohibitorum des 16. Jahrhunderts*, p. 324 ff.). These are the only Indexes that state, not which books are forbidden, but which are allowed. And among the permitted books are works which were expressly forbidden in other Indexes. We know also that the sister of the duke of Bavaria, herself a devout Catholic, recommended the reading of Luther's famous table sermons to her brother. Lasso used even Lutheran melodies in his German psalm compositions. But the most distinct evidence of the liberties he could permit himself are the blasphemous chanson texts which he set to music and which would have done honor to a Rabelais. Satire against religion and the clergy of such an extreme character is not to be found in the repertoire of chansons composed by Netherlands musicians of the period and published in the Netherlands.
[22] Phalèse 1559, Lib. V, No. 2.
[23] *Ibid.*, Lib. II, No. 2.
[24] Wieder, *De schriftuurlijke Liedekens*, p. 78.

care et non iudicabimini,[25] where we find the following phrase about the hypocrite who sees the mote in his brother's eye, but not the beam in his own eye. "Hypocrita ejice primum trabem de oculo tuo et tunc videbis ejicere festucam de oculo fratris tui."

To console Dying Man, Scriptural Sense and Figured Demonstration offer the city of Nineveh as an example of great sinners who were forgiven by God's eternal mercy after offered repentance.

We have a great motet by Clemens non Papa dedicated to Nineveh; the composer sets to music the scene of repentant Nineveh alarmed by Jonas's sermon calling for repentance.

Timor et tremor venit in Niniven civitatem magnam per quae scelera plebis indicitur ieiunium et luctuosa turba induitur cilicio. Contigit autem regem nobilem de solio suo descendere, ut esset humilior cunctis lugentibus. Et praecepit per universum regnum omnes viri et sexus femineus non gustent quicquam, boves et pecora non pascantur herbis terrae, pueri et vituli non sugant matrum ubera, sed clament in fortitudine tribus diebus, ne periclitentur ut Zodoma.[26]

The whole scale of religious emotions and ideas represented in the dramatic performances of Ghent is brought into play in Clemens's motets.

There is another work by Clemens non Papa whose text suggests the spirit of the Reformation. It is the cry of woe over Babylon. "Ve tibi Babylon et Syria precingite vos saccis et cilicio et plangite filios vestros et dolete, quoniam appropinquavit contritio vestra." [27]

From the fourteenth century on heretics used Babylon as well as Babel as synonyms for the Church. In the time of the Reformation this became very common. F. C. Wieder, in his study of the songs of the reformers, quotes one poet who, in seeking God, exclaims: "Alas, where shall I go to seek Him, I shall find Him nowhere in the Babylonic city." [28] In the oldest collection of letters written by the martyrs of the Anabaptist movement [29] we also find Babylon as a synonym for the Church.

The symbol of the New Gospel is Jerusalem and the Daughter of Zion. Such figures of speech as "Jerusalem lies quite destroyed" and "I must go to Jerusalem," "Zion's daughter must be happy, for God comes as her bridegroom" are very common.[30] A poet of the time says: "You know well, I hope, whom I mean when of Babel or Syon I sing." [31]

[25] Waelrant 1554, Lib. I, No. 11.   [26] Susato 1553, Lib. I, No. 14.
[27] *Ibid.*, Lib. II, No. 17.   [28] Wieder, *De schriftuurlijke Liedekens*, p. 27.
[29] "Het Offer des Heeren," 1570, in *Bibliotheca Reformatoria Neerlandica*, II, 115, 228, 592.
[30] Wieder, *De schriftuurlijke Liedekens*, p. 46.
[31] *Ibid.*, p. 77.

There are several motets on Jerusalem in Clemens's work, and their texts become very meaningful if connected with the symbolic use of Jerusalem during the Reformation. We cite one example: "Jerusalem, Jerusalem cito veniet salus tua; quare dolore consumaris numquid consiliarius non est tibi, quia innovavit te dolor, salvabo te et liberabo te et noli timere. Civitas Jerusalem noli flere quoniam doluit dominus super te, gaude et letare, salvabo te et liberabo te et noli timere." [32]

Let us quote from a few more texts which may hint at the composer's temper. The following brings to mind the Last Judgment, where there is no hope but in God. "O fili dei roga patrem tuum pro famulo tuo, ne peream in die iudicij . . . Quoniam tribulatio proxima est et non est qui adiuvet sed tu domine." [33]

Deeply moving is the text wherein the composer's muse joins in the affliction of her favorite. "Adesto dolori meo deus . . . cecidit in luctum cithara mea et cantatio mea in plorationem." [34] "O domine multi dicunt animae meae non est salus ipsi in deo eius, sed tu domine susceptor meus es." [35]

Then, again, Clemens uses Psalm 117, so eminently true for the man of the Reformation, who puts his trust in God alone without fear of what man might do to him. "Impulsus eversus sum, ut caderem et dominus suscepit me, dominus adiutor meus et ideo non timebo quid faciat mihi homo." [36] Or he sets to music Jeremiah's ever-great lamentation: "Caligaverunt oculi mei a fletu meo, quia elongatus est a me, qui consolabatur me. Videte omnes populi si est dolor similis sicut dolor meus." [37]

Significant, too, in the light of contemporary events is Clemens's motet on the true martyr, who does not long for earthly glory or fear the judges' threat. Clemens has used this text twice, once for four voices [38] and another time for six. [39] "Hic est vere martir, qui pro Christi nomine sanguinem suam fudit, qui minas iudicum non timuit nec terrene dignitatis gloriam quaesivit, sed ad celestia regna foeliciter pervenit."

All in all, this certainly is not the language spoken by a man who feels sure and safe or has inner peace because he believes in the promises of his Church. It is rather the stirring language adopted by a sincere and restless seeker of God. All these texts, instead of dealing with the great intermediary between God and man, the Church, speaks of the immediate relation be-

[32] Phalèse 1559, Lib. I, No. 2.
[33] Susato 1553, Lib. III, No. 1.
[34] *Ibid.*, Lib. VI, No. 7.
[35] Phalèse 1554, Lib. IV, No. 13.
[36] Waelrant 1556, Lib. II, No. 10.
[37] Phalèse 1559, Lib. II, No. 5.
[38] *Ibid.*, Lib. III, No. 8.
[39] *Ibid.*, Lib. VII, No. 14.

tween God and the human soul, a main theme of reformatory thinking.

The choice of Biblical personalities points in the same direction. Clemens has twice set to music the scene of the Prodigal Son, once for four voices,[40] once for eight.[41] In contemporary plays the story of the Prodigal Son was used as a simile for the reformation of the Church; [42] we find it so used in the songs of the Netherlands reformers.[43] To comfort the fighters and martyrs for the new faith, these songs often presented the great sufferings of Biblical heroes like Jacob, David, Daniel, and Stephen. We find Jacob,[44] David,[45] Daniel,[46] and Stephen [47] celebrated in Clemens's motets. It is significant that in his works containing hidden chromaticism Clemens glorified the great sufferers David, Job,[48] and Rachel. Lazarus raised by Jesus is also a symbol—the symbol of eternal hope—used in plays of the reformers.[49] In Clemens's great pseudo-Biblical motet *Qui consolabatur me*, consisting of text parts taken from Jeremiah and the Song of Songs, we find the quasi parodistic use of the *Pater noster* tune.[50]

[40] *Pater peccavi* in Susato 1547, Lib. III, No. 11, and other sources; the earliest date of publication is 1546.

[41] Phalèse 1555, Lib. VIII, No. 14; reprinted in Commer I.

[42] The humanist Grapheus, rector of the Latin school in the Hague, who had to seek refuge in Germany to escape the Inquisition, wrote a play on the Prodigal Son: *Acolastus*. See Kalff, *Geschiedenis der Nederlandsche Letterkunde*, III, 15.

[43] Wieder, *De schriftuurlijke Liedekens*, p. 31.

[44] Videns Jacob . . . Phalèse 1559, Lib. I, No. 8.

[45] Cf. p. 26.

[46] Cf. p. 12. Melanchthon, too, uses the story of Daniel as an allegory: ". . . as Daniel was thrown before the lions because of God's word, so we have to take upon us the wild wrath of the enemy because of God's word." Melanchthon, *Opera*, XIII, 472.

[47] "Lapidabant Stephanum," Susato 1553, Lib. I, No. 22.

[48] In the Antwerp Index of 1570 we find *Een Duytsche Historie van den verduldigen Job* (Reusch, *Die Indices librorum prohibitorum*, p. 313). In Rouen the representation of the *Mystère de Job* was forbidden (Mâle, *L'Art religieux de la fin du moyen âge*, p. 484). Melanchthon in his "Repetitio Confessionis Augustanae," in *Opera*, XXVIII, 390, cites Job and David as examples of undeserved suffering; their fate proves that the just are not vindicated by external success, but by God's word.

[49] Play of Lazarus's death and how Jesus raised him from the grave (Kalff, *Geschiedenis der Nederlandsche Letterkunde*, III, 22). In 1543 Jos. Klug published in Wittenberg, the center of the Reformation, Joh. Sutellius, *Historia von Lazaro . . . Itzt zurzeit des Sterbens zu trost den krancken und den sterbenden Menschen ausgelegt und gepredigt* . . . On the Antwerp Index of 1570 we find the *Historie van Lazarus redivivus per Joannem Sapidum Selestadium* (Reusch, *Die Indices librorum prohibitorum*, p. 313).

[50] See again the Antwerp Index of 1570 noting a *Pater noster int sotte*—that is, a parody of the Pater noster—in Reusch. *Die Indices librorum prohibitorum*, p. 312. Moreover, the *Pater noster* seems to have served as a basis for theological comments regarded as heretical by the Church. On Paul IV's Roman Index of 1559 Savonarola's *Exposicion del Pater noster* is listed (*ibid.*, p. 234). On the Antwerp Index of 1570 we find two other interpretations of the *Pater noster*, the one by Matthias Bywant (*ibid.*, p. 314), the other by Erasmus (*ibid.*, p. 315).

One of the great documents of the time is Sebastian Castellio's tract *Concerning Heretics.*[51] Castellio's flaming protest against the persecution of heretics was occasioned by the burning of Michael Servetus on October 23, 1553, where Calvin played the role of the informer. In this tract we discover again all the images, figures, and parables which we found in the songs and plays of the heretics and in the motets of Clemens non Papa. Again the persecutors are compared to the Sodomites, to the Babylonians, to the hypocrites.[52] Again the persecuted are symbolized by the great figures of the Old and the New Testament celebrated in Clemens's motets: Job, David, Daniel, and Stephen. To quote in more detail: Job is called "that model of patience" and to him is compared Michael Servetus, who received the news of his verdict with the same equanimity as Job did the ill tidings of the messengers.[53] David is cited as the father of the persecuted. Castellio extols him because he patiently endured Saul's persecution and did not desire revenge when chance delivered Saul into his hands.[54] In the dedication to William of Hesse, with which Castellio accompanied the French version of his tract, Daniel is held up as an example of unjust persecution for alleged heresy, and Castellio adds: "Would that good kings and princes would diligently consider this account . . . !" Also, in his *Reply to Calvin* Castellio quotes the story of Jesus's raising of Lazarus. And as in Clemens's motets, so in Castellio's writings we hear time and again the warning of the Last Judgment.[55]

All this evidence tends to crystallize the impression that there is a current of reformatory thinking in Clemens's work. Clemens on the other hand has composed a sufficient number of texts of purely and definitely Catholic character to convince us that he was a true member of the Roman Catholic Church.[56] Moreover, we will find several of the texts quoted here in the

---

[51] Bainton, *Concerning Heretics.* This tract appeared in 1554 anonymously. Bainton shows convincing evidence that it comes from Castellio's pen.

[52] *Ibid.,* p. 249; see also Bainton's excerpts of Castellio's *Reply to Calvin* (p. 269): "They call the papacy 'Babylon.' " See, moreover, pp. 224 and 273 on "hypocrites" and "hypocrisy."

[53] *Ibid.,* p. 285.

[54] *Ibid.,* p. 251. John Knox, too, in a letter of 1560, gives David as an example of the innocently persecuted (see p. 112).

[55] *Ibid.,* pp. 251, 253, 259, 213.

[56] Also, in the same year, 1550, when Clemens composed the votive motet of the brothers Schetz, he stayed for a longer time in 'sHertogenbosch with the fraternity of St. Mary, the Illustre Lieve Vrouwe Broederschap, and composed for the *fratres* a mass and a Mary motet (Bernet-Kempers, *Jacobus Clemens non Papa und seine Motetten,* p. 17). From the accounts of the fraternity we know that Clemens must have been there from September until Christmas, 1550, while we may assume from the Schetz motet that he was in Antwerp in the spring of the same year. 'sHertogenbosch

publications of other genuinely Catholic composers. But if we compare his text repertoire to, let us say, the ones of Nicolas Gombert or Palestrina, it is manifest where the difference lies. In the text repertoire of Gombert and Palestrina, texts like the ones cited above are found only in isolated instances, while the overwhelming majority of their works is of an unambiguous Roman Catholic character, being dedicated to the celebration of the Virgin, the Saints, the holidays, the liturgy, and the whole stable and hieratic world of the Roman Catholic Church. In Clemens's motets the texts mirroring the religious conflicts of the time and the new ideas of the Reformers are an interdependent unit; they reveal something of the inner drama of his time, nothing of which can be deduced from the texts which Gombert and Palestrina set to music.

Waelrant's Choice of Texts

The case of Hubert Waelrant seems clearer. Though connected with the Cathedral of Antwerp,[57] which was dedicated to the Virgin Mary, he com-

---

is about sixty miles from Antwerp. It is interesting that among the nonecclesiastical members of the fraternity we should find some of those Netherlands aristocrats with whom Gaspar Schetz was intimate, men like the count of Egmont, the count of Horne, moreover, Prince William of Orange, men who fought for the establishment of Netherlands freedom, for tolerance, and even forthright for the new religion. In accepting such men in their midst the fraternity started a movement which logically ended in the seventeenth century with the extraordinary decree that half the members of this Roman Catholic fraternity should belong to "the new religion" (Smits, *De Kathedraal van 'sHertogenbosch*, pp. 47–48). 'sHertogenbosch had been the scene of revolt against the clergy as early as 1516, 1517, 1518, and 1525. The Brotherhood of the Life in Common, which had started a most significant prereformatory movement, had a settlement there; Erasmus studied with them for several years (Pirenne, *Histoire de Belgique*, III, 185, 305, 340). In spite of the appearance to the contrary we may therefore assume that the spiritual and religious atmosphere in 'sHertogenbosch was not very different from that in Schetz's house in Antwerp, of which we shall hear more, presently.

[57] It is known that Waelrant was engaged as tenor at the Cathedral of Antwerp in the years 1544 and 1545. After having left the service of the Cathedral, Waelrant established himself in an independent position as teacher, composer, and publisher in Antwerp. It seems to be unknown that in later years he was called in as an expert in the matter of tuning the church bells, as attested by the archives of the Cathedral of Antwerp (1562–1563).

It is interesting to compare the social positions of Gombert and Crecquillon with those of Clemens non Papa and Waelrant. Both Gombert and Crecquillon had high functions in the service of Charles V. Undoubtedly this imposed certain restrictions upon these composers from which Clemens and Waelrant were free. It is pertinent to note that Gombert's and Crecquillon's contributions to the secret chromatic art are very modest in number as well as in artistic daring. Moreover, the compositions in which they use the technique are composed on texts of an unobjectionable Catholic character. Bernet-Kempers has disproved earlier assumptions that Clemens held positions in Charles V chapels or at the Cathedral of Antwerp. Our own findings show that in the spring of 1550 Clemens was in Antwerp, while he is known to have been

posed not one work of Mariolatry or Saint worship. Though one of the
outstanding masters of his time, he wrote no masses, no hymns, no Magnificats, in short not one work dedicated to the liturgy of the Roman Catholic
Church. Among his motets there is none of a definitely Catholic character.
Five of the few motets preserved are based on Psalms, which Luther called
the "Bible within the Bible," and which were a "pillar of the Reformation" [58] in all its branches and denominations. While this in itself does not
give any indication of Waelrant's attitude toward the religious movements
of his time, since the Psalms were also used by the Roman Catholic
Church,[59] an examination of the tetralogy of the motets devoted to the life
of Jesus may yield clearer results.

Both the Augsburg and the Helvetic Confessions reject prayers to the
Saints or to the Blessed Virgin. Both stress the unique and central importance of Christ. It is therefore doubly significant that Waelrant not
only did not compose any music addressed to the Saints or to Mary but
also did compose a cycle of motets dedicated exclusively to Jesus.

Waelrant chooses from Jesus's life the Adoration of the Three Magi,
John the Baptist's prophecy, Jesus's baptism, Jesus's teaching of love and
forgiveness, and Jesus's appearance to his disciples and his sending abroad
the apostles. He could just as well have chosen the twelve-year-old Jesus
in the temple, Jesus's temptation by Satan in the desert, Jesus's crucifixion,
and Mary and Magdalena at the empty grave. Waelrant's selection of scenes
and teachings from Jesus's life seems an almost complete representation of
the essentials of the Anabaptists' creed, one of the strongest reform movements in Flanders and especially strong in Antwerp at that time.

The Anabaptists "strove to reproduce in themselves the life of Christ."

---

in 'sHertogenbosch at the end of the same year for several months. This supports the
supposition that Clemens could not have held a fixed position at that time. The account books of the fraternity of 'sHertogenbosch reveal that he received remunera-
tions not for practical services such as singing or choir leading, but for his compositions
offered to the brethren. We may assume that he also received generous remuneration
from the brothers Schetz for his composition in their honor. At no other time did a
composer have a safer chance of supporting himself even without a position than in
those days of flourishing culture and commerce in the Netherlands. The comparative
social independence of Clemens non Papa and Waelrant offers one more explanation
for the fact that just these two composers should have dedicated themselves to the
secret chromatic art with its bold progressive tendencies and its reformatory implications.
[58] Briggs, *History of the Study of Theology*, II, 106.
[59] It should be noted, however, that according to Douen (*Clément Marot et le psautier
huguenot*, I, 1) the singing of psalms was considered heretical as early as 1531; that in
the Netherlands it was explicitly forbidden by a decree of 1562, and that most of the
heretics, who were burned for their faith died with a psalm on their lips (see the
enumeration of martyrs and psalms, *ibid.*, pp. 3 ff.).

They believed that "no institution—sacred or secular—could mediate between soul and God, who must approach each other through Jesus Christ." They claimed for themselves the name "brethren" or "disciples." [60] They taught universal toleration and freedom of worship and lived together—for instance, in Moravia—in great communal settlements. They did not believe in baptizing children, but they did baptize adults. They laid great stress on Jesus's outpouring of the Holy Spirit upon his disciples, believing that only the spirit, the "inner light," could bring immediate revelation to the faithful at any time. They also emphasized that Jesus sent the apostles on a universal mission, and they tried to follow this order in their own lives. One of the most typical features of Anabaptism is the wandering preacher; many of their greatest representatives, men like Hans Denck, Conrad Gebel—both belonging to the Erasmus circle—or the famous Melchior Hoffmann and others, lived as wandering preachers.

Looking back to Waelrant's motet cycle, we find in the center of his tetralogy John the Baptist and his baptism of Jesus, when he was an adult, on the one hand, and Jesus's teaching of love and forgiveness on the other. Waelrant chooses a text wherein Jesus uses the word "brother," the name by which the Anabaptists called themselves. At the beginning we find the most familiar scene of Jesus's childhood, the Adoration of the Three Magi. Did Waelrant want to indicate that it is not the baptism of the young Jesus which was reported in the Gospel? At the end we do not see Christ crucified (incidentally, the Anabaptists disliked all painted representations of religious subjects, particularly of the Crucifixion), but, instead, we see Christ appearing to his disciples, blessing them with the Holy Spirit, and ordering them to go out and preach the Gospel to every creature.

The first tract of the Anabaptists published in the Netherlands and written in the Flemish tongue is Melchior Hoffmann's *Die Ordonnantie Godts*, which appeared first in 1530 and was republished several times.[61] Hoffmann's *Ordonnantie* begins with a quotation from St. Matthew's Gospel (28:18), narrating Jesus's sending out of the apostles. Hoffmann, in his comments on this chapter, stresses (1) the universality of the apostles' mission, meant for all nations, tongues, and creeds; (2) the sacrament of baptism for all who want to enter into communication with Christ; (3) the significance of the Holy Spirit. These three ideas are illustrated by three scenes: (1) the apostles lead mankind out of Satan's realm; (2) Jesus goes

---

[60] *Encyclopaedia of Religion and Ethics*, under "Anabaptism."
[61] *Bibliotheca Reformatoria Neerlandica*, VI, 133 ff.; this text is printed after the edition of 1611 in Amsterdam.

to the Jordan to be baptized by John the Baptist; (3) during the baptism the heavens open and the Holy Ghost descends upon Jesus in the form of a dove; God acknowledges Jesus as His Son. Let us compare the texts of Waelrant's tetralogy with Hoffmann's tract which was so widely known in the Netherlands throughout and even beyond the sixteenth century. In *Recumbentibus* Waelrant emphasizes the universality of the apostles' mission ("euntes in mundum universum praedicate Evangelium omni creaturae"). Part 2 of the same motet describes the new powers given to the faithful: they shall expel demons, speak in new tongues, and destroy serpents [62] ("demonia ejicient, linguis loquentur novis,[63] serpentes tollent"). To be faithful does not suffice. The faithful need the sacramental confirmation of baptism. This part of the motet begins with the words "Qui crediderit et baptizatus fuerit, salvus erit."

In *Venit fortior* Waelrant portrays Jesus's being baptized by John. As he rises from the waters of the Jordan the heavens open and the Holy Ghost in the form of a dove descends upon Jesus while a voice sounds from above: "Thou art my beloved Son."

. . . in diebus illis venit Jesus à Nazareth Galileae et baptizatus est à Johanne in Jordane. Part 2: Et statim ascendens de aqua vidit coelos apertos et spiritum sanctum tamquam columbam descendentem et manentem in ipso et vox facta de coelis: tu es filius meus dilectus in te complacui.

Scene for scene, idea for idea, Waelrant's tetralogy parallels Hoffmann's tract.

If we examine the words which Waelrant points out by means of hidden modulation, we find again that he chooses the two main points of the Anabaptists' creed: the mysterious power of baptism and the sending of the apostles to preach the Gospel to *every creature*. The power of the apostles to effect miraculous cures *in Christ's name* is also emphasized by a secret modulation.

There is an even closer connection between the secret technique of modulation and the Anabaptist creed. As the art of hidden chromaticism admits of two interpretations, one for the common people and one for the initiated, so the Anabaptist distinguished between two interpretations of the Bible: the one literal and used by the common people, the other figurative

---

[62] In writings and songs of the Reformers the "serpent" appears time and again. From Adam's fall to the crucifixion of Jesus everything bad is traced back to the "serpent's seed."

[63] In the meetings of the Anabaptists in the Netherlands everyone who felt urged to do so could rise and speak. This was called "prophecy" (Wieder, *De schriftuurlijke Liedekens*, p. 54). The faithful spoke "in new tongues."

and reserved for the initiated. We quote from another tract of an Anabaptist, from Henrick Rol,

Die Slotel van dat Secreet des Nacht-
maels, onses Heren Jesu Christi,
welcke omsluyt dat rechte verstant,
dat daer verborgen isz: Geschreven
doer eynen Henrick Rol, om des Ge-
loofs wille, anno 1536 verbrant tot
Maestricht.

The Key of the Secret of the Lord's
Supper comprising the right meaning
hidden in it. Written by Henrick Rol,
burned for belief's sake in Maestricht
in 1536.

Dat woordt Gotz is al duyster ende
onbegrypelijk even als God selve isz.
. . . God spreickt dat niemant en kan
verstaen, ende zijn woorden sijn al
parabolen den menschen die jn haar
vernufft sijn verlaten. . . . Daerum
seyt Christus, Matth. 13. V isz gegeven
te verstaen de mysterien oft verbor-
gentheden des rijckes Gotz, mer den
anderen jn parabolen, dat sy siende
niet en sullen sien. . . . So gebruyckt
de geyst sijn ampt, ende openbaert hen
die mysterien Gotz, dat sy Gotz sin
verstaen, ende die hebben dan macht
van Gotz woordt te spreken, want sy
hebben den meyster van binnen, die
leyt hen jn alle waerheyt.⁶⁴

God's word is dark and inconceivable
even as God himself. God speaks so
that nobody can understand, and his
words are parables for those who are
abandoned in their reasoning. Therefore Christ says, Matthew 13: "It is
given unto you to know the mysteries
of the kingdom of heaven, but to them
it is not given. Therefore I speak to
them in parables: because they seeing,
see not . . ." So the spirit uses his
power and reveals God's meaning.
They then have the power to speak
of God's word, for within themselves
they have the master teaching them all
truth.

In another place the author speaks of the "illuminated" in contrast to the
"common folk." ⁶⁵

There are other indications that Waelrant was heretically minded. In
1881 G. Becker ⁶⁶ called attention to Waelrant's part in the composition and
publication of Clement Marot's Psalms, the official version of the Calvinist Church. In 1555 Waelrant published the fifty psalms by Jean Lovys in
Marot's French rhymed translation. In 1556 he published Jean Caulery's
compositions of Marot's psalms and chansons by Marot and Eustorg de
Beaulieu,⁶⁷ in spite of the fact that Marot's name had appeared on the Index

⁶⁴ *Bibliotheca Reformatoria Neerlandica*, V, 59.
⁶⁵ *Ibid.*, p. 67: "de verlichte menschen" and "dat volck." This differentiation applies
to a spiritual rather than a social hierarchy, since the Anabaptists made it abundantly
clear that they thought the simple and uneducated people were more open to the
truth than the sophisticated.
⁶⁶ Becker, *Hubert Waelrant et ses psaumes*.
⁶⁷ Becker, *Jean Caulery et ses chansons spirituelles*.

in 1554.[68] Waelrant himself composed eight psalms by Marot, and Becker points out that one of Marot's French psalms in Waelrant's collection of 1556 was composed by Clemens non Papa, whose musical setting of the one-hundred-and-fifty psalms in the Flemish language is well known under the name *Souterliedekens.*

Becker also mentions the fact that the motet books of Waelrant were on the Prohibitory Index, while Waelrant's *Primo libro de madrigali et canzoni Francezi (sic)* of 1558 was confiscated by the Inquisition in Mons in 1568.[69]

Waelrant was connected with Johannes Laet (Latius). From the prefaces of their musical publications it is evident that Waelrant is the editor and Laet the printer. Laet, however, printed not only music but also books, some of them religious. It is interesting that we find Johannes Laet, Waelrant's partner, on the *Indices librorum prohibitorum* of the sixteenth century. The Antwerp Index of 1570 contains this note: "Een Hantboexken van devotien, sine nomine auctoris. Antverpiae apud Joannem Latium anno 56." Laet printed this book stamped as heretical by the Inquisition at the same time that he printed Waelrant's compositions and editions.

Was Waelrant a Calvinist? Was he an Anabaptist? Did he change from one to the other at different times in his life? One thing seems certain: he had heretical inclinations. But his connection with the cathedral in Antwerp, as attested by the archives of the cathedral, proves that he kept up his relations with the Church. He belonged, thus, to the large group of people with divided loyalties, if not to the group of secret heretics. This, then, at last explains why a composer so eminently gifted as Waelrant should have composed so little.

Church music dominated the musical scene in the Netherlands. Evidently shaken in his belief in Catholicism, Waelrant is a unique figure among his fellow composers in the Netherlands, being the only one among them who, though greatly gifted, did not contribute one single work to the liturgy of the Roman Catholic Church. His experiences with the Inquisition, on the other hand, may have warned him against engaging too much in the composition of "heretical music."

No doubt the time of the Reformation produced artists who sacrificed their inner conviction in order to be free to create. It seems that we may see in Waelrant the reversed picture—a man who sacrificed his creative genius to his faith.

[68] Reusch, *Die Indices librorum prohibitorum,* p. 143.
[69] Sandberger on Waelrant in *Allgemeine deutsche Biographie,* and van den Borren, *Biographie Nationale Belgique.*

Religious Background 127

Listenius's and Coclico's Testimony and the Protestant Ideal of Style

In view of the preceding considerations, it seems noteworthy that the only two documents having a direct bearing on the secret chromatic art should stem from Protestant sources. Both Listenius and Coclico were Protestants. But then, why should Coclico denounce the secret chromatic art, and why should Listenius pass over it in such a strangely vague manner? We may add one more point to the interpretations already given. It was a central idea of the Reformed Church service to bring the religion to the people. To this end the Bible was translated into the vulgar tongues, theological tracts were written in the vernacular, the Latin disappeared more and more from church music, and simplicity and clarity in writing and teaching were urged time and again by Luther, by Melanchthon, and by numerous other Protestant educators. If we compare Coclico's denunciation of the secret chromatic art with Melanchthon's condemnation of a sophisticated literary style, the parallel is striking. In his work on the elements of rhetoric Melanchthon warned against an artificial style, against the search for new words, against anything which might cause obscurity or ambiguity: "diligenter fugiendum est genus sermonis inusitatum" (beware of an unaccustomed manner of speech [70]). Exactly as Melanchthon, in 1542, protested against a "genus sermonis inusitatum," so, ten years later and for the same reasons, Coclico objected to a "musica inusitata." Both demanded simplicity and clarity. Therefore, too, Listenius passed over the whole matter lightly and assured the reader that no circumlocutions and no ambiguities were necessary to explain his example of *cantus fictus*.[71]

Thus, the secret chromatic art finds itself in a paradoxical situation: camouflaged in order to escape notice on the part of the orthodox, it is rejected by the Reformers because of the ambiguities involved in that camouflage. The short life of this art is undoubtedly also conditioned by this circumstance.

The Religious Attitude of the Family Schetz

Up to this point we have based our argument on inner evidence alone. Among the works under investigation there is only one which gives us a

[70] See p. 139 for the full text of this passage.
[71] It is evident from a study of Listenius's tract that he was inspired by the ideal of simplicity, brevity, and clarity. One has but to compare his accounts of solmization and mutation with the explanations of preceding theorists. In the introduction to Chapter X on the church modes he remarked: "Ego ne videar supervacaneis verbis, materiam plus obscurare quam illustrare, breviter quod ad rem ac negotium spectat . . . dicam."

concrete indication as to who the people were for whom this music was written. We found that Clemens's motet *Jesus Nazarenus* was composed for the brothers Gaspar, Melchior, and Balthasar Schetz, the heads of the renowned Flemish trading firm Gaspar Schetz and Brothers.[72] Waelrant, too, was in contact with this Antwerp family; in 1556 he dedicated one of his editions of French chansons to Conrad Schetz, the youngest of the brothers. If we could ascertain anything about the religious attitude of the family Schetz, it might elucidate the situation considerably. I shall give a synopsis of the facts I could ascertain.

Erasmus Schetz, the father of the four brothers, was noted for his interest in the humanistic movement and for his intimate friendship with Erasmus of Rotterdam and other humanists.[73] Schetz's friendship with Erasmus began in 1525. We shall see later that to be a friend of Erasmus in those years, that is, after the introduction of the Spanish Inquisition in the Netherlands, was in itself an act of courage and an indication of liberalism. There are about seventy letters extant of the correspondence between Erasmus Schetz and Erasmus of Rotterdam.[74] They deal for the most part with business affairs, since Erasmus chose Schetz as his financial agent and adviser. In these letters we come to know Erasmus, the scholar, as a shrewd businessman, and Erasmus, the merchant, as a man of high culture. More than that, we find that Schetz belonged to those men whom we characterized at the beginning of this chapter as "possessed by a deep loyalty toward the Church, but painfully aware of the utter imperfection of her servants." In a letter to Erasmus, July 12, 1531, Schetz complained bitterly about the "greed of some, even most, of the theologians of this age who, under the pretext of religion and dignity, pillage and plunder as much as they can." [75] In another letter Schetz strongly condemned the use of force in matters of faith.[76] He was anxious to see the quarrel between Charles V and the Protestant countries settled by peaceful means.[77]

---

[72] See pp. 32 ff.

[73] Van der Aa, *Biographisch Woordenboek der Nederlanden* and Ehrenberg, *Das Zeitalter der Fugger.*

[74] Erasmus, *Opus epistolarum;* ed. by P. S. Allen. Vols. VI–X.

[75] *Ibid.,* IX, 286 ff.: "Est tam ardens per hoc seculum aliquorum, ymmo plurimorum, theologorum avaritia ut, quoquo valent, expilent et rapiant quod possunt, ac id religionis et dignitatis pretextu . . ."

[76] *Ibid.,* p. 11 (August 13, 1530): "Utinam dum de fide agitur, catholice potius, hoc est gladio spiritus, quam vi et ferro . . . belligeretur!"

[77] *Ibid.,* p. 95: "Comitiarum Augustarum . . . finis est, sed non tam felix ut cristiana res exigit, dum nil vel parum parturierint concordiae." This refers to the rather fruitless negotiations between the emperor and the Protestants at the Diet of Augsburg in 1530.

At that early date Schetz had the vision to predict that the movement of the Reformers would continue to expand if no reconciliation was effected.[78] Erasmus of Rotterdam trusted his namesake sufficiently to vent his anger without restraint when the narrow-minded opposition of Roman Catholic theologians irritated him too much. Once he confessed even to regret that he had written a single word against the Lutherans.[79] In this correspondence Erasmus Schetz appears to be broad-minded, tolerant, and liberal and not without understanding for the cause of the Reformation and the motives behind it.

We have evidence that Gaspar Schetz (1513–1580), the oldest and the most influential of Erasmus's sons, had, to say the least, the same liberal outlook as his father. At first we have to record the strange fact that Gaspar studied with Helius Eobanus Hessus, a Protestant humanist and friend of Ulrich Hutten, at Erfurt (1535) and later (1540) at Marburg; that he was introduced to Hessus by Melanchthon,[80] the great collaborator of Luther; that the friendship between the Protestant poet and the Catholic merchant's son must have been rather intimate, for in 1540 Helius dedicated his translation of Homer's *Iliad* to Gaspar, prefixing a poem in honor of the young scholar; to which Gaspar replied in a long poem, which was printed at the end of the edition.[81]

Yet, one might assume that Gaspar was a loyal member of the Roman Catholic Church, particularly after Philip II had invested him with such great power and in 1564 had made him treasurer of the Netherlands. However, we find Gaspar at the beginning of the Netherlands troubles (1565) on the side of the discontented Netherlands nobility.[82] In 1577 he opposed

[78] *Ibid.*: "Verendum est, nisi quam primum adornetur hoc celebrandum concilium, omnes reliquas orbis catholicas provintias evangelicis se seditioso tumultu addicturas."
[79] *Ibid.*, p. 461: "Theologi pro quibus steti talem referunt gratiam ut me poeniteat ullum scripsisse verbum adversus Luteranos."
[80] From Melanchthon's letters to Hessus it is evident that not only he but also Luther thought highly of the latter's poetical talent. (Melanchthon, *Opera*, I, 573, 1081.)
[81] Erasmus, *Opus epistolarum*, X, 346; see also Wauters, *Biographie nationale Belgique*, VIII, 314 ff. Erasmus entertained the highest opinion of Hessus as evidenced by the lavish praise which he bestowed upon him in a letter (D. Erasmus, *Opus epistolarum*, IX, 269) wherein he also wrote: "Ego ob dogmatum varietatem nulli amicitiam renunciavi, praesertim iis quos mihi singularis eruditio conciliavit: in quibus te vel imprimis numero, cui contigit quod M. Tullio fuit negatum . . ."
[82] Here an incident should be recorded which took place at a dinner party at Gaspar's house. Among the guests were Baron Montigny, count of Berghes, and Count Egmont. When they were speaking of Cardinal Granvella, favorite of Philip II and adviser of Margaret of Parma, governess of the Netherlands, the complaint about his insolence and his extravagance was general. The conversation turned to the bad example set by the wearing of expensive liveries by the cardinal's servants and Count Egmont declared that his own servants should appear in future clad in a plain livery. Soon the

Don Juan, the new governor, and in 1579 he participated in the mission which was to compose the differences between Philip II and the Belgian provinces. In the apology written at this occasion he showed courage in defending the misdemeanors of his countrymen, pointing out to the king the cruelty, the greed, and the insolence of the governors, the generals, and the Spanish soldiery for the past eleven years. Moreover, Gaspar predicted the impossibility of exterminating Calvinism in Holland and Zeeland. Most biographical accounts of Gaspar concur in the opinion that in spite of all this he was a loyal member of the Roman Catholic Church.[83] While this, perhaps, appeared to be true, it was not necessarily true in substance. Our doubts are based on a most trustworthy source, the confidential dispatches sent by Sir Thomas Gresham to the British State Department. From this reporter we know that Gaspar gave essential information to the Reformed Queen, Elizabeth, that he received financial rewards for his secret service [84] to the Queen and—most important—that he "favored" the Queen's religion.[85] The trustworthiness of this testimony is guaranteed not only by the personality of Sir Thomas Gresham but also by the fact that he, a Protestant himself, lived often and for long stretches of time in Gaspar's house and had a chance to know thoroughly the mind of his "very friend."

That the two great composers of the secret chromatic technique, Clemens non Papa and Hubert Waelrant, should have had intimate artistic relations with the family Schetz cannot but help to confirm our thesis as to the religious background of this novel style.

The Religious Situation in the City of Antwerp

Moreover, the whole situation in Antwerp in matters of religion corrobo-

servants of all Flemish nobles wore the same simple attire embroidered only by a fool's cap and, more often, by a cardinal's hat worn on the loose sleeve then in use for servants. This contributed to making the cardinal ridiculous, and years later Philip II reproached Count Egmont bitterly with it. (Burgon, *The Life and Time of Sir Thomas Gresham*, I, 276.) Montigny, whose name is mentioned in this incident, was known for his demonstrations of frivolity in religious matters. He openly ate meat during Lent and did not hesitate to declare that he was "fed up with masses." Pirenne, *Histoire de Belgique*, III, 433.

[83] *Biographie nationale Belgique*; A. J. van der Aa, *Biographisch Woordenboek der Nederlanden*; Ehrenberg, *Das Zeitalter der Fugger*, I, 369.

[84] "The intelligence with which Schetz supplied Gresham, and the frequent services which that eminent financial officer was able to render his friend, were of a nature so little calculated to redound to his advantage, had Gresham's letters by any accident been intercepted, that after a certain period his name is invariably indicated . . . by a cypher. When transmitting a letter of Schetz it was always with a request that 'for dyvers respects as soon as the Queene had considered them, they might be burnt.'" Burgon, *The Life and Time of Sir Thomas Gresham*, p. 367.

[85] *Ibid.*, p. 365.

rates the conclusions drawn. Since the early days of the Reformation Antwerp had been the center of all heretical movements in the Low Countries. It was in Antwerp that the first trial against a Lutheran monk was established;[86] it was there that the first victims of the Inquisition were burned in public.[87] In 1522, against the counsel of his advisers, Charles V established the Spanish Inquisition in the Netherlands, since the mild Episcopal supervision proved incapable of dealing effectively with the heretics. The Spanish Inquisition was an instrument, not of the Church, but of the State. The emperor nominated the Inquisitors and outlined their powers, which were considerable. They could, merely by denunciation, cite, arrest, and imprison all persons suspect of heresy; they could torture them into confession, confiscate their goods, banish them for a time or perpetually from any or all parts of the country, have them executed—and all this without recourse to the established order of law and without the right of appeal on the part of the accused.

After the establishment of the Inquisition the Dominicans and the Carmelites started a systematic hate campaign against Erasmus, who enjoyed a great popularity in the country, particularly in Antwerp. Martin Zipaeus, one of those belonging to the Erasmian circle, recommended to his correspondents that they hide their reformatory opinions in their letters as carefully as he had hidden Luther's books in his library.

The placard of 1529 went to the extreme of decreeing the death penalty for anyone who even discussed religious matters, except theologians, or who, knowing a person to be a heretic, would not inform the authorities of it. The Anabaptists, whose number had increased steadily in Antwerp, were banished from that city in 1534. The heretical movements, however, could not be eliminated; they went underground. Those who were convicted of heresy often preferred death to retraction; their "spiritual testaments" were published by a great number of clandestine printing establishments in Antwerp and were passed from hand to hand. Heretical books were printed under innocent titles, with forged approbations, or without place, date, and publisher. The people, of high and of low degree, took to reading the Bible to an unprecedented extent. There were literally scores of printers in Antwerp alone who engaged in the publication of new editions of the Bible, and most of them were listed on the Index of the Theo-

---

[86] See the remarks on Jacobus Praepositus on p. 113.
[87] This sketch of the religious situation in Antwerp is based mainly on the excellent representation of Pirenne, *Histoire de Belgique*, III, 344 ff.

logical Faculty of Louvain in 1546. There we find twenty editions of Latin Bibles (three of them published in Antwerp), three editions of German Bibles (all of them published in Antwerp), two editions of French Bibles (both published in Antwerp), three editions of the New Testament in Latin (two of them published in Antwerp), sixteen editions of the New Testament in German (eleven of them published in Antwerp), three editions of the New Testament in French (all of them published in Antwerp).[88] It is noteworthy that the Antwerp printers excelled in the publication of editions of the Bible in the vulgar tongues.

The placard of 1540 stated that the "cursed and perverted sects continue to multiply and that the situation grows from bad to worse." Charles V increased the terror and installed special Inquisitors for all provinces of the Netherlands. The new system was proclaimed by the placard of 1550. And now an amazing thing happened: the city of Antwerp protested energetically. The mayors of the city declared that the whole commerce of Antwerp would be ruined by such a measure, that the numerous foreign merchants, adhering to sundry creeds, would leave the city, that the famous exchange of Antwerp would be closed. The emperor, always in need of money, could not close his ears to such arguments. He exempted the foreign merchants in the new edict, he replaced the name "Inquisitor" by "ecclesiastical judge"; he pretended to be unaware of the fact that the mayors of Antwerp had accepted the edict only as far as it would not infringe upon the old privileges of the free city of Antwerp, that the mayors were not even present when the placard was proclaimed, and that the proclaimer stammered out the edict in such a manner that nobody could understand a word of it. The situation was paradoxical. Charles spared exactly that city which was the central seat of heresy; he was forced to do so because of the very people who were the most to blame for all the troubles. For there is no doubt that it is the foreign merchants, those of Germany in particular, who spread the heretical ideas in Antwerp.

In this connection it is worth while to record the fact that Waelrant dedicated his musical publications exclusively to merchantmen, among whom there were two Germans, Wilhelm Trainer of Ratisbon and Marcus Welser of Augsburg.[89] The latter is a less-well-known member of the famous Welser family, one branch of which was Protestant.[90] And another circumstance is highly significant. The booksellers of Antwerp had

[88] Reusch, *Die Indices librorum prohibitorum des 16. Jahrhunderts,* pp. 33–35.
[89] Sandberger, *Hubert Waelrant,* in *Allgemeine deutsche Biographie.*
[90] Ehrenberg, *Das Zeitalter der Fugger,* I, 199. I have been unable to find pertinent information about either Trainer or Marcus Welser of Augsburg.

a special privilege: they could not be arrested in Antwerp proper. If the authorities wanted to seize an Antwerp bookseller because he was dealing with forbidden books, they had to lure him out of the city.[91]

Conclusion

We have attempted to connect with one another the single fragments of historical information that we could gather. Let us now look at the emerging mosaic as a whole: there were a few Roman Catholic composers of religious music in the Netherlands of 1550 who employed a novel technique, which seems the more daring, since the great school of Netherlands composers of that period was largely conservative. This new technique had been rejected by the Roman Catholic Church and was hardly used by those composers who had high functions within either the Church or the State. A very small group of composers used it, nevertheless, concealing it in a most astonishing camouflage. The passages in which the new technique appears are set to words of high religious emotion and belong to texts which have a distinctly reformatory ring. The scenes chosen by the composers were the same as those that were represented in contemporary reformatory plays and in reformatory tracts and songs. These same composers were engaged in setting to music and publishing a psalm version officially approved by a heretical sect and disapproved by the Church. They worked with a printer whose name appeared on the Index. Some of their works were confiscated by the Inquisition. One of them failed to choose even a single text devoted to the liturgy of the Roman Catholic Church. One of the works containing the secret technique was composed for a wealthy and distinguished Flemish family whose members were in many ways connected with the liberal movements in the country and showed understanding and even sympathy for the Reformation, though only in such manner as was compatible with their security. This family, as well as one of the two most important composers of the group, lived at the central seat of heresy of the Low Countries, the city of Antwerp, which successfully fought the establishment of the Spanish Inquisition within its walls at exactly the time when the new art was flourishing. It is in the light of this evidence that we have to examine every fact which otherwise might have a neutral character. If we accept the assumption that the composers of the secret chromatic art harbored reformatory feelings and ideas, the hidden nature of the new art gains a deeper perspective. Far from merely indulging in the joy of artful play, these composers attempted to create

---

[91] Reusch, *Der Index der verbotenen Bücher*, I, 100n.

a technique which would give them new means of expression for a new religious feeling and at the same time protect themselves from suspicion and persecution. Since chromaticism is a child of the Italian Renaissance, the secret chromatic art seems not only a combination of Italian and Netherlands technique but also a synthesis of the ideas of the Renaissance and the Reformation.

IX: THE MEANING OF DOUBLE MEANING IN THE SIXTEENTH CENTURY

The art-historian will have to check what he thinks is the *intrinsic meaning* of the work or a group of works, to which he devotes his attention, against what he thinks is the *intrinsic meaning* of as many other documents of civilization historically related to that work or group of works, as he can master: of documents bearing witness to the political, poetical, religious, philosophical, and social tendencies of the personality, period or country under investigation. Needless to say that, conversely, the historian of political life, poetry, religion, philosophy, and social situations should make an analogous use of works of art. It is in the search for *intrinsic meanings* or *content* that the various humanistic disciplines meet on a common plane instead of serving as handmaidens to each other.—E. Panofsky, *Studies in Iconology*, Introductory.

ONE OF the outstanding characteristics of the secret chromatic art is its ambiguity. It allows of two readings: one is literal; the other is implied.

This musical double talk finds its counterpart in almost every field of human thought and creative activity in the sixteenth century. It constitutes one of the most puzzling traits in the physiognomy of this period. So far as I know this phenomenon has not yet been made the topic of a comprehensive investigation, though many writers have touched upon it in one field or another. To treat the problem as it deserves to be treated would mean to write another book. To leave it out completely would deprive our study of its full illumination. It is impossible to grasp the implications of the secret chromatic art if we do not realize that the whole thought of the time [1] was pervaded by the subtle play of meaning and double meaning.

The present chapter is insufficient and incomplete—nobody can realize

---

[1] I should like to make it clear from the very outset that many, indeed, most of the phenomena mentioned in this chapter, though relevant to the Renaissance, are not exclusively peculiar to this period. In the course of this disquisition I will have to refer time and again to medieval, to ancient, and to Eastern models for many of the devices employed during the period under discussion. The man of the Renaissance was passionately interested in everything secret and esoteric and studied all available models wherever he could find them. However, new and original techniques were evolved, old concepts were changed and reinterpreted, and the persistent appearance of double meaning in every field of human endeavor indicates that duplicity became almost a habit of mind with the man of the Renaissance. Nevertheless, in singling out this widespread attitude for closer analysis we are aware of the fact that it represents only one facet in the spiritual physiognomy of the time.

this more clearly than does the author. It may, nevertheless, suffice for our limited purpose, which is to hint at the background of what seems at first not more than a peculiar musical technique.

In the fifteenth and sixteenth centuries a tremendous surge of new religious, philosophical, scientific, and artistic ideas clashed with one of the most intolerant systems of intellectual policing, which covered every area of human creativeness and interfered with every new idea of consequence. The invention of the printing press and the possibility of spreading every new idea to all corners of Europe gave new impetus to the spirit of revolt from Rome and constituted a serious challenge to the firm grip of the Roman Catholic Church on the souls and minds of the faithful. The Church answered with the establishment of the Index, which listed all books considered heretical or dangerous by the Fathers of the *Santo Ufficio*.

It is a most illustrious society of artists, writers, philosophers, theologians, scientists, and politicians which fills the silent lists of the numerous Indexes of the Cinquecento. We find here not only the outspoken heretics, but almost every independent thinker of the age, even though he may have professed the Catholic religion publicly and loudly. We meet Cardinal Bembo, the philosophers Pico della Mirandola and Pietro Pomponazzi, the architect Leon Battista Alberti, the courtier Baldesar Castiglione, the politician Machiavelli, the poet Torquato Tasso, the uncouth Rabelais, the witty and wise Erasmus, the ill-mannered Pietro Aretino, the skeptical Cornelius Agrippa, the physician Theophrast Paracelsus, the bibliographer Conrad Gesner, the eminent statesman Sir Thomas More, and numerous other highly original personalities. While a potential danger was felt in every free intellectual activity, the main defense of the Church was directed against new ventures in the field of theology.

Theology

From the beginning the Inquisition recognized the danger of the secret heretics and the subtle skeptics who sought protection in double meaning and subterfuge. In the preamble of the Index drawn up by the faculty of theology of the University of Louvain in 1546 we read a sharp condemnation of translators of the Bible who by a seemingly innocent marginal remark distorted the true meaning of the Bible and stirred up the people to all kinds of religious doubts and disobedience.[2] The same body of professors remarked in the Index of the year 1550 that there must be prohibited not only those books which are notoriously heretical but also those which

[2] Reusch, *Die Indices librorum prohibitorum*, p. 31.

under the veil of assumed sincerity attract the simple and plain people, only to mislead them.[3] And again in their Index of 1558 we find a bitter denunciation of those "false preachers" (II Corinthians 11) who dare not show openly their heresies, but try to introduce them by subtle and hidden means into their writings.[4]

The integrity of the Church dogma was compromised by a growing tendency toward a double interpretation of the Bible. Pico della Mirandola (1463–1494) held that the Bible had a literal meaning and a secret meaning, the latter closed to the *volgo profano*. The literal meaning can be grasped by the "occhio nudo" (the naked eye), but the discovery of the hidden meaning of the Bible needs the "intelletto esperto" (the expert intellect).[5]

Savonarola, whose friend and admirer Pico was, believed firmly in the hidden meaning of the Bible. To him "every image, every allegory, every parable, every figure, has not one, but a thousand meanings. Meanings each of the same authority with its plainest and most literal significance . . ."[6]

Sebastian Franck, in his *Chronica*, of 1531, called the Scriptures a book sealed with seven seals, which is "so composed of the words of God that none may understand it save His children, with whom He speaks in parables and mysteries, in order that they only may perceive who are born of Him. This obscure speech is sealed to all who are without, that is, to all the world."[7] The Anabaptists adhered to the same creed, differentiating between a literal and a figurative interpretation of the Bible, as we saw in the preceding chapter.

The philosopher-monk Thomas Campanella in his *Defense of Galileo* against the charge of having violated the Scriptures, pointed out the ambiguous character of the Bible. The Scriptures contain, he said, "a mystical meaning for the wise as well as an obvious meaning for the vulgar." Thereupon he proceeded to interpret all statements in the Scripture apparently contradicting the new scientific ideas as written according to the limited understanding of the "vulgar."[8]

These are only a few of the exponents of the double or multiple interpretation of the Scriptures. They were inspired by very diverse motives: Pico della Mirandola by his desire to reconcile pagan philosophy with

---

[3] *Ibid.*, p. 46 ". . . mais aussi ceulx qui soubz umbre de sincerite ou pretext de pure ou facille religion attirent par fraude et abuz le simple peuple . . ."
[4] *Ibid.*, p. 49.   [5] Anagnine, *Giovanni Pico della Mirandola.*
[6] Villari, *The History of Girolamo Savonarola*, p. 113.
[7] Bainton, *Concerning Heretics*, p. 186.
[8] *The Defense of Galileo of Thomas Campanella*, trans., ed. by Grant McColley, p. 27.

Christian faith, Savonarola by his efforts aimed at a fundamental reform of the Church, Sebastian Franck by his mystical belief in an invisible spiritual Church, and Campanella by his enthusiasm for the new science. Since they remained in the Roman Catholic camp and had to justify their views, they had to resort to the theory of an esoteric meaning of the Scriptures which would support their beliefs.

The idea of a multiple interpretation of the Bible was old. The scholastics distinguished between a literal, a figurative, a moral, and an anagogical sense,[9] of which the last one was often considered to embody the mystic, the esoteric meaning. Thus the new interpretation of the Scriptures was founded upon a legitimate basis. New, in the Christian tradition, were not only some of the motives behind the fresh surge of hermeneutics in the fifteenth and the sixteenth centuries and, of course, many of the results but also some of the methods. One has only to look at that strange piece of exegesis, Pico's interpretation of the first word of the Old Testament, *Bereshit*, out of which he construed a prophecy of Christ's advent by the cabalistic method of substitution and numerical interpretation of letters.[10] Agrippa of Nettesheim, Paracelsus, Reuchlin, and especially Pico della Mirandola studied the Cabala. Pico called it "that secret revelation of the Law which Moses and his successor Joshua Navin . . . reserved for the initiated only, since they thought it not possible 'to cast pearls before swine,' to reveal its mystery to the mob . . ." [11]

It is highly interesting to observe that the Protestants discarded the doctrine of the multiple interpretation of the Bible. Having left the Roman Catholic Church and having succeeded early—unlike the Anabaptists—in establishing political security, they saw no need of justification by a supposedly hidden meaning of the Bible. Melanchthon, in his work on rhetoric,

---

[9] An old verse explains the fourfold sense thus:
> Littera gesta docet; quid credas, allegoria;
> Moralis, quid agas; quo tendas anagogia.

In a well-known example the fourfold sense is illustrated by defining Jerusalem literally as "city," figuratively as "the Church," according to the moral meaning as "the moral order," according to the anagogical meaning as "everlasting life." The tradition of the fourfold sense of the Scriptures went back to Thomas Aquinas and the early Fathers, who had taken it over from Origen and Philo, while Philo, in turn, was influenced by the ancient tradition of Jewish exegesis as well as by the Platonic and Stoic theory of interpretation of Homer. (Caplan, "The Four Senses of Scriptural Interpretation and the Mediaeval Theory of Preaching," *Speculum*, IV [1929], 282 ff.)

[10] Anagnine, *Giovanni Pico della Mirandola*, p. 188. Incidentally, his belief in the cabala as representing a prophecy of Christ's advent was one of those thirteen theses "which savored of heresy." To defend himself he wrote his *Apologia*, which, however, did not save him from being forced into full submission (Lea, *History of the Inquisition*, III, 573).

[11] Anagnine, *Giovanni Pico della Mirandola*, p. 104.

expressly rejected a belief in any kind of ambiguity or obscurity, any attempt to interpret a secret language; he even specifically refuted the methods of Bible interpretation used by cabalists and Anabaptists and stated flatly that this kind of thought and speech was professed by heretics.

Fugienda est in sermone peregrinitas, et illam licentiam gignendi novum sermonem, nullo modo permittamus nobis, qua in scholis immodice utuntur. . . . Quia notae res omnes verbis exponi notis et significantibus possunt. Exempla extant infinita in omnibus artibus, ubi saepe inepte finguntur nova vocabula. . . . Amaverunt tale dicendi genus et haeretici, ut Valentinianus excogitavit quadrigas αἰώνων. Nec minus sunt inepti Judaeorum Cabalistae, qui novis verbis repertis, mira mysteria promittunt, cum meras nugas doceant, et nostro tempore Anabaptistae, prodigiosis figuris utuntur. Tali orationi vix unquam subsunt res ullae cognitionae dignae aut utiles. . . . Certissimum enim indicium est monstrosae mentis, oratio monstrosa, quare diligenter fugiendum est genus sermonis inusitatum. . .[12]

Avoid sophistication in your mode of expression; we shall under no circumstances permit ourselves the license of creating a novel style which they use so excessively in the schools [of the Scholastics]. . . . For, all known things can be expounded by known and clear words. There are innumerable examples extant in all professions, where new terms are invented, often quite foolishly. . . . The heretics, too, loved this kind of speech. Valentinianus, for example, contrived the term of the four ages. Not less absurd are the Jewish cabalists, who by devising new words prophesy miraculous mysteries, while they teach sheer nonsense; and in our time the Anabaptists use prodigious allegories. There are hardly any things worth knowing or useful underneath such a style. . . . The surest indication of an unnatural state of mind is an unnatural style. Therefore, carefully avoid any uncommon manner of speech.

Social Criticism

In the field of social and political criticism of the Renaissance—as in much satire earlier and later—we find that outstanding men had recourse to the device of double meaning.

When Erasmus wanted to say what he thought about this world and its institutions, secular and ecclesiastical, he was careful to put his ideas into the mouth of Folly, "for," says Folly, "I do not feign one thing in my face while I hold something else in my heart."[13] This is, of course, exactly what Erasmus did—feign one thing in his face while holding some-

[12] Melanchthon, *Philippi Melanthonis Opera*, ed. by C. G. Bretschneider, XIII, 462.
[13] The *Praise of Folly* by Desiderius Erasmus, trans. from the Latin . . . by H. H. Hudson; the first edition appeared in 1512 under the title *Encomium moriae*.

thing else in his heart. He feigned folly, but in his heart he wanted to slash out against the madness and the hypocrisy of the age. Both tendencies are clearly manifest in the Preface, a masterpiece of cunning and dissimulation, in which Folly and Erasmus seem to change parts constantly. While Folly tries to ridicule the whole undertaking, presenting it as a scholarly sport and spiritual recreation, Erasmus hints at the serious background of it. Evidently it is Folly who says: ". . . what an injustice it is, when we allow to each way of life its own recreation, that none should be permitted to studies." And Erasmus observes: "Especially when literary trifles may lead to serious matter, and fooleries may be so handled that a reader who is not altogether a fathead may garner more of profit from them than from the bristling and pompous arguments of some whom we know." Folly continues, "this liberty has always been permitted to men of wit, that in their jests they may poke fun at the general manners of men with impunity"; to which Erasmus remarks, "For this reason I wonder a little at the tenderness of ears in these times, which can tolerate nothing, almost, but solemn forms of address. . . . Besides, he who spares no class of men would seem to be angry at no person, but at the vices of all. . . . Saint Jerome indulged in this kind of writing, and with greater freedom and sharpness." Frightened by the adduction of so solemn an authority, Folly is quick to reassure the "judicious reader . . . that my end is pleasure rather than censure," and "I take care to set out things that are ridiculous rather than foul. Still, if there is anyone whom the work cannot please, he should at least remember this, that it is a fine thing to be slandered by Folly," to which Erasmus agrees: "Since I have feigned her speaking, it was of course necessary to preserve decorum in her character."

There is no mistaking the tone of earnestness and of heartfelt concern with which Erasmus satirizes theology and theologians in his *Moria*. Few sentences in Erasmus's writings seem to come so genuinely from the very depth of his heart and mind as, for example, his bitter denunciation of the endless and hairsplitting theological arguments concerning the last things, "this speaking with unclean lips about holy things, which are rather to be worshiped than expounded." [14]

At the end of his work Erasmus dismisses his audience in exactly the same manner as he had welcomed it. He makes a series of statements, one neutralizing the other so as to allow of a double interpretation as to what he really wanted to convey. First he blames everything which may seem

[14] *Ibid.*, p. 83.

"too saucy or too glib" on Folly, who, after all, is but a woman.[15] Then he lifts his finger and reminds his audience of the Greek proverb "Even a foolish man will often speak a word in season." Finally, he admits with a smile that "perhaps" this proverb "does not extend to women."

But these wily maneuvers could not appease the theologians. Erasmus grew so concerned about the attacks opened upon him by them that he chose a letter of criticism from Martin Dorp, theologian of the University of Louvain, as a suitable occasion for an answer. This answer was added to later editions of the *Moria*, and in 1540 it was included in the edition of Erasmus's works among the *Apologiae*. It numbers twenty-five printed pages.[16] An indication of how seriously the *Moria* was taken by Erasmus's contemporaries may be seen in the fact that Dorp reproved it in his letter, together with Erasmus's critical edition of the New Testament according to the Greek sources, and his edition of Saint Jerome's writings. In Erasmus's *Apologia* we find such amazing statements as these: "First, let me tell you quite frankly that I almost regret the publication of the *Moria*." [17] In another passage he pleads "perhaps" guilty to the charge that Folly is too frivolous a person to discuss such serious matters.[18] To see Erasmus seek cover in the foxholes of regret and revocation with nothing left for posterity but an "almost" and a "perhaps" to guess his true mind, this truly is a miserable sight. But then, Erasmus understood that this was the price he had to pay if he wanted to be left alone with his studies. "I wish," he sighs, "to have all men placated, if it were possible." [19]

That Erasmus constructed the Preface and the Conclusion of the *Moria* with the intention of having a possible alibi is evident from the letter to Dorp, in which he quotes them as witnesses to his good intentions.[20] But he takes only those sentences from the context which Folly speaks, not those in which we find Erasmus himself, true and unadulterated.

Not even the *Apologia* appeased the theologians. We see that Erasmus took up his pen more than once in renewed defense of his *Praise of Folly*.[21]

[15] *Moria*, the Latinized version of the Greek word, is feminine.
[16] *Opus epistolarum*, ed. by P. S. Allen, II, 90 ff. The letter was written from Antwerp in 1515, three years after the publication of the *Encomium moriae*.
[17] *Ibid.*, p. 92: "Primum igitur ut ingenue dicem, aeditae Moriae propemodum me poenitet."
[18] *Ibid.*, p. 94: "Quod si respondebis personam quam induxi leviorem esse quam ut sub illius praetextu de rebus seriis disputetur, hanc culpam fortassis agnoscam."
[19] *Ibid.*, p. 107: ". . . cupiam, si liceat, universos mortales habere placatos."
[20] *Ibid.*, p. 105.
[21] *Ibid.*, p. 169, letter to a theologian in Bergen of December, 1517; *ibid.*, p. 183, letter of January, 1518, to another theologian in Louvain.

"I wonder," he exclaims, "why of all people only monks and theologian are offended." [22] But he promises more moderation hereafter.[23]

It was in England, during his stay at Sir Thomas More's home, that Erasmus wrote his *Encomium moriae*. He dedicated the book to his host, to whom he alluded in the punning manner of the humanists by the title of his work. More possibly conceived the first idea of his *Utopia* while reading the *Praise of Folly*.[24] In his amazingly daring representation of a new community, More created a positive counterpart to Erasmus's criticism of contemporary society.

As Erasmus had put his opinions into the mouth of Folly, so More had the account of the Utopian state given by Raphael Hythlodaye,[25] a traveler from the fabulous oversea island Utopia, while he himself was portrayed as being one of the listeners who participated in criticism and discussion. In a most perplexing manner he has mixed serious description of community life, education, religion, culture, and economics with half fantastic, half-humorous notions. And More dismissed his readers—exactly as did Erasmus—in a way which left them uncertain as to what the author thought himself.

When Raphael had thus finished his discourse [the concluding sentences run] though many things occurred to me in the manners and laws of this people which seemed sufficiently absurd, as their art of war, their notions of religions etc. but principally (what seemed the foundation of the rest) their living in common without the use of money, by which all nobility, splendour, and majesty, in the common opinion the true ornaments of a nation, would be destroyed; yet perceiving him to be weary and being uncertain whether he

[22] *Ibid.*, p. 183: "Illud demiror, cur omnium soli monachi et theologi offendantur."
[23] Ibid., ". . . in ceteris posthac agam moderatius."
[24] Ruegg, "Des Erasmus 'Lob der Torheit' und Thomas More's 'Utopie,'" in *Gedenkschrift zum vierhundertsten Todestage des Erasmus von Rotterdam*.
[25] The name Hythlodaye, as derived from Greek roots, has been explained as meaning "fashioner of deception," "artist in visions" (see George Sampson's edition of the *Utopia*, p. 24n). But it seems to have passed unnoticed that the name of the fabulous stranger in itself constitutes an ambiguity. Whereas the name Hythlodaye alludes to the fanciful character of the tale, Raphael, in Hebrew, means "the divine healer" and may well point to the philosophical and moral background of the work. In the apocryphal narrative of Tobias, Raphael appears as the messenger of the Lord's help, delivering Sarah from her plague and Tobit from his blindness (*Cyclopaedia of Biblical, Theological and Ecclesiastical Literature*). This agrees exactly with the description of Raphael given in the introduction to *Utopia*. There the seafarer is compared with Ulysses (Hythlodaye) on the one hand and with Plato (Raphael) on the other. Throughout the book More has invented his names in a meaningful manner. He was not the only one who employed this technique. We shall find it used by Gringoire and by Marot. The whole age enjoyed playing on the meaning of names. Erasmus gives outstanding examples of this technique in his letters to Leo X and to the humanist Beatus Rhenanus (*Opus epistolarum*, II, 61 ff., 79 ff.).

ould easily bear contradiction (for I remembered he had noticed some who
eemed to think they were bound to support the credit of their wisdom, by
inding something to censure in all other men's inventions), I only commended
he constitution and the account he had given of it, in general terms; and,
eading him to supper, said I would find some other time for examining this
ubject more particularly. Indeed, I shall be glad to embrace an opportunity of
o doing. Meanwhile, though it must be confessed he is a very learned man, and
ne who hath acquired great knowledge of the world, I cannot assent to every
hing he hath said. Yet I freely confess, there are many things in the common
vealth of Utopia, which I wish, but have no hope of seeing adopted among
ıs.[26]

If More intended to puzzle and divide his readers as to what he himself
hought and stood for, he succeeded admirably.[27] *Utopia* has been regarded
ıs "one of the great sphinxes of world literature." There exist two schools
of thought; one sees in the *Utopia* a serious outline of an ideal state; the
other is inclined to dismiss it as a mere play of fancy.[28] It is an interesting
fact, however, that many outstanding contemporaries of Sir Thomas seem
to have taken the *Utopia* very seriously.[29] So did the Index Congregations.
Both Erasmus's *Encomium moriae* and More's *Utopia* are to be found on
sixteenth-century Indexes.

Philosophy

In philosophy one main escape for the free thought of the time was the
doctrine of the twofold truth, the idea that there was one kind of truth
in religion and another equally valid one in philosophy. The doctrine of
the twofold truth had a long history; throughout the Middle Ages it was
connected with the name of the famous Arabic philosopher, Averroës
(1120–1198). Averroës lived and taught under circumstances which were

[26] *Memoirs of Sir Thomas Moore, with a New Translation of His Utopia* . . . by
Arthur Cayley, the Younger Esq., II, 145.
[27] In conversation, too, More seems to have enjoyed puzzling his partners. He made
a friend say to him: "Ye use to look so sadly when ye mean merrily, that many times
men doubt whether ye speak in sport, when ye mean good earnest" (Chambers,
Thomas More, p. 18).
[28] Ruegg, "Des Erasmus 'Lob der Torheit' und Thomas More's 'Utopie'"; see also
Chambers, *Thomas More*, p. 23.
[29] For a selection of contemporary opinions see Dermenghem, *Thomas Morus et les
Utopistes de la Renaissance*. That there was good reason for More to be very cautious
in airing his views is evident from a letter to his friend, the humanist Budé, who
suggested the publication of More's letters in a volume of Budé's correspondence.
More asked his friend to wait a while, until he had revised his letters, since he feared
not only that some passages were badly phrased in Latin, but also that what he had
written on peace and war, morality, marriage, the clergy, the people, etc., was not
always "so cautious and guarded that it would be wise to expose it to captious critics"
(Routh, *Sir Thomas More and His Friends*, p. 115).

very similar to the situation of a European intellectual in the sixteenth century. In the twelfth century Islam organized a systematic persecution of all philosophy and free thought. Trials were established because of alleged atheism, books were burned and sometimes their authors, too.[30] Against the background of such events Averroës wrote his *Harmony of Philosophy and Theology,* in which he attempted to prove the fundamental agreement between religion and philosophy.

Averroës nowhere stated the theory of the *duplex veritas* clearly and as a principle.[31] He did believe, however, in the doctrine of a double meaning of the Koran. The literal sense of the Koran represents the exoteric meaning; the esoteric meaning is to be disclosed by interpretation. Only the "learned in philosophy" are able and justified to find out the hidden meaning of the Koran. "But one who is not learned should take it exoterically; an interpretation in his case is unbelief, for it leads to infidelity." [32]

It has been asserted that the doctrine of the double meaning of the Scriptures has nothing whatever to do with the doctrine of the double truth.[33] It seems to me, however, that the theory of the double meaning of the Scriptures can be stretched to a point where it is in essence nothing but a disguised theory of double truth. This point is reached when a contradiction between philosophy and religion is resolved by the declaration that the findings of philosophy are true (because they rest on a logical foundation) and all opposition to religion is only apparent, since interpretation, if applied correctly to the Scriptures, will verify the results of philosophical reasoning. I believe that Averroës, with a reservation as to the three principles of faith—the belief in God, in prophecy, and in the happiness or the misery of the next world—had reached just this point. In his *Harmony of Philosophy and Theology* he says:

. . . rational investigation is not contrary to Law,[34] for truth cannot contradict truth,[35] but verifies it and bears testimony to it. . . . We hold it to be an established truth that, if the Law is apparently opposed to a truth proved by philosophy, it admits of an interpretation according to the canons of the Arabic language. . . . The aim of this discourse is to bring together intellectual and traditional science. Indeed, we would even say that no logical conclusion will be

[30] Renan, *Averroës et l'averroïsme,* pp. 22–23.
[31] Mauser, "Das Verhältnis von Glauben und Wissen bei Averroës," in *Jahrbuch für Philosophie und spekulative Theologie,* 1910–1911.
[32] Quoted from Mohammad Jamil-Ur-Rehman, *The Philosophy and Theology of Averroës,* p. 50.
[33] Ueberweg, *Grundriss der Geschichte der Philosophie,* III, 321.
[34] Averroës uses the concept of Law as synonymous with that of religion.
[35] This is the nearest I can find in Averroës's tract to an expression which would suggest a belief in the existence of two kinds of truth.

found to be opposed to the Law, which when sifted and investigated in its different parts will be found in accordance, or almost so,[36] with it.

It may be on account of passages like this one that the doctrine of the two-fold truth has been ascribed to Averroës. In any event, he and the theory of the double truth exercised a great influence upon European thinkers in the Middles Ages and the Renaissance. His teachings dominated the Italian universities of Bologna, Ferrara, Naples, and especially Padua.[37]

It is in Padua, and later in Ferrara and Bologna, that we find Pietro Pomponazzi (1462–1525), teacher of natural philosophy and one of the most eminent exponents of the doctrine of the twofold truth in the philosophy of the Renaissance. Though holding many views that conflict with those of Averroës, he agrees with him in the conviction that the Scriptures contain many things which cannot be taken literally, *non possunt intelligi ut litera sonat.* He believed in the *sensus mysticus,* in the mystical meaning, that is wisely hidden from the masses, who cannot grasp things immaterial.[38] Pomponazzi referred explicitly to Averroës in comparing religious language to poetry, which may not be taken literally either, but which contains hidden truth, *ut verba sonant non sunt possibiles, intus tamen veritatem continent.*[39] Pomponazzi's writings are puzzling in the extreme if one takes them at face value. They lose their contradictory character if one admits his conscious use of ambiguous language to cover his daring and often downright blasphemous ideas.[40] The very title of one

[36] I wish to emphasize these three words "or almost so." They remind one slightly of the style Erasmus uses when treating of problems of similar delicacy. Mauser (*op. cit.*) draws attention to Averroës's statement that there may be cases where a philosophical demonstration is contradicted by one passage of the Koran if taken literally. In this case Averroës is of the opinion that the common people are obliged to believe in the literal sense as representing the revealed truth. Mauser maintains that this attitude represents practically the doctrine of the twofold truth, since it results in the thesis that one and the same theory may be true according to belief and false according to philosophy.
[37] The reader interested in Averroës's influence upon medieval thought is referred to Mandonnet, *Siger de Brabant et l'averroisme latin au XIIIe siècle.*
[38] It is quite common for Pomponazzi to distinguish in his discussion between the general opinion, *secundum vulgares,* and the philosophical opinion, *secundum philosophos.* (Douglas, *The Philosophy and Psychology of Pietro Pomponazzi,* p. 297.) As to Pomponazzi's somewhat complicated relations with Averroës see Renan, *Averroës et l'averroisme,* pp. 276 ff.
[39] Quoted by Douglas, *The Philosophy and Psychology of Pietro Pomponazzi,* p. 287.
[40] "In his treatise *De incantationibus* he argued away all miracles. The bones of a dog would effect cures as readily as the relics of a saint if the patient's imagination entertained the same belief in them. Like Peter of Abano, moreover, he held that everything is according to the order of nature; revolutions of empires and religions follow the course of the stars; thaumaturgists are but skilful physicists who foresee the occult influences at work and profit by the suspension of ordinary laws to found new religions; when the influences cease, miracles cease, religions decay, and incredulity

of his most important works was meant to mislead the theologians. In his treatise on immortality he undertook to prove the mortality of the soul, as was correctly observed by the Master of the Holy Office.[41] Of course, Pomponazzi conducted his argument in a most careful manner and, after having discussed the problem from all angles, bowed devoutly before the Apostolic seat and subjected himself in this as in all other matters to the superior wisdom of the Mother Church.[42] Agostino Nifo and Marsilio Ficino concluded philosophical treatises in almost exactly the same manner.[43]

Pomponazzi's sincerity in acknowledging the superior wisdom of the Church is open to doubt. In the notebooks of one of his students, who took down his lectures, he is said to have given this advice to his students: believe in philosophy as much as your reason dictates; believe in theology as much as the Church dictates. To do otherwise would mean your death at the stake.[44] In another passage the student reports that Pomponazzi quoted Aristotle to the effect that nobody can in his mind concede the truth of two ideas that contradict each other, for contradictory opinions are incompatible in thinking; we can concede them with our mouths, but never in our minds.

Highly illuminating is Pomponazzi's own comment upon the reason which may have prompted the religious legislator to assume the theory of immortality: the legislator, aiming at the common good, sanctioned the theory of the soul's immortality, herein concerning himself, not with the truth, but only with morality, in order to induce men to virtue—and the politician ought not to be blamed for that.[45] This statement is of central importance in view of what follows. At the conclusion of this book, as we

would triumph if renewed conjunctions of the planets did not cause fresh prodigies and new thaumaturgists. All this was far worse than anything for which Cecco d'Ascoli suffered, but Pietro escaped his fate by cautiously excepting the Christian faith." (Lea, *History of the Inquisition*, III, 575.)

[41] "In fact the only work which gave him serious trouble was his treatise *De immortalitate animae*, written after the Lateran denunciation in 1516, which, Prierias informs us, ought rather to have been entitled *De mortalitate* . . . The thin veil . . . cast over its infidelity did not save the book in Venice, where the patriarch had it publicly burned and wrote to Cardinal Bembo to have it condemned in Rome. Bembo read it with great gusto, pronounced it conformable with the faith, and gave it to the Master of the Sacred Palace, who reached the same opinion. The latter's successor in Office, however, Prierias, was less indulgent." *Ibid.*, pp. 575–576.
[42] *Ibid.*   [43] *Ibid.*
[44] Francesco Fiorentino, *Studi e ritratti della Rinascenza.*
[45] "Legislator . . . intendens communi bono, sanxit animam esse immortalem non curans de veritate, sed tantum de probitate, ut inducat homines ad virtutem, neque accusandus est politicus." (Quoted by Betzendörfer, *Glauben und Wissen bei den grossen Denkern des Mittelalters*, p. 196.)

shall see presently, Pomponazzi glorified religion as the only source of illumination as to the problem of immortality; in the statement quoted above, however, he discredits this same source in that it advocates a philosophical theory for opportunistic reasons only. This reasoning takes on added significance in the light of Averroës's condemnation of it, which carries a special weight coming as it does from one who pleaded constantly for tolerance in religious matters and, moreover, was regarded as an enemy of religion throughout the Middle Ages. Averroës writes: ". . . if a man believes that there is no happiness or misery in the next world, and that the teaching is only an artifice to safeguard the life and property of the people from one another and that there is no goal for men other than this life, then he certainly is an unbeliever." [46] To anyone conversant with Averroës's ideas it must have been evident that Pomponazzi gave no unclear indication of the state of his mind when he repudiated even what Averroës did not dispute. Perhaps it was in answer to this opinion of Averroës that Pomponazzi said: ". . . it must be taken into account that there have been many who have known the soul to be mortal, but have dissembled their belief, because of reserve or as a moral precaution." [47]

In his attempt to speak his mind and at the same time to safeguard himself from being denounced as a heretic Pomponazzi uses in principle the same methods as did Erasmus. He conducts his argument by way of contradictions which he does not try to reconcile. Thus, he stimulates the reader to discover for himself the true mind of the author. In the last chapter, for example, Pomponazzi declares the problem of the immortality of the soul to be a neutral one, since "no natural reasons can be adduced proving that the soul is immortal and less proving that the soul is mortal." He quotes Plato, who says "that to be certain of anything, when many are in doubt, is for God alone." After having thus taken the stand of the skeptic, Pomponazzi moves to the antithesis: "Yet it does not seem to be fitting nor expedient that man should lack such certainty. For if he were in doubt on this matter, he would also have actions uncertain without end." [48] And in the next paragraph the skeptic is transformed into a dogmatist:

Wherefore, if those reasonings seem to prove the mortality of the soul they are false and mere semblances, since the first light and the first truth show the op-

---

[46] Quoted from Mohammad Jamil-Ur-Rehman, *The Philosophy and Theology of Averroës*, p. 46.
[47] Quoted by Douglas, *The Philosophy and Psychology of Pietro Pomponazzi*, p. 268.
[48] Pomponatius, *Tractatus de immortalitate animae*, trans. by W. H. Hay II.

posite. If some then seem to prove its immortality, they are indeed true and clear, but not light and truth. Wherefore this way alone is very firm, unshaken and lasting: the rest are untrustworthy.

Moreover every art ought to proceed by things proper and fitting to that art; for otherwise it is faulty and proceeds not according to the rule of art, as Aristotle says in the first book of *Posteriora* and of *Ethica*. But that the soul is immortal is an article of faith, as is plain by the Apostles' and the Athanasian Creed; therefore it ought to be proved by things proper to faith. The principle by which faith is supported is revelation and the canonical scriptures. Therefore it is proved only truly and properly by these; but other reasons are foreign and are supported on a proof not proving what is intended. Therefore it is not surprising if philosophers disagree among themselves about the immortality of the soul, when they rely on arguments foreign to the conclusion and fallacious; but all followers of Christ agree, since they proceed by proper and infallible things, since these cannot be except according to one mode. Wherefore one must assert without doubt that it is immortal.[49]

But doubt is stirred in the reader's mind by Pomponazzi's very next sentence, which is full of implications that must have been easily grasped by those familiar with the philosophical currents of the time.

But one must not go that way which the wise men of this age have gone, who, when they call themselves wise, become fools. For whoever goes this way, as I think, will waver always uncertain and wandering; whence I believe that, even though Plato wrote so many and such great things about the immortality of the souls, yet I think he did not have certainty.[50]

It is one of Pomponazzi's subtleties to appeal to Plato when chiding the modern followers of Plato.

In the heading of this chapter Pomponazzi promises to posit "the final conclusion in this matter, which, in my opinion, seems must be maintained without doubt."[51] What is the final conclusion? Is the soul mortal; is it immortal? Are we to judge according to "natural reasons" or according to religion? Is religion a reliable authority as to the truth of the idea of immortality? Is human reason a competent judge in this question? Are we to strive for certainty in this problem, or is certainty not desirable? Is certainty possible at all concerning a metaphysical problem like this or is it "for God alone"? To each of these questions two answers, one contradicting the other, may be found in Pomponazzi's treatise. Sometimes his manner of writing reminds me of one of the tricky musical compositions of his day in which either certain notes or certain rests had to be disregarded if one was to arrive at the real score as conceived by the com-

[49] *Ibid.*   [50] *Ibid.*   [51] *Ibid.*

poser. Similarly, Pomponazzi seems to invite the reader to disregard certain opinions uttered in the treatise and thus to arrive at his real meaning. Since the coexistence of opposite opinions in one mind is logically inadmissible, which opinions may Pomponazzi want us to disregard, the ones based upon reason or the others based on revelation?

His readers seem to have concluded that Pomponazzi wanted them to neglect the opinions based on revelation. For three years after the treatise had gone to press Pomponazzi was forced to add a strange theological comment to it, not only because "in the future many might be led into error," but because already now "some people have greatly erred from the path of truth, inasmuch as they assumed that I felt the soul was mortal." But Pomponazzi calls God to witness that this was not his considered opinion about the soul.[52] The theological comment was composed by the Reverend Father Chrysostomus, who carefully refuted every argument brought forward in favor of the mortality of the soul, and the words just quoted were written by Pomponazzi in the Preface to the comment of the padre. The whole affair was handled in a very subtle and admirable manner, Pomponazzi addressing the padre as his friend, and the padre praising Pomponazzi in a dedicatory letter and expressing only mildly his misgivings about Pomponazzi's treatise. At the end we find the approbations of the vicar-general and of the Inquisitor of Bologna, which made it clear that Pomponazzi was forced to the solemn revocation by the same ecclesiastical authorities who ordered Chrysostomus to compose his theological refutation of the tract.[53] Both the vicar-general and the inquisitor commend Chrysostomus's arguments which "invalidate the cunning subtleties of the philosophers and illuminate faith. Since they were published and accepted by Pomponazzi, the book was given the imprimatur." [54]

A man reveals himself not only in his ideas but also, and perhaps even more, in his style. The public for which Pomponazzi wrote was aware of the meaning of style and the necessity of reading between the lines. Leonardo Aretino, a fifteenth-century humanist, had this to say on the matter:

[52] "Animadvertens . . . ex iis quae scripsimus in libro de immortalitate animi non solum multos in posterum in errorem induci posse, sed etiam nonnullos magnopere a veritatis via aberasse, quippe qui me mortalem esse animum sentire arbitrati fuerint. . . . Libens cum fidei firmandae gratia: tum ut facile omnibus liqueret, deo teste, non eam de animo sententiam meam esse libens admisi . . ." Pomponatius, *De immortalitate animae*, Bologna, 1525. The comment and the approbations are dated as of 1519.
[53] This is intimated by Chrysostomus himself when he writes: "Tantum demandatum mihi opus ab Rever. D. D. Laurentio Flischo vicelegato et Rever. vicario . . . Joanne de Bonoiae ordinis praedicatorum Vicario Rever. inquisitoris exequi intendo . . ." *Ibid.*
[54] *Ibid.*

Intent is grasped not only from words, which may be feigned, but from the
expression in the face and eyes of the speaker . . . I also seem to notice the
same in the letters of a good writer . . . in which besides words and sound,
there is something behind, a tacit indication of the mind which, as from the
movement of the speaker's eyes, you may catch, in a writer, from the very
vibration of his discourse.[55]

Martin Luther wrote in a clear and strong style. He had nothing to hide.
His break with the Church was open. Michel de Montaigne, one of the
most honest and outspoken men of the time, wrote in a wonderfully simple,
lucid, and straightforward manner.[56] Pomponazzi's speech is careful, slow
moving, and involved; it is full of hints and implications, of alternate explanations and evasive formulas.

That Pomponazzi in his own day was suspected of "feigned intent" is
evident from Father Chrysostomus's dedicatory address, in which he attempts to whitewash the philosopher with regard to these suspicions:

I thought it not unuseful to make one allowance in your favor, and this is that
none of the faithful, be they learned or ignorant, shall harbor a wrong opinion
of you because you have written such a treatise. For, indeed, I know that you
would not say one thing with your mouth and think another in your heart, since
you are by nature opposed to dissimulation and to falsehood.[57]

I cannot concur with Father Chrysostomus in pronouncing Pomponazzi
sincere. The contradictions in which Pomponazzi gets entangled are too
striking, too obvious, too irreconcilable. His constant changes, emphasizing
once the truth of religion, then again the truth produced by reasoning,
seem to be but a smoke screen behind which to save his philosophical convictions. A man who declares philosophy the gods' greatest gift to mankind and the philosophers the gods of this earth,[58] a man who proclaims
that all who do not participate in philosophy belong to the category of
beasts [59] cannot denounce in good faith his philosophical findings as "false
and mere semblances." He does so, and he is justified in doing so, because

[55] Quoted by Taylor, in his *Thought and Expression in the Sixteenth Century*.
[56] Characteristically enough, we do not find any predilection for allegory in Montaigne's writing, while an early interest in symbolism and allegory on the part of
Luther decreased with growing age and maturity. The stand of the Reformation
against hermeneutics also belongs here, see p. 138.
[57] ". . . putavi non inutile fore unum permittere in tui favorem: et est. Quod fidelium
nullus doctus aut imperitus de te sinistre opinari habet eo quod huiusmodi tractatus
composueris. Novi siquidem te naturaliter simulationis et mendacii inimicum nec unum
corde detines alterum vero ore depromis." (Pomponatius, *De immortalitate animae*.)
[58] Betzendörfer, *Glauben und Wissen bei den grossen Denkern des Mittelalters*, p. 195.
[59] ". . . revera qui de philosophia non participat, bestia est." (Quoted by Douglas,
The Philosophy and Psychology of Pietro Pomponazzi, p. 297.)

"to do otherwise would mean," in his own words, "death at the stake." It is to the historian of philosophy, however, that we have to leave the final judgment of so complex a phenomenon as Pomponazzi's philosophy and personality.[60]

Science

Science was in exactly the same situation as the philosophy of the time. The greatest scientific discoveries of the Cinquecento were made in the field of astronomy. They had to appear in the twilight of a hypothetical truth. The Church held on dogmatically to the view that the earth was the immobile center of the universe, around which sun and planets described their circles. Andreas Osiander, who in 1543 supervised the last stages of the printing of Copernicus's lifework, *De revolutionibus orbium coelestium,* supplied a Preface of his own, viewing the new heliocentric world system as a mere hypothesis. This cryptic Preface, which was written under the name of Copernicus himself, allowed doubts in the minds of many readers as to the actual relation of the new theory to physical reality.[61] But in this case we are in the fortunate position of having unequivocal evidence as to the true intentions behind this procedure. In a letter of April 20, 1541, Osiander wrote these illuminating sentences:

The peripatetics and theologians will be readily placated if they hear that there can be different hypotheses for the same apparent motion; that the present hypotheses are brought forward, not because they are in reality true, but because they regulate the computation of the apparent and combined motion as conveniently as may be. . . . In this way they will be diverted from stern defense and attracted by the charm of inquiry, first their antagonism will disappear, then they will seek the truth in vain by their own devices, and go over to the opinion of the author.[62]

Modern research on Copernicus has proved beyond the shadow of a doubt that he believed firmly in the physical reality of his theory. He was, however, acutely aware of the danger of professing his views publicly. This is evident from the dedication of his book, wherein he states that he

---

[60] A conclusive representation of Pomponazzi's personality and philosophy has not yet been written. One great shortcoming of Douglas's account is the complete lack of consideration of the time and the background against which Pomponazzi developed his ideas. Even the most independent philosopher does not live in a vacuum. How much more imperative is a consideration of the circumstances, when the philosopher lives in an age which does not grant him independence of thought!

[61] Armitage, *Copernicus, the Founder of Modern Astronomy,* p. 85, and Johnson, *Astronomical Thought in Renaissance England,* p. 114.

[62] Reprinted from Rosen, *Three Copernican Treatises,* p. 23, by permission of Columbia University Press.

refrained from publication for thirty-six years and even considered the possibility of keeping his ideas secret, of reserving them for an esoteric circle of friends, as did the Pythagoreans with their philosophy.[63] When, in the year of his death, he finally consented to publication, he only yielded to the continued pleas of his friends.

Half a century later Galileo Galilei found himself in the same plight. He wrote to Johannes Kepler in 1597: "I am since many years already a follower of the Copernican theory. It explains to me the reasons of many phenomena which are quite incomprehensible according to the views commonly accepted. I have collected many arguments for the refutation of the latter, but I dare not publish them." [64]

However, Galilei's volcanic temperament did not allow him to devote his life quietly to research without an attempt at publication. Among his many writings he published in 1613 a book on the sunspots, in which he defended the Copernican theory. In 1616 the Inquisition brought an action against Galilei, and he had to pledge himself in writing to cease teaching and believing in the correctness of the Copernican theory, which in the same year was condemned by the Index Congregation as heretical. But in 1632 he published the *Dialogue concerning the Two Chief Systems of the World, the Ptolemaic and the Copernican*, which caused the Inquisition to put Galilei on trial, and this time seriously. Galilei had expressly chosen the form of dialogue in order to have an alibi before the Inquisition. After all, it was not he who spoke; he only reported the conversations of friends, which had taken place many years ago. He did not need to identify himself with any opinion uttered.[65] Moreover, in the introduction to the *Dialogues* Galilei maintained that the aim of the present publication was to show that the Roman Catholic censors, in condemning the dangerous theories of Copernicus, were fully aware of all the scientific reasons favoring it; that if Rome was contented with the idea of the immobility of the earth it was not because of ignorance, but for reasons of piety and of religion, in order to keep to the fore man's insufficiency as compared with God's omnipotence.

[63] The work was dedicated to Pope Paul III. It was introduced by a laudatory letter from Cardinal Nicholas Schönberg. In the dedication another friend of Copernicus, who himself was a cleric, was mentioned, the Bishop of Culm. "The combination of bishop, cardinal, and pope was intended to provide a stout bulwark against Roman Catholic assaults." (Rosen, *op. cit.*, p. 27.)

[64] Quoted by Wolf, *A History of Science*, p. 29.

[65] Galilei referred to the dialogue character of his book in protesting his innocence during the trial. (*Dialog über die beiden hauptsächlichen Weltsysteme* . . . trans. by E. Strauss, p. lxxii.)

Galilei's dissimulation was too obvious. The Inquisition saw through it. To study the documents of the trial against Galilei means to witness one of the most humiliating scenes in the painful story of man's struggle for freedom of thought.

Art

Essentially, science is hostile to double meaning; only pressure from without can divert it from its main aim, which is to establish facts and to interpret them as clearly as possible. Art, however, has often, indeed almost always, the desire to hide in visual form deep meanings. This is certainly true for sixteenth-century art. So Hieronymus Bosch (1450–1516), a contemporary and countryman of Erasmus, gave in one of his finest paintings, the "Haywagon," what seems to be a pictorial interpretation of mankind as seen by Erasmus's *Folly*. The haywagon is a symbol of the vanity of this world; everyone, from pope and emperor down to monk, citizen, and peasant, makes his bid to get a share from the hay on the wagon. High in the clouds Christ appears, the distressed witness of humanity's march on the road to ruin.[66] Bosch's triptych, the "Haywagon" belongs to the category of Netherlands proverb paintings, in which Pieter Brueghel, the Elder (1516–1569), Bosch's spiritual pupil, excelled. These paintings represent the surface of the world to the unreflective spectator, but to the penetrating mind they disclose a philosophy of life. "The enigma of the most inexplicable scenes, the most fantastic buildings, the strangest creatures disappears in the light of the proverb which, each time, is hidden behind them." [67] The subsequent history of the interpretation of Bosch's "Haywagon" illustrates the ambiguity of this art. The picture has undergone different interpretations in modern times; some critics, for example, have sought to illuminate it by the Biblical tag "all flesh is like grass." Only when Tolnay offered as a key to the picture the old Flemish proverb: "the world is a mountain of hay; everyone picks of it as much as he can get," did every figure and every detail in the picture come to make sense.

It is astonishing to see the close parallel between the ideas and the technique of this art of proverb painting and the secret chromatic art. Clemens non Papa and Waelrant are contemporaries of Pieter Brueghel. As they hint at the chromatic interpretation by some anomaly of sound, so Brueghel hints at a deeper interpretation—for example, in his picture of the seven cardinal virtues, by some small anomaly in the representation

[66] De Tolnay, *Hieronymus Bosch*, p. 25.
[67] De Tolnay, *Pierre Brueghel l'Ancien*, p. 35.

of the virtues. Brueghel gives to the virtues all the symbolic attributes usual at the time. By omitting one of them, he hints at the "second face" hidden behind the mask of virtue.[68] Brueghel's work is full of enigmas and has challenged the curiosity and keenness of many a historian of art. One peculiar feature in a number of his paintings is that he conceals the main event in such a way that it passes almost unnoticed. In his "Fall of Icarus" the main action is hardly hinted at by the two legs that just show, the rest of the body having already disappeared under the water. In his "Jesus Bearing the Cross" the principal motive is so well hidden among the various scenes represented in the picture, that the beholder can find it only with the greatest difficulty. It seems to me that Brueghel thus gave an artistic expression to the idea, so far spread in the sixteenth century, that the world had an outer and an inner reality and that the great and really important events were noticed only by the initiated, if by anyone.[69] The scene in which Jesus is bearing the cross is the only one in the picture which includes no spectators.[70]

There is another similarity with the technique employed in the secret chromatic art. We found that chromatic passages were outwardly concealed, but pointed out by an almost mathematical symmetry of the form. Though the scene in which Jesus is bearing the cross contains no spectators in the painting and is almost lost in the numerous actions going on around it, it stands exactly in the center of the picture.[71]

Recent research has given good reasons for the supposition that Brueghel belonged to the group of Flemish libertines gathering around Henry Nicolaes, who in his *Speculum justitiae* took the position, so well known to us from the sources discussed in the preceding chapter, that the sinner can be redeemed through God's mercy alone. The libertines, moreover, believed that all religions are equivalent symbols of one fundamental truth, which even in the Scriptures has found only an allegorical representation. The Flemish libertines, while deviating substantially from the Roman Catholic dogma, did not break openly with the Church; they were nevertheless persecuted.[72] To us it is important to observe that in Flemish paint-

---

[68] *Ibid.*, p. 20.

[69] Glück, in his *Pieter Brueghel the Elder*, p. 14, interprets this habit as a manifestation of Brueghel's "opinion of the world, which he considered to be topsy-turvy and wrong-headed blind to the importance even of the most momentous occurrences."

[70] Jedlicka, *Pieter Brueghel, der Maler in seiner Zeit*, p. 170.

[71] *Ibid*, p. 180. Jedlicka shows how Brueghel time and again uses symmetry in form and correspondence in color and composition in order to hint at the meaning hidden under the surface of the things represented.

[72] De Tolnay, *op. cit.*, pp. 9 ff. and Jedlicka, *op. cit.*, pp. 140 ff.

ing, as in music, an esoteric attitude accompanies secret heretical tendencies.

While the key to the understanding of Netherlands painting is often found in popular tradition, for example, in the proverb, in Italian art this key is provided by the classical tradition, revived by the humanistic movement. The plastic arts of the Italian Renaissance abound with signs, emblems, symbols and allegories whose meanings are not obvious. However, in the last decades, stimulated by the work of A. Warburg [73] and the investigations of K. Giehlow,[74] iconographic [75] research has made vigorous strides.[76] Such Renaissance symbols as Father Time, Blind Cupid, Hercules standing at the Cross-Roads, and other Renaissance images have been subjected to a penetrating analysis by E. Panofsky.[77] Panofsky has stressed the fact that the revival of classical motifs and classical themes is "only one aspect of the Renaissance movement in art." Another equally important one is what he calls the "reinterpretation" of classical images, which were invested with new meaning and symbolism. Panofsky shows the immense interest and the fertility of the Renaissance artist in evolving new personifications and allegories,[78] but what interests us most is his distinction between medieval and Renaissance symbolism. The medieval scholastic tried to translate a complicated system of ideas into the clear and effective language of the picture. The humanist's intent was to hide ideas, generally simple ones, in pictorial enigmas.[79]

The humanists were fascinated by Egyptian hieroglyphic writing; stimulated by it they developed an intricate picture writing of their own, in praise of which Alberti said that it was understandable for all nations, but only for the initiated among them.[80] The German humanist Pirkheimer translated the late ancient writer Horapollon's work on the Egyptian hiero-

---

[73] Warburg, *Gesammelte Schriften.*
[74] Giehlow, "Die Hieroglyphenkunde des Humanismus in der Allegorie der Renaissance," in *Jahrbuch der Kunsthistorischen Sammlungen des Allerh. Kaiserhauses,* 1915.
[75] "Iconography is that branch of the history of art which concerns itself with the subject matter or meaning of works of art, as opposed to their form." Panofsky, *Studies in Iconology,* p. 3.
[76] I have already drawn attention to the work of the Warburg Institute in this field in my essay "The Goddess Fortuna in Music," *Musical Quarterly,* XXIX (January, 1943), 1.
[77] *Ibid.,* and the same author's *Hercules am Scheidewege und andere antike Bildstoffe in der neueren Kunst.*
[78] *Studies in Iconology,* pp. 69 ff.
[79] *Hercules am Scheidewege* . . . p. 26.
[80] *Ibid.* In 1521 Cesare Cesariano, who completed the Cathedral of Milan, had his Italian edition of Vitruvius published in Como. In his comment to the second book he mentioned the hieroglyphics and stated that this riddle writing was held in highest esteem, particularly by scholars, because they did not want the divine word to be understood too easily by all men. (Volkmann, *Bilderschriften der Renaissance.*)

156 *Double Meaning*

glyphics from the Greek. Pirkheimer's friend, Albrecht Dürer, illustrated this translation and took over many of its symbols. We find them also in Dürer's illustrations of the prayerbook, the triumphal procession, and the triumphal arch for Maximilian I.[81]

Mantegna was furnished with the *invenzione* for his *Realm of Comus* by Pietro Bembo and Giovanni Jacopo Calandra.[82] Ghiberti was advised in the choice of subjects for the doors to the Baptistery in Florence by the humanist Leonardo Aretino.[83] Commenting on Raphael's *Stanza della Segnatura* Suida writes: "One would misconstrue the intellectual atmosphere of the time if one assumed that the invention of the subjects was the task merely of the painter," and he points out that Raphael belonged to a circle of scholars, such as Conti, Sadoleto, Inghirami, Bembo, Gióvio, Castiglione, who had an important voice in the determination of the subjects.[84]

A most lively intercourse, and even intimate collaboration, between humanists and artists was an outstanding feature of artistic life in the fifteenth and sixteenth centuries. The innumerable academies may have contributed to this. There artists, musicians, poets, and scholars came together; stimulating discussions on all kinds of topics helped develop the world of ideas which all of them attempted to express through their different mediums. G. F. Hartlaub, who has tried to interpret the mysterious signs and representations in the paintings of Giorgione,[85] came to the conclusion that they were alchemistic symbols which were guarded and passed on by secret societies and sodalities flourishing in Italy at that time. Artists were often members of these sodalities and received commissions for paintings and portraits from them.[86] Intellectual circles in the sixteenth century took a passionate interest in alchemy.

The picture language of alchemy was ambiguous so as to elude the un-

[81] Giehlow, "Die Hieroglyphenkunde des Humanismus in der Allegorie der Renaissance," in *Jahrbuch der Kunsthistorischen Sammlungen des Allerh. Kaiserhauses*, 1915.
[82] Panofsky, *Studies in Iconology*, p. 153.
[83] Taylor, *Thought and Expression in the Sixteenth Century*, I, 53.
[84] Suida, *Paintings and Drawings by Raphael*. From the sixteenth century on Raphael's great frescoes, particularly the "School of Athens" have been submitted to a series of divergent interpretations. One of the most recent investigations has been made by Gutman in his "The Medieval Content of Raphael's 'School of Athens,'" *History of Ideas*, II (1941), 4.
[85] Hartlaub, *Giorgiones Geheimnis*.
[86] Hartlaub, *Giorgione und der Mythos der Akademien*. Hartlaub carried on this research in the following studies: "Arcana artis; Spuren alchemistischer Symbolik in der Kunst des 16. Jahrhunderts," *Zeitschrift für Kunstgeschichte*, Vol. VI (1937), and "Signa Hermetis; Zwei alte alchemistische Bilderhandschriften," *Zeitschrift für Kunstwissenschaft*, IV (1937).

derstanding of the uninitiated, who were interested merely in the synthetic production of gold, not in the deeper, "hermetic" philosophy of alchemy, which consisted in the belief that the process of the purification of the cosmos could be furthered by the purification of man. To this end man had to go through the different grades of initiation which, incidentally, Hartlaub believes to be the topic of Giorgione's painting of the "Three Philosophers."

There is, indeed, reason to assume that much of the painting of the sixteenth century was esoteric and was meant to be so. Cesare Ripa, whom Panofsky [87] calls the dean of the iconologists of the sixteenth century, in the Preface to his *Iconologia*,[88] promises to reveal the meaning of those "images which are made to signify something else than one can perceive with the eye." [89] He states as the reason for the invention of these images the desire to prevent the ignorant from understanding and penetrating into the deeper reasons of things as the learned do.[90]

That painters used pictorial symbols which were not clearly understood in their own day even by the experts is proved by Vasari. He tried to interpret a certain symbol used by his teacher Michelangelo,

which was three coronals or circlets, interwoven in such sort that the circumference of one crossed alternately through the centres of the other two. This Michelangelo used either because he meant to signify that the three arts of Sculpture, Painting, and Architecture were so bound and united that each received benefit and ornament from the other, and neither can nor ought to be divided; or perhaps (he being a man of so high a genius) because he had some more subtle meaning in view.[91]

Vasari, however, is unable to indicate what this more subtle meaning was.

Seen against the background of the general tendency toward hidden meanings, the strange technique of dual images which arose in the period of the Counter Reformation, seems but a curious, though fascinating, off-shoot.[92] Whereas the paintings discussed heretofore show their duplicity by hiding an invisible spiritual face under the visible surface, here we have

---

[87] *Studies in Iconology*, p. 89.
[88] *Iconologia di Cesare Ripa Perugino*. For earlier editions of 1613 and 1645 see Panofsky, *Studies in Iconology*, Bibliography, nos. 284–285.
[89] "Le Imagini fatte per significare una diversa cosa da quella, che si vede con l'occhio . . ."
[90] ". . . accioche non egualmente i dotti, & l'ignoranti potessero intendere & penetrare le cagioni delle cose . . ."
[91] Giorgio Vasari, *Lives of Seventy of the Most Eminent Painters, Sculptors, and Architects*, IV, 245.
[92] I wish to thank Dr. E. Panofsky for having called my attention to the art of dual images.

to do with paintings and drawings which contain two visible pictures in one according to the way the beholder looks at them. The main representative of this art is Giuseppe Arcimboldo (1530–1593) of Milan, who served as court painter under the emperors Ferdinand I, Maximilian II, and Rudolph II. He painted the portraits of the "Four Seasons" from suitable flowers, vegetables, and so forth.[93] "At a distance they appeared to be figures of men and women; but on a nearer view the Flora disappeared in a heap of flowers and leaves, and the Vertumnus was metamorphosed into a composition of fruits and foliage."[94]

A pupil of Arcimboldo painted a visionary landscape with rocks and trees and a dream castle, with a farm and farmers, a ploughman and a sower, with water and boats on which fishermen are busy drawing in their nets. If the position of this painting is shifted by ninety degrees from the normal, it is transformed into the gigantic head of a bearded man wearing a cap and feather.[95]

Similar surprises are hidden in those images which make sense only if looked at obliquely,

> perspectives which, rightly gazed upon,
> Show nothing but confusion—eyed awry,
> Distinguish form.[96]

These images, produced by distorting the perspective, were known under the name "anamorphosis."[97] The earliest specimens date back to about 1530. It was a Flemish artist who, around 1546, hid the portrait of Edward VI in a landscape by means of distorted perspective.[98] Dr. Erwin Panofsky draws my attention to the big shapeless object seen in the foreground of Holbein's "Ambassadors" in London. This, when looked upon obliquely, turns out to be a Death's head and is meant as a stern reminder: *Memento mori.*[99] At the same time, however, it is the signature of the artist (Hohl-Bein, hollow bone).[100]

[93] "The Summer" is reproduced in the catalogue of the exhibition of *Fantastic Art, Dada, Surrealism,* ed. by A. H. Barr, Jr.; "the Winter," in Venturi, *Storia dell'arte italiana,* IX, 499.
[94] Lanzi, *The History of Painting in Italy;* trans. by Thomas Roscoe, II, 505.
[95] This painting is reproduced in the catalogue mentioned in note 93, above.
[96] Shakespeare, Richard II, Act II, Scene 11. (Panofsky, *The Codex Huygens and Leonardo da Vinci's Art Theory,* p. 93n.)
[97] Waetzold, *Hans Holbein der Jüngere,* p. 218.
[98] *Ibid.*
[99] For a detailed interpretation of the idea of death in its relation to the "Ambassadors" see Waetzold, *Hans Holbein der Jüngere.*
[100] Waetzold failed to observe the autograph character of the death's head.

On the surface it may appear that the dual-image art provides the closest parallel to the secret chromatic art in that it contains two possible visual readings even as the secret chromatic art allows of two sound versions. This is, indeed, a similarity, but an external one. There seems no inner necessity behind the dual-image art comparable with the religious earnestness of the secret chromatic art. The dual images seem to represent the tendency of the sixteenth century toward duplicity in a playful and fanciful and even tricky aspect rather than in its real seriousness as expressed in the work of a great thinker and artist like Pieter Brueghel.

Poetry and Imaginative Literature

An important source of inspiration for the plastic arts was opened by the study of ancient and modern poets such as Ovid, Lucretius, Lucian, Virgil, Dante, Petrarch, Politian, and others whose works furnished suitable scenes and subjects.[101] Raphael expressed the feeling of the Renaissance painter when paying homage to poetry in his "Parnassus," where he portrayed among others Homer, Sappho, Dante, and Petrarch. The poetry of the fifteenth and sixteenth centuries shared a love of allegory and hidden meaning with the plastic arts of the time. How closely related the symbolic language of art and speech was in the view of the Renaissance artist is indicated by Ripa, when in the preamble to his *Iconologia* he observes that he does not intend to deal with those images which the orator uses, but only with those belonging to the realm of painting.

The avowed idols of the poets were Dante and Petrarch. "Dante, who defined poetry as the art 'which publishes the truth concealed beneath a veil of fable,' frequently interrupts the story to bid his reader note the meaning underneath the figures of his verse." [102] And Petrarch, in a letter to his brother, reveals the allegorical meaning of his eclogue *Parthenias*. "In fact, it is difficult to understand his eclogues without a key to the symbolism of their language." [103] Both Dante and Petrarch interpreted the great creations of classical poets in an allegorical fashion. This view was wholly shared by the humanists of the era, as is exemplified by Erasmus: "As divine Scripture has little fruit for him who sticks to the letter, so the

[101] Besides poetry, philosophy inspired and influenced artists like Titian and Michelangelo. See the chapters on "The Neoplatonic Movement in Florence and North Italy" and "The Neoplatonic Movement and Michelangelo" in Panofsky, *Studies in Iconology*.
[102] Symonds, *Renaissance in Italy*, I, 886.
[103] Taylor, *Thought and Expression in the Sixteenth Century*, I, 14–15.

Homeric and Virgilian poetry will be found helpful if one remembers that it is all allegorical—*eam totam esse allegoricam*—which none denies whose lips have so much as tasted the learning of the ancients." [104]

François Rabelais, who admired Erasmus and knew More's *Utopia*, indulged in the use of allegory and of ambiguities of all kinds in surprising and often burlesque interpretations of poems, of riddles, of self-invented sibyllic oracles, and even of the Scriptures. He followed Erasmus and More in using a technique for deliberately confounding the reader as to his true intentions. In the prologue to the first book of *The Lives, Heroic Deeds and Sayings of Gargantua and His Son Pantagruel* he addresses the "most noble and illustrious drinkers" and tells them that the jests, mockeries, lascivious discourse, and recreative lies which they will find in his book are all like so many Sileni: [105] little boxes,

> painted on the outside with wanton toyish figures . . . to excite people unto laughter, as Silenus himself . . . was wont to do; but within those capricious caskets were carefully preserved and kept many rich and fine drugs . . . with several kinds of precious stones, and other things of great price.

And put the case, that in the literal sense you meet with matters that are light and ludicrous, and suitable enough to their inscriptions; yet must not you stop there, as at the melody of the charming syrens; but endeavour to interpret that in sublimer sense, which possibly you might think was spoken in the jollity of heart . . .

---

[104] Quoted in *ibid.*, p. 168.

[105] Rabelais avowedly borrows the idea of the Sileni from Plato's *Symposium*. He quotes Alcibiades as comparing Socrates with the Sileni. "For to have eyed his outside, and esteemed of him by his exterior appearance, you would not have given the peel of an onion for him, so deformed he was in body, and ridiculous in his gesture. He had a sharp pointed nose, with the look of a bull, and countenance of a fool; he was in his carriage simple, boorish in his apparel, in fortune poor, unhappy in his wives, unfit for all offices in the commonwealth, always laughing, tippling, and merry, carousing to every one, with continual jibes and jeers, the better by those means to conceal his divine knowledge. But opening this box, you would have found within a heavenly and inestimable drug, a more than human understanding, an admirable virtue, matchless learning, invincible courage, inimitable sobriety, certain contentment of mind, perfect assurance, and an incredible disregard of all that for which men commonly do so much watch, run, sail, fight, travel, toil and turmoil themselves." There is little doubt that Rabelais and his contemporaries were also well aware and much impressed by Alcibiades's characterization of Socrates's manner of speech: ". . . his words are ridiculous when you first hear them; he clothes himself in language that is as the skin of the wanton satyr—for his talk is of pack-asses and smiths and cobblers and curriers, and he is always repeating the same things in the same words, so that an ignorant man who did not know him might feel disposed to laugh at him; but he who pierces the mask and sees what is within will find that they are the only words which have a meaning in them, and also the most divine, abounding of fair examples of virtue and of the largest discourse, or rather extending to the whole duty of a good and honorable man." Quoted from Jowett's translation of *The Works of Plato*, III, 355.

After this introduction, adorned with a goodly number of stories, jokes, and quasi-learned quotations, Rabelais executes a sudden about-face.

Do you believe [he asks his readers] do you believe upon your conscience, that Homer whilst he was couching his Iliads and Odysses, had any thought upon those Allegories, which Plutarch, Heraclides, Ponticus, Eustatius, Cornutus squeezed out of him. . . . If that is your faith, you shall never be of my Church; who hold that those mysteries were as little dreamed of by Homer, as the Gospel Sacraments were by Ovid, in his *Metamorphosis*.

And Rabelais insists that he, too, writing his "jovial new Chronicles" did not think of "more than you, who possibly are drinking (the whilst) as I was." And at this point Rabelais makes his exit and leaves the perplexed reader alone. But after having gone through five books of the descriptions of Gargantua's and Pantagruel's fantastic exploits and fabulous adventures, the reader is dismissed by the "Priestess of the Holy Bottle" with a sermon on the topic "that the greatest treasure and most admirable things, are hidden under ground; and not without reason." [106] While Rabelais thus is engaged in the deceitful art of double talk, he does not mind taking a good shot at the philosophers of his day, who follow the same trade so well that "it is . . . henceforth to be found an enterprise of much more easy under- taking, to catch lions by the neck . . . than to entrap such philosophers in their words." [107]

In the revised edition of the first two books of Gargantua and Pantagruel, in 1542, Rabelais used the name "sophists" when he meant to insult the theologians at the Sorbonne.[108] So his countryman Gringoire said *Meresote*, i.e., *mère sotte*, foolish mother, when he chose to ridicule the Mother Church; [109] so Castellio spoke about the "world," when he meant the pope; [110] so Clément Marot used the name *Ysabeau* when speaking about the Church.[111] The use of a code name—on the interpretation of which

[106] Quoted from the Bibliophilist Society's edition of *The Works of Rabelais*.
[107] *Ibid.*, p. 342.
[108] Incidentally, Rabelais, who himself, for ten years, had lived as a friar, did not dare publish the first edition of his narration under his true name. On the other hand, he wanted to make sure the success would be his, if there should be any. So he used his name in an anagram: *Alcofribas Nasier*. His invectives against Church, clergy, and monasticism put Rabelais's books on almost all Indexes. He is also known to have been in frequent contact with Calvinists and Protestants and had in 1547 to flee France. (Haupt, *Luther and Rabelais*, pp. 46–47.)
[109] Douen, *Clément Marot et le psautier huguenot*, I, 62.
[110] Bainton, *Concerning Heretics*, p. 185.
[111] Douen, *Clément Marot et le psautier huguenot*, p. 64, quotes Marot's *Rondeau* "De l'inconstance de Ysabeau," which was the reason for Marot's being thrown into jail. "Ysabeau," which is a soubriquet for "Elizabeth," is derived from the Hebrew

depended the meaning of all the rest—corresponds to the use of a code-note in the secret chromatic art.

In the introduction to the *Roman de la Rose* (1527) Marot spoke of the "literal" and the "mystic" ways of understanding. He said of the author of the medieval *Roman:*

. . . bien peult estre que ledict auc-teur ne gettoit pas seulement son pen-ser et fantasie sus le sens litteral, ains plus tost attiroit son esprit au sens alle-goric et moral, comme lung disant et entendant lautre.

. . . it can very well be that the said author did not only direct his thought and imagination toward the literal meaning, but rather drew his mind to the allegorical and moral meaning, as though saying one thing and meaning another.

And as if he had already said too much, he added cautiously:

Je ne veulx pas ce que je dis affermer, mais il me semble quil peult avoir ainsi faict.

I do not want to affirm what I say, but it seems to me that he could have done it in this way.

But in elaborating on this view he continued:

Doncques qui ainsi vouldroit interpre-ter le Rommant de la Rose, ie dis quil y trouveroit grand bien, proffit et util-ité cachez soubz lescorce du texte. . . . Fables sont faictes et inventées pour les exposer au sens mystique. . . . Si nous ne creusions plus avant que lescorce du sens litteral, nous naurions que le plai-sir des fables et des histoires, sans ob-tenir le singulier proffit de la nouvelle pneumaticque, c'est assauoir venant par linspiration du Sainct Esprit quant à lintelligence morale.[112]

Therefore, he who would interpret the *Roman de la Rose* would find great profit and usefulness, I say, hidden un-der the bark of the text. . . . Fables are made and invented in order to ex-pose them to the mystic meaning. . . . If we do not go deeper than the bark of the literal meaning, we would have only the pleasure of the fables and stories, without obtaining the singular profit of the pneumatic gospel coming through the inspiration of the Holy Ghost as for the moral intelligence.

Twenty years later Sibilet, in his *Art poétique françois,* (1548) calls the technique of poetry, in almost the same words,

une escorce . . . qui couvre artifi-ciélement sa naturéle sève et son ame naturélement divine.[113]

a bark . . . which artfully covers its natural sap and its soul which by na-ture is divine.

"Elisheba" and means the worshiper of God, alias the Church. Marot composed other allegories of a distinct satiric character. See Lenient, *La Satire en France . . . au XVIe siècle,* pp. 163 ff.   [112] Douen, *op. cit.,* p. 74.
[113] Quoted by Willey, in *Tendencies in Renaissance Literary Theory,* p. 16. Willey quotes a number of Renaissance authors to the same effect.

In poetry, however, the art of double meaning can assume a reversed meaning. Whereas usually double meaning is brought into play to hide the real purpose from the vigilant eye of the inquisitorial critic, allegory sometimes is used in poetry to persuade all varieties of moralist objectors that the colorful, pagan-like surface of the poem has a deeper spiritual and moral meaning. "Virgil, whom the middle ages would not have relinquished, though a General Council had condemned him, received the absolution of allegorical interpretation." [114]

This attitude was also taken by Erasmus. He saw the foundation of a Christian life in Christ, but he opened his house hospitably to all great spirits of the past. He insisted that a Christian may enjoy the whole pagan literature if it be read at the right age, in the right manner, with the right selection, and if—and this is his main point—everything is related to Christ.[115] He found that all literature, Christian and pagan alike, consists of a simple sense and a mystic sense, which he compared to body and soul. He exhorted the reader to leave the literal sense behind and hasten toward the mystery which is hidden in the writings of the poets, of Plato and his school, but particularly in the divine Scriptures, which are well-nigh like those Sileni of Alcibiades in that under a base and almost ridiculous cover they enclose the divine will unadulterated.[116] He justified ancient mythology by giving it a moralized-allegorical meaning. In this manner he interpreted the stories of Prometheus, of Circe, of Tantalus, Sisyphus, Hercules, but just as well the Biblical tales of Eve, Goliath, and Samson. "Of what use is it," he asked, "to read the books of the Kings and the Judges or the history of Livy, if you do not see the allegorical meaning in either?" [117]

In spite of the ecclesiastic condemnation of allegory as a means of condoning paganism on the part of the Council of Trent,[118] Torquato Tasso used the same device and invented an allegory for the avowed purpose of saving his romantic epic, the *Gerusalemme liberata*, from the pitiless eye

[114] Symonds, *Renaissance in Italy*, I, 886; see also Willey, *op. cit.*, p. 10.

[115] "Breviter omnem ethnicam literaturam delibare profuerit, si quidem id fiat, ut dixi, et annis idoneis, et modice, tum cautim, et peregrinantis non habitantis more: postremo, quod est praecipuum, si omnia ad Christum referantur." See *Militis Christiani Enchiridion, Omnia Opera Des. Erasmi Roterodami ... Cum Prefatione Beati Rhenani ...* V, 8.

[116] "Idem observandum in omnibus literis, quae ex simplici sensu et mysterio, tanquam corpore atque animo constant, ut contempta litera, ad mysterium potissimum spectes: cuius modi sunt literae poetarum omnium, et ex Philosophis Platonicorum: maxime vere scripturae divinae, quae fere Silenis illis Alcibiadeis similes, sub tectorio sordido ac pene ridiculo, merum numen claudunt." *Ibid.*, p. 25.

[117] "Quid interest, regum aut iudicum libros legas, an Livianam historiam, modo in neutra spectes allegoriam?" *Ibid.*

[118] Panofsky and Saxl, *Classical Mythology in Mediaeval Art*, pp. 228–280.

of the Inquisition. Tasso's letters give a complete account of the demands presented by the Inquisitor Silvio Antoniano, of Tasso's concessions made against his better insight, and of his sudden idea to save the "offensive" scenes of love and incantation by investing them with an allegorical meaning. In a letter to Gonzaga, Tasso writes: "To tell your Excellency frankly the truth, I had no idea of allegory at all when I started on my poem. . . . But when I was well beyond the middle of my work, and when I became aware of the difficult times, I began also to think of allegory as something that could remove any difficulty." [119] In his allegory he intends to reconcile not only Plato's and Aristotle's poetic principles but also the concepts of moral philosophy with those of Christian theology. He asks Gonzaga to secure the advice of good theologians, because he himself feels unsafe in handling theological problems. Tasso does not seem too happy about the whole affair. He calls himself a hypocrite and a politician of necessity, since it is only with the shield of allegory that he can protect "gli amori e gl'incanti." [120]

Aside from this "political" use of allegory, hidden meaning is an essential part of Renaissance poetry. A contemporary critic, Lorenzo Giacomini Tebalducci Malespini, speaking on Torquato Tasso before the Accademia degli Alterati in Florence,[121] stated that he found extreme clarity in poetry

[119] "Jo, per confessare a Vostra Signoria Illustrissima ingenuamente il vero, quando cominciai il mio poema non ebbi pensiero alcuno d'allegoria. . . . Ma poi ch'io fui oltre al mezzo del mio poema, e che cominciai a sospettar de la strettezza de'tempi, cominciai anco a pensare a l'allegoria come a cosa ch'io giudicava dovermi assai agevolar ogni difficoltà." See Torquato Tasso, *Gerusalemme liberata*, I, 38. In this excellent critical edition Solerti gives the authentic documents on the development of the idea of allegory as a means of appeasing the Inquisition.
[120] "Farò il collo torto e mostrerò ch'io non ho avuto altro fine che di servire al politico; e con questo scudo cercherò d'assicurare ben bene gli amori e gl'incanti." *Ibid.*, p. 37.
[121] The Accademia degli Alterati was founded in 1569. Its professed aim was the cultivation of the Italian language. Aside from Dante and Petrarch, Tasso was held in highest esteem. The academicians wanted to offset the unfavorable impression created by the warfare, which the Accademia della Crusca in Florence conducted against Tasso's *Gerusalemme liberata*. (Maylender, *Storia delle Accademie d'Italia*, I, 154 ff.) The famous and influential Accademia della Crusca had given its favor to Lodovico Ariosto and played him off against Torquato Tasso. Soon two literary parties came into being. Pamphlets were written by the partisans of either group and the discussion developed into the most passionate literary controversy of the sixteenth century. The interpretation of the Crusca's attitude as given by Donadoni (*Torquato Tasso*, II, 20 ff.) seems to suffer from oversimplification. Donadoni makes it appear as if the main motive of the Crusca in adopting Ariosto and rejecting Tasso was the one-sided preference given by the academy to the Florentine vocabulary and language. The reading of the original discussions, however, seems to prove that two ideals of style stood behind the great controversy. The Crusca was against the refined and esoteric manner of writing which his friends praised as the particular merit of Tasso's style. The Crusca's stand boils down to this simple statement: "La chiarezza è virtù, e'l con-

a grave offense, because it is nothing else but pleasantness overdone, intelligibleness driven to a point where the listener has no chance to find out something for himself. The refined reader, he continued, will repudiate the kind of poetry in which he sees himself treated like a child. Aware of this, Torquato Tasso avoids the commonplace and loves the new, the unusual, the unexpected, the admirable, in concepts as well as in words. To keep away from vulgar style and from excess of clarity, he ingeniously interweaves various poetic figures, sudden breaks, turns, circumlocutions, hyperboles, ironies, metaphors. Malespini compares this style with a steep and stony path where the weak get tired and the less cautious sometimes stumble; he contrasts it with that style which is similar to a sloping and slippery or plain and muddy public highway. This style, noble, strange, and removed from vulgar intelligence, was loved and followed by those famous wise men,[122] who therefore were said to have spoken their own language in another language.[123]

It is amazing to see the degree to which this description of a refined poetic style corresponds with the definition of *musica riserbata* as given by Nicola Vicentino; we find in both the same differentiation between commonplaceness and refinement, between a style accessible to everyone and a style intelligible only to a select circle. Both Vicentino and Tasso lived at the court of Ferrara, though at different times, and the discussed documents prove that one aesthetic theory prevailed at this court in both poetry and music.

This attitude, however, is not peculiar to the court of Ferrara; we have seen that it is part and parcel of Renaissance aesthetics. Undoubtedly the humanists had much to do with the rise of this aesthetic ideal, which flourished especially well, but not exclusively, in the atmosphere of the court.

I have had a chance to examine what is probably the unique copy of a collection of Latin poems in honor of King Ferdinand I and Emperor Charles V by Joannes Bockenrodt of Worms.[124] Every possible ingenuity of humanistic artifice is contrived in these poems destined for the exclusive taste of the court. Great events in both Ferdinand's and Charles's

---

trario è vizio," clarity is virtue, its opposite is vice. (See *Apologia del Sig. Torquato Tasso in difesa della sua Gierusalemme liberata*.) To us this controversy proves once more that the idea of an esoteric art had not only its partisans but also its declared adversaries in the sixteenth century.

[122] By "those famous, wise men" Malespini understood the great thinkers of antiquity known to have been esoteric, such as Pythagoras.

[123] *Prose Fiorentine raccolte dallo Smarrito accademico della Crusca*, I, 63.

[124] Bockenrodt, *Admiranda quaedam poemata, vatis undecunque rarissimi*. I wish to thank Mr. Paul Gottschalk for his friendly permission to study this early book.

careers are celebrated in hexameters, and the year is indicated in the text of the poems by capitalized Roman letters, which thus serve the double function of letters and of numerals. Acrostics and allegory flourish. The climax of artifice is reached in a poem which is dedicated to Ferdinand and which reveals its peculiar structure by rows of conspicuous capital letters wandering through the different lines in geometrical patterns. If one reads the letters arranged along these patterns, one arrives at another, the "inner" poem, drawing out the patterns, one comes to the innermost sanctum and finds four hexagons in the form of a cross, eight equilateral quadrangles, and one square, each of which has a symbolic meaning: the four hexagons in the form of a cross signify the four Gospels and the four kingdoms over which Ferdinand reigned and in which he was to defend the Gospel; the eight equilateral quadrangles represent the eight grades of the beatitude through which he was to come to the Kingdom of God, and the square is a symbol of his solid, strong, and constant personality.

In such an example, the humanistic art of double meaning has changed to a mere *jeu d'esprit*. This is most clearly indicated by the unusual fact that the solutions of all the enigmas were printed in the book along with the enigmatic poems. Nevertheless, a *tour de force* like this is only the extreme of a habit of mind which was widespread; the use of double meaning was not rare, but a literary method which found acceptance with both writers and readers.

The degree to which ambiguity and double meaning had become an integral part of Cinquecento thought is shown by the fact that even in conversation it was considered to manifest the greatest elegance and finesse. This we learn from Baldesar Castiglione, who in teaching the courtier how to strive for perfection in conversation, maintained that "of the ready pleasantries that are contained in a short saying, those are keenest, that arise from ambiguity"; [125] that "another very pretty form of pleasantry is that, which consists in a kind of *innuendo*, when we say one thing and tacitly imply another"; [126] that it is fine to describe "an evil thing in polite terms"; [127] that "those witticisms also are very clever in which we take from our interlocutor's lips something that he does not mean"; [128] that "it is also fine to explain or interpret a thing jocosely"; [129] that "moreover it is a fine thing to use metaphors seasonably"; [130] that "we often use a word in which there is a hidden meaning remote from the one we seem to intend." [131] All this

---

[125] Castiglione, *The Book of the Courtier;* trans. by L. Eckstein Opdycke, p. 132.
[126] *Ibid.*, p. 143.   [127] *Ibid.*, p. 144.   [128] *Ibid.*, p. 145.
[129] *Ibid.*, p. 148.   [130] *Ibid.*, p. 150.   [131] *Ibid.*

shows the transference of the literary ideal of refinement and subtlety to the neighboring art of sophisticated conversation.

Cryptography

It is natural that an age so deeply imbued with the love of the secret should be interested in the art of secret writing. The ancient Hebrews, Hindus, Greeks, and Romans had secret codes, partly for practical, partly for esoteric purposes. The ancient codes chiefly consisted in the substitution of letters, such as the substitution of each letter by the next one in the alphabet (Emperor Augustus's secret code) or by the fourth following letter (Julius Caesar's code).[132] In the Middle Ages the interest in cryptography was rather limited. The ancient method of substitution of letters by other letters in a simple and logical fashion was taken over. No new systems of cryptography were evolved.[133] Medieval physicians, chemists, alchemists, and astrologers developed an independent code of signs, which does not belong to cryptography—in the strict sense of the term—though we find it included in Renaissance treatises on the subject.

The Renaissance witnessed a great revival of interest in cryptography and a considerable expansion of cryptographic methods. One source of this fresh interest was undoubtedly the new secret diplomacy stimulated by the institution of permanent embassies at foreign courts and the growing necessity of having secret codes for the transmission of messages. Another source, however, was the fascination which everything secret exercised on the mind of the Renaissance scholar. Men of many nations and various backgrounds, such as the German Trithemius (1462–1516), the Italian Girolamo Cardano (1501–1576), the Frenchman Blaise de Vigenère (1522–1596), Giovanni Battista della Porta of Naples (1535–1615), began to write and publish treatises on cryptography. Let us look into one of the Renaissance studies on cryptography. Porta writes a treatise in five books on the subject. In the Preface he confesses that always, by nature, he has felt attracted to the secret and the occult and that he now wants to show how one can express one's ideas in a hidden manner and how one can decipher hidden messages.[134] Porta's cryptographic methods are distinctly different

---

[132] Meister, *Die Anfänge der modernen diplomatischen Geheimschrift*, p. 4.
[133] The cipher used in the Voynich MS, partly deciphered by W. R. Newbold, who attributed the manuscript to Roger Bacon, seems to be one of few exceptions. John M. Manly has proved Newbold's method of decoding untenable; the key to the cipher has not yet been found (Manly, *Roger Bacon and the Voynich MS, Speculum*, VI, 1931, pp. 345 ff.).
[134] *De furtivis literarum notis vulgo de ziferis libri quinque.* . . . The first edition of this work appeared in 1563.

from those employed during the Middle Ages. Whereas the codes of the Middle Ages use the device of substituting letters and thus exhibit their secret character by the fact that the letters make no sense, Porta concentrates on codes whose secretiveness is hidden in a meaningful, but innocent, surface message. Bacon, in his *Advancement of Learning*, Book VI, chap. 1, in treating of cryptography, mentions this method still as a new invention: "There is a new and useful invention to elude the examination of a cipher; viz., to have two alphabets, the one of significant, and the other of non-significant letters; and folding up two writings together, the one conveying the secret, whilst the other is such as the writer might probably send without danger." In other words, the Renaissance cryptographer resorts to double meaning in his efforts to find an effective camouflage for the transmission of a secret message. The change that took place in the representation of the secret writing is exactly parallel to the change that we observed in the representation of the enigmatic in music. The medieval method of posing a musical riddle was to point it out quite openly by an allegorical motto; the secret chromatic art on the other hand conceals the secret reading in an inconspicuous surface reading. I cannot describe Porta's highly interesting work in detail, but I wish to draw attention to a masterpiece of double faced letter writing attributed by Porta to Petrarch. If this letter is read in the normal manner, it contains praise and good wishes for a friend; if it is read backward, word for word, it indulges in severe blame and ill wishes.[135]

Among the many codes which Porta communicates we find also a musical secret writing in which every note stands for a letter and which is thus capable of carrying messages.[136] Of course, Porta treats also of the finer art of dissimulation by allegory, metaphor, and amphibology.[137]

While Renaissance cryptography furnishes us with a new confirmation of the importance of double meaning as a means for hiding an esoteric message, it proves, if viewed from another angle, the degeneration of double meaning as a technique of communication. The surest sign of decay in an esoteric tradition is the divulgence of the secret or the means of preserving it.[138] The very act of publishing a cryptography reveals that the genuine desire of guarding the secret gives place to scientific analysis on the one hand and an attitude of showmanship on the other.

[135] *Ibid.*, Book V, chap. i.   [136] *Ibid.*, chap. xvi.
[137] *Ibid.*, Book I, chap. v.
[138] As Rabelais remarks philosophically "subtilty suspected, subtilty foreseen, subtilty found out, loses the essence and very name of subtilty, and only gains that of blockishness." (Rabelais, *The Works*, Book V, p. 598.)

Double Meaning as a View of the World

In our search for the meaning of double meaning in theology, philosophy, social criticism, science, art, poetry, and cryptography of the sixteenth century we have encountered many motives: double meaning as a screening device to protect the thinker and his ideas; double meaning as a scheme planned to prevent meaning from being misunderstood and abused on the part of the uninitiated and incompetent, the *profanum vulgus;* as a *jeu d'esprit* in literature and conversation; as a view of the world (Bosch, Brueghel, and in much serious poetry). It is this last and deepest conception to which we wish to devote our final attention.

Erasmus, in his *Praise of Folly*, gave clear expression to this idea, when he let Folly say:

. . . the fact is that all human affairs, like the Sileni of Alcibiades, have two aspects, each quite different from the other; even to the point that what at first blush (as the phrase goes) seems to be death may prove, if you look further into it, to be life. What at first sight is beautiful may really be ugly; the apparently wealthy may be poorest of all; the disgraceful, glorious; the learned, ignorant; the robust, feeble; the noble, base; the joyous, sad; the favorable, adverse; what is friendly, an enemy; and what is wholesome, poisonous. In brief, you find all things suddenly reversed, when you open up the Silenus.[139]

Were it not for the difference in style and mood, these words could have been spoken by Hamlet. Hamlet's heart was torn asunder by just this insight into the double-faced character of man and the world. It was his fate to experience the complete reversal of human affairs. The adored father falls; the satyr-like uncle reigns; the mother marries her husband's murderer; the son takes his mother to task, procrastinates where he should act, acts where he should wait, and brings deadly hurt where he means to love. To meet the reversed world on its own ground, Hamlet reverses his own behavior, puzzling friend and foe alike, using double talk as defense and weapon, but also as a genuine expression of the paralyzing discovery of the world's deceitful double aspect. The Italian *Cinquecento* had produced

[139] Erasmus, *The Praise of Folly*, p. 36. A similar philosophy in a humorous vein is expressed by a contemporary Latin poem, which Orlando di Lasso set to music and which appeared in a posthumous edition of his motets in 1597 (see *Gesammelte Werke*, Vol. XI, No. 295): "In quoscunque locos videam contraria cerno: illi nigra placent, illi sed displicet album, mulier illa viro vult vivere foedere iuncta. Musica cantores amat et celebratur ab ipsis: est incredibilis penitus mutatio rerum; sic breve quod legitur longum pronuntiat ille: quot quot sunt homines, totidem sententiae habentur." To depict in tones the reversed order of things, Lasso gives throughout the piece long notes to short syllables and vice versa: "sic breve quod legitur longum pronuntiat ille."

Hamlet's great antipode, the man who saw the world's faithlessness, il-
loyalty, and double face even as did Hamlet, but who accepted it coldly,
analyzed it scientifically, and based on it his recommendations for political
action. I speak of Niccolò Machiavelli. In the famous Chapter XVIII of
The Prince (1513) he teaches the future ruler how to use double talk
and two-faced appearance for political success. While he recommends the
breaking of promises and of agreements whenever opportune, he admon-
ishes the ruler seriously to take great care that "he should *seem* to be all
mercy, faith, integrity, humanity, and religion. And [he continues signifi-
cantly] nothing is more necessary than to *seem* to have this last qual-
ity. . ." [140]

With a frankness unheard of before Machiavelli advises the prince: "You
must know, then, that there are two methods of fighting, the one by law,
the other by force: the first method is that of men, the second of beasts;
but as the first method is often insufficient, one must have recourse to the
second. It is therefore necessary for a prince to know well how to use both
the beast and the man. This was covertly taught to rulers by ancient writers, who relate how Achilles and many others of those ancient princes
were given to Chiron the centaur to be brought up and educated under
his discipline. The parable of the semi-animal, semi-human teacher is meant
to indicate that a prince must know how to use both natures, and that the
one without the other is not durable.

A prince being thus obliged to know well how to act as a beast must imitate the fox and the lion, for the lion cannot protect himself from traps,
and the fox cannot defend himself from wolves. Those that wish to be only
lions do not understand this . . . those that have been best able to imitate
the fox have succeeded best. But it is necessary to be able to disguise this
character well, and to be a great feigner and dissembler."

The aggressiveness of Machiavelli's concept of double meaning is high-
lighted by the images which he uses to elucidate his political philosophy:
the image of the centaur, who is half beast and half man, and the image of
the ruler, who must unite in himself the opposing natures of the lion and
the fox. And like all thinkers of the sixteenth century who believed in double meaning Machiavelli, too, distinguishes between the "vulgar," who are

[140] Does this not remind us of that classical advice which Pomponazzi gave his students:
"Believe in philosophy as much as your reason dictates; believe in theology as much
as the Church dictates. To do otherwise would mean your death at the stake."
Machiavelli wrote *The Prince* in 1513. Pomponazzi wrote his treatise *On the Immortality of the Soul* in 1516. The one lived in Florence and was exclusively interested
in politics. The other taught at Bologna and was absorbed in philosophical and ethical
problems. But both are related by their attitude toward religion and their use of double
meaning as a shield and—particularly in the hands of Machiavelli—as a sword.

to be deceived by appearances, and the "few," who are able to see through the appearance of things and to discover their substance. Whereas the philosophy appeals to the "few," Machiavelli advises the prince to disregard the "few" and to build his power upon the vulgar, who are many and who are easily deceived. "Let a prince therefore aim at conquering and maintaining the state, and the means will always be judged honourable and praised by every one, for the vulgar is always taken by appearances and the issue of the event; and the world consists only of the vulgar, and the few who are not vulgar are isolated when the many have a rallying point in the prince." Machiavelli teaches the prince to know, to accept, and to meet on its own terms that same world that breaks Hamlet. What to Machiavelli is cold and—as it were—scientific reality is to Hamlet the bitter tragedy of life. The motif of the deceiving duplicity of man and world recurs time and again in Shakespeare's work.[141]

What Hamlet had to learn in his prime, King Lear experienced in his old age. His mistaking the double-tongued speech of his daughters, Goneril and Regan, for truth, ruined his life; the late recognition of Cordelia's true affection, misunderstood because it was reserved, sweetened his death. His fate is reflected mirror-like in Gloucester's experience with his sons Edmund and Edgar. The part played by the fool is essentially identical with the one taken by Erasmus's Folly. He belies his name by the wisdom of his observations, and he belies his wisdom by the foolishness with which he puts it forward.[142]

[141] It may be observed in passing that Shakespeare's drama is teeming with figures who either partly or fully correspond to Machiavelli's ideal of the prince, men like Jago, Edmund, or Richard III, who boasts that he will even "set the murderous Machiavel to school" (third part of Henry VI, act III, scene II). Machiavelli is known to have had a tremendous influence upon the imagination of the Tudor dramatists and of Shakespeare in particular. But no outside influence will ever account for the inimitable way in which these men come to life in Shakespeare's creations.

[142] Rabelais, in the third book of *Gargantua and Pantagruel*, writes: "I have often heard it said, in a vulgar proverb, 'The wise may be instructed by a fool . . .' You know how, by the advice and counsel, and prediction of fools, many kings, princes, states, and commonwealths have been preserved, several battles gained, and divers doubts of most perplexed intricacy resolved . . .

"As he, who narrowly takes heed to what concerns the dexterous management of his private affairs, domestic businesses . . . whose frugal spirit never strays from home; who loseth no occasion whereby he may purchase to himself more riches . . . is called a worldly-wise man, though perhaps, in the judgement of the intelligences which are above, he be esteemed a *fool*; so, on the contrary, is the most like (even in the thought of most celestial spirits) to be not only *sage*, but to *presage* events to come, by divine inspiration, who, laying quite aside those cares which are conducible to his body or his fortunes, and as it were departing from himself, rids all his senses of terrene affections . . . all which neglects of sublunary things are vulgarly imputed to *folly* . . .

In *Timon of Athens* [143] Shakespeare couples the concept of human duplicity with the concept of Fortuna's double face. In a manner rarely used in other plays Shakespeare puts the underlying idea motto-like in front of the tragedy in the form of a picture which is developed by the poet and the painter as a common creation, the poet clearly having the lead.

Poet: I have upon a high and pleasant hill
       Feign'd Fortune to be throned; the base o' the mount
       Is rankt with all deserts, all kind of natures,
       That labour on the bosom of this sphere
       To propagate their states: amongst them all,
       Whose eyes are on this sovereign Lady fixt,
       One do I personate of Lord Timon's frame,
       Whom Fortune with her ivory hand wafts to her:
       Whose present grace to present slaves and servants
       Translates his rivals.

Painter: 'Tis conceived to scope
       This throne, this Fortune, and this hill, methinks,
       With one man beckon'd from the rest below,
       Bowing his head against the steepy mount
       To climb his happiness, would be well exprest
       In our condition.

Poet: Nay, sir, but hear me on.
       All those which were his fellows but of late,—
       Some better than his value,—on the moment
       Follow his strides, his lobbies fill with tendance,
       Rain sacrificial whisperings in his ear,
       Make sacred even his stirrup, and through him
       Drink the free air.

Painter: Ay, marry, what of these?

Poet: When Fortune, in her shift and change of mood,
       Spurns down her late beloved, all his dependants,
       Which labour'd after him to the mountain's top,
       Even on their knees and hands, let him slip down,
       Not one accompanying his declining foot.

Painter: 'Tis common:
       A thousand moral paintings I can show,
       That shall demonstrate these quick blows of Fortune's
       More pregnantly than words.

"The like we see daily practised amongst the comic players, whose dramatic rolls, in distribution of the personages, appoint the action of the *fool* to him who is the wisest of the troop." (Rabelais, *The Works*, pp. 344–345.)

[143] Doubts have been raised as to the extent of Shakespeare's share in the authorship of *Timon of Athens*. However this may be, we are interested in *Timon* as a document of the time.

This little scene is illuminating in many respects. It is another testimony of the intimate community of ideas and symbols on the part of poet and painter of the time. How life stimulates the poet to invent a fable and how the fable stimulates the painter to imagine scene and action are shown here by Shakespeare most vividly. The concept of Fortuna, as it appears here, is another evidence of the international character of ideas and symbols in the Renaissance.[144]

But nowhere does Shakespeare's belief in the fateful ambiguity of life find so direct and moving a testimony as in his sonnets. The sixty-sixth sonnet expresses this philosophy, as in a last will, with a clarity of vision which he has who is reconciled to death. It is in this sonnet that we find words which might furnish the chapter heading for our description of this aspect of intellectual and artistic life in the sixteenth century: "And art made tongue-tied by authority." This is the wording of the poem:

> Tired with all these, for restful death I cry,—
> As, to behold Desert a beggar born,
> And needy Nothing trimm'd in jollity,
> And purest Faith unhappily forsworn,
> And guilded Honour shamefully misplaced,
> And maiden Virtue rudely strumpeted,
> And right Perfection wrongfully disgraced,
> And Strength by limping Sway disabled,
> And Art made tongue-tied by authority,
> And Folly, doctor-like, controlling Skill,
> And simple Truth miscall'd Simplicity,
> And captive Good attending captain Ill:
>   Tired with all these, from these would I be gone,
>   Save that, to die, I leave my love alone.

Again and again the sonnets speak of the world's Janus face. In sonnet 35 we read:

> Roses have thorns, and silver fountains mud;
> Clouds and eclipses stain both moon and sun,
> And loathsome canker lives in sweetest bud.[145]

[144] This applies just as well to the Middle Ages; see the author's *The Goddess Fortuna in Music, Musical Quarterly*, XXIX (January, 1943), 1.

[145] The sonnets 93–96 are devoted to the depiction of the duplicity of love. The old lament over love's deceptions finds new expression in these verses (sonnet 93):
> So shall I live, supposing thou art true,
> Like a deceived husband; so love's face
> May still seem love to me, though alter'd new;
> Thy looks with me, thy heart in other place: . . .

But in the process of deciphering the true face of men and things, the poet cannot escape the insight into the duplicity of his own self. I quote from sonnet 62:

> Methinks no face so gracious is as mine,
> No shape so true, no truth of such account;
> And for myself mine own worth do define,
> As I all other in all worths surmount.
> But when my glass shows me myself indeed,
> Beated and chopt with tann'd antiquity,
> Mine own self-love quite contrary I read;
> Self so self-loving were iniquity.

And again, and more sharply, the poet reveals the double nature of his self in sonnet 144:

> Two loves I have of comfort and despair,
> Which like two spirits do suggest me still:
> The better angel is a man right fair,
> The worser spirit a woman colour'd ill.
> To win me soon to hell, my female evil
> Tempteth my better angel from my side,
> And would corrupt my saint to be a devil
> Wooing his purity with her foul pride.
> And whether that my angel be turn'd fiend
> Suspect I may, yet not directly tell;
> But being both from me, both to each friend
> I guess one angel in another's hell:
> Yet this shall I ne'er know, but live in doubt,
> Till my bad angel fire my good one out.[146]

In this sonnet Shakespeare adds a new idea to the philosophy of man's double nature: the duplicity in man's heart is not a static fact, but a dynamic process. In the struggle between the two selves within man only death can act as umpire.[147]

And sonnet 96 explains the deceiving power of love's "second" face:
> . . . As on the finger of a throned queen
> The basest jewel will be well esteem'd,
> So are those errors that in thee are seen
> To truths translated and for true things deem'd . . .

[146] All quotations are taken from the Shakespeare Head Press Edition.

[147] I am aware of the interpretation which Shakespeare research has given to this sonnet. The fact that the "man right fair" is thought to be a blond young man of noble rank and the "woman colour'd ill," a "dark lady" does not contradict my interpretation, I believe. Shakespeare's being torn between two such extremes as he describes in the sonnet presupposes his harboring these two extremes in his own self.

Conclusion

We are at the end of our road. In looking back to our point of departure we see the secret chromatic art and the *musica reservata* change from a strange and isolated phenomenon in the history of music to one little facet in a great pattern of the cultural history of the time. The idea of a musical style reserved for the few, offering one face, the outside, to the world, another one, the inside, to the initiated, now appears to be completely in harmony with the strong esoteric trends of the time. Moreover, the secret chromatic art seems to unite all motives underlying the appearance of double meaning. There is the motive of seeking protection from the Inquisition, since chromaticism was frowned upon by the Church; there is the hiding of an esoteric religious message in the choice of texts and in the selection of words distinguished by secret modulations; there is the hidden humor and the pleasure in the attempt to match wits with the Inquisition; there is the delight of the expert in the ability to clothe secret meaning in inconspicuous form, and the playfulness which goes with every sophisticated technique. At the bottom of it all, however, is the serene joy of the creative artist in the consciousness that no oppression, cruel as it may be, can ever enslave man's spirit, destined to be free.

BIBLIOGRAPHY

Aa, A. J. van der. Biographisch Woordenboek der Nederlanden. 12 vols. Haarlem, 1877.

Abert, A. A. Die stilistischen Voraussetzungen der "Cantiones sacrae" von Heinrich Schütz. Berlin, 1935. "Kieler Beiträge zur Musikwissenschaft."

Altmeyer, J. J. Les Précurseurs de la réforme aux Pays-Bas. 2 vols. Brussels, 1886.

Ambros, A. W. Geschichte der Musik. 5 vols. Breslau and Leipzig, 1862–1882.

Anagnine, Eugenio. G. Pico della Mirandola; sincretismo religioso-filosofico, 1463–1494. Bari, 1937.

Armitage, Angus. Copernicus, the Founder of Modern Astronomy. London [1938].

Avella, Padre Fra Giovanni d'. Regole di musica. Rome, 1657.

Bacon, Francis. Advancement of Learning. London, 1605.

Bainton, R. H. Concerning Heretics. New York, 1935.

Bartha, Dénes. Benedictus Ducis und Appenzeller. Wolfenbüttel-Berlin, 1930.

Becker, Georg. Hubert Waelrant et ses psaumes. Paris, 1881.

—— Jean Caulery et ses chansons spirituelles. Paris, 1880.

Bermudo, Juan. Declaración de instrumentos musicales. Ossuna, 1555.

Bernet-Kempers, K. P. Jacobus Clemens non Papa und seine Motetten. Augsburg, 1928.

Betzendörfer, Walter. Glauben und Wissen bei den grossen Denkern des Mittelalters. Gotha, 1931.

Bibliotheca Reformatoria Neerlandica. 10 vols. The Hague, 1903–1914.

Bockenrodt, Joannes. Admiranda quaedam poemata, vatis undecunque rarissimi. Cologne, 1533.

Borren, Charles van den. Guillaume Dufay. Brussels, 1926.

—— Hubert Waelrant. Brussels, 1938. "Biographie Nationale Belgique."

—— Inventaire des manuscrits de musique polyphonique qui se trouvent en Belgique. Reprint from *Acta musicologica*, 1933–1934.

—— Polyphonia sacra. Nashdom Abbey, 1932.

Bosco, Simon à. Tertius liber modulorum quatuor quinque, et sex vocum . . . n.p., 1555. Eitner 1555i.

—— Quintus liber modulorum, quinque vocum . . . n.p., 1556. Eitner 1556g.

Bottrigari, Ercole. Il desiderio; overo, De' concerti di varii strumenti musicali. Venice, 1594; Berlin, 1924.

Bragers, A. P. Chant Service Book. Boston, 1941.

Briggs, C. A. History of the Study of Theology. 2 vols. London, 1916.

Bruno, Giordano. Del infinito universo e mondi. Venice, 1589.

Burgon, J. W. The Life and Times of Sir Thomas Gresham, Knt. Founder of the Royal Exchange. 2 vols., London, 1839.

Burtius, N. Nicolai Burtii . . . musices opusculum . . . Bonn, 1487.

Cametti, Alberto. Palestrina. Milan, 1925.

Campanella, Tommaso. The Defense of Galileo of Thomas Campanella; trans. and ed. by Grant McColley. Northampton, Mass. [1937]. "Smith College Studies in History."

Caplan, H. "The Four Senses of Scriptural Interpretation and the Mediaeval Theory of Preaching," *Speculum*, Vol. IV (1929).

Castiglione, Baldassare, conte. The Book of the Courtier. Trans. by L. Eckstein Opdycke. New York [1929].

Chambers, R. W. Thomas More. New York [1935].

Chrysander, Friedrich. "Lodovico Zacconi als Lehrer des Kunstgesanges," in *Vierteljahrsschrift für Musikwissenschaft*, Vols. VII, IX–X, 1891–1894.

Coclico, A. P. Compendium musices . . . Nuremberg, 1552.

—— Musica reservata; consolationes piae ex psalmis Davidicis . . . Nuremberg, 1552.

Commer, Franz. Collectio operum musicorum Batavorum saeculi XVI. 12 vols. Berlin and Mainz, 1844–1858.

Copernicus, Nicolaus. Three Copernican Treatises; trans. with Introduction and notes, by E. Rosen. New York, 1939.

Coussemaker, C. E. H. de. Scriptorum de musica medii aevi nova series. 4 vols. Paris, 1864–1876.

Crevel, Marcus van. Adrianus Petit Coclico. The Hague, 1940.

Cyclopaedia of Biblical, Theological, and Ecclesiastical Literature. New York, 1894.

Dermenghem, Emile. Thomas Morus et les utopistes de la Renaissance. Paris [1927].

Des Prez, Josquin. Werken; ed. by A. Smijers. Leipzig and Amsterdam, 1921 ff.

Dèzes, Karl. Prinzipielle Fragen auf dem Gebiet der fingierten Musik . . . Berlin, 1922.

Donadoni, Eugenio. Torquato Tasso. 2 vols. Venice, 1928.

Douen, Orentin. Clément Marot et le psautier huguenot. 2 vols. Paris, 1878.

Douglas, A. H. The Philosophy and Psychology of Pietro Pomponazzi. Cambridge, 1910.

Ehrenberg, Richard. Das Zeitalter der Fugger. 2 vols. Jena, 1912.

Eitner, Robert. Bibliographie der Musik-Sammelwerke des XVI. und XVII. Jahrhunderts. Berlin, 1877.

Elsner, Emilie. Untersuchung der instrumentalen Besetzungspraxis der weltlichen Musik im 16. Jahrhundert in Italien. Berlin, 1935.

Encyclopaedia of Religion and Ethics; ed. by I. Hastings. New York, 1922.

Eppstein, Hans. Nicolas Gombert als Motettenkomponist. Würzburg, 1935.

Erasmus, Desiderius. Omnia opera Des. Erasmi Roterodami. . . . 10 vols. Basel, 1540.

—— Opus epistolarum Des. Erasmi Roterodami; ed. by P. S. Allen. 10 vols. Oxford, 1906.

—— The Praise of Folly; trans. by H. H. Hudson. Princeton [1941].

Fantastic Art, Dada, Surrealism; ed. by A. H. Barr, Jr. New York, The Museum of Modern Art, 1936.

Ficker, Rudolf von. Beiträge zur Chromatik des 14.–16. Jahrhunderts; Beihefte, "Denkmäler der Tonkunst in Oesterreich," II, 1914.

Finck, Hermann. Practica musica. Wittenberg, 1556.

Fiorentino, Francesco. Studi e ritratti della Rinascenza. Bari, 1911.

Galilei, Galileo. Dialog über die beiden hauptsächlichsten Weltsysteme . . . trans. by Emil Strauss. Leipzig, 1891.

Giehlow, Karl. "Die Hieroglyphenkunde des Humanismus in der Allegorie der Renaissance," in *Jahrbuch der kunsthistorischen Sammlungen des Allerh. Kaiserhauses*, Vienna, 1915.

Giunti, I. Biblia Sacrosancta Testamenti Veteris et Novi . . . Lyon, 1546.

Glareanus, Henricus, Dodekachordon. Basel, 1547.

—— Isagoge in Musicen . . . Basel, 1516.

Glück, Gustav. Pieter Brueghel the Elder. London [1936].

Guicciardini, Lodovico. Belgicae . . . descriptio. Amsterdam, 1660. The first edition appeared in 1560.

Gutman, H. B. "The Medieval Content of Raphael's 'School of Athens.' " *Journal of the History of Ideas*, II (1941), 4.

Haas, Robert. Aufführungspraxis der Musik. Potsdam, 1931. "Handbuch der Musikwissenschaft."

Hartlaub, G. F. "Arcana Artis, Spuren alchemistischer Symbolik in der Kunst des 16. Jahrhunderts," *Zeitschrift für Kunstgeschichte*, VI (1937).

—— Giorgiones Geheimnis. Munich [1925].

—— "Giorgione und der Mythos der Akademien." *Repertorium für Kunstwissenschaft*, 1927.

—— "Signa Hermetis; zwei alte alchemistische Bilderhandschriften," *Zeitschrift für Kunstwissenschaft*, Vol. IV (1937).

Haupt, D. E. Luther und Rabelais. Langensalza, 1890.

Hervagius, J. Concordantiae majores sacrae Bibliae . . . Basel, 1552.

Huber, Kurt. Ivo de Vento. Lindenberg, 1918.

Ingegneri, Angelo. Della poesia rappresentativa. Ferrara, 1598.

Jacobsthal, Gustav. Die chromatische Alteration im liturgischen Gesang der abendlaendischen Kirche. Berlin, 1897.

Jamil-Ur-Rehman, Mohammad. The Philosophy and Theology of Averroës; translated. Baroda, 1921.

Jedlicka, Gothard. Pieter Bruegel; der Maler in seiner Zeit. Erlenbach, Zurich, and Leipzig [1938].

Jeppesen, Knud. Die mehrstimmige italienische Laude um 1500. Leipzig-Copenhagen, 1935.

Johnson, F. R. Astronomical Thought in Renaissance England. Baltimore, 1937.

Kalff, Gerrit. Geschiedenis der nederlandsche Letterkunde. 7 vols. Groningen, 1906–1912.

—— Geschiedenis der Nederlandsche Letterkunde in de 16de Eeuw. 2 vols. Leiden [1889].

Kinkeldey, Otto. Orgel und Klavier in der Musik des 16. Jahrhunderts. Leipzig, 1910.

180 *Bibliography*

Kriesstein, Melchior. Selectissimae necnon familiarissimae cantiones . . . Augsburg, 1540. Eitner 1540g.

Kroyer, Theodor. Die Anfänge der Chromatik im italienischen Madrigal des XVI. Jahrhunderts. Leipzig, 1902.

Lanzi, L. A. The History of Painting in Italy; trans. by Thomas Roscoe. 3 vols. London, 1854–1888.

Lasso, Orlando di. Gesammelte Werke; ed. by F. Haberl und A. Sandberger. Leipzig, 1894–.

—— Orlando Lasso Prophetiae Sibyllarum; ed. by H. J. Therstappen. *Das Chorwerk*, 48. Wolfenbüttel-Berlin, 1937.

—— Sacrae lectiones novem ex Propheta Job . . . Venice, 1565.

Lea, C. H. History of the Inquisition. 3 vols. New York, 1922.

Lenient, C. F. La Satire en France . . . au XVIe siècle. 3d ed. 2 vols. Paris, 1886.

Levitan, J. S. "Adrian Willaert's Famous Duo, Quidnam ebrietas," *Tijdschrift der Vereeniging voor nederlandsche Muziekgeschiedenis*, XV, 1938, 166 ff.

—— Ockeghem's Clefless Compositions, *The Musical Quarterly*, XXIII (1937), 4.

Liber Usualis. Tournai, 1938.

Liliencron, Rochus von. Die Chorgesänge des lateinisch-deutschen Schuldramas im XVI. Jahrhundert, *Vierteljahrsschrift für Musikwissenschaft*, VI (1890), 309 ff.

Lindenburg, C. W. H. Het Leven en de Werken van Johannes Regis. Amsterdam [1939].

Listenius, Nicolaus. Musica Nicolai Listenii. Nuremberg, 1549. Facsimile-edition by G. Schünemann, Berlin, 1927. *Veröffentlichungen der Musik-Bibliothek Paul Hirsch*, Vol. 8.

Lowinsky, Edward. E. Das Antwerpener Motettenbuch Orlando di Lasso's und seine Beziehungen zum Motettenschaffen der niederländischen Zeitgenossen. The Hague, 1937. Reprint from *Tijdschrift der Vereeniging voor nederlandsche Muziekgeschiedenis*, XIV–XV.

—— "The Goddess Fortuna in Music," *The Musical Quarterly*, XXIX (January, 1943), 45–77.

—— "The Function of Conflicting Signatures in Early Polyphonic Music," *The Musical Quarterly*, XXXI (April, 1945), 227–260.

Lowinsky, Eduard, and Eduard Reeser. Zur Ausgabe der Motette "Fremuit spiritus Jesu" von Clemens non Papa, *Tijdschrift der Vereeniging voor Nederlandsche Muziekgeschiedenis*, XV (1937), 106–108.

Luscinius, Ottomar. Musurgia. Basel, 1536.

Machiavelli, Niccolò. The Prince. New York [1940].

Mâle, Emile. L'Art religieux de la fin du moyen âge. Paris, 1925.

Mandonnet, P. F. Siger de Brabant et l'averroïsme latin au XIIIme siècle. 2 vols. Louvain, 1908–1911.

Manly, J. M. Roger Bacon and the Voynich-MS, *Speculum*, VI (1931), 345 ff.

Mauser, M. "Das Verhältnis von Glauben und Wissen bei Averroës," in *Jahrbuch für Philosophie und spekulative Theologie*, Berlin, 1910–1911.

Maylender, Michele. Storia delle accademie d'Italia. 5 vols. Bologna, 1926.

Meister, Aloys. Die Anfänge der modernen diplomatischen Geheimschrift. Paderborn, 1902.

Melanchthon, Philipp. Philippi Melanthonis Opera; ed. by C. G. Bretschneider. 28 vols. Halle, 1834–1860.

Moderne, Jacques. Secundus liber cum quinque vocibus . . . Lyon, 1532. Eitner 1532c.

Montanus, Joannes, and Ulrich Neuber. Novum et insigne opus musicum, sex, quinque, et quatuor vocum . . . 3 vols. Nuremberg, 1558–1559. Eitner 1558b, 1559a. (The second and third volumes appear under the name *Magnum et insigne opus musicum.*)

—— Quintus tomus evangeliorum . . . quinque vocum . . . Nuremberg, 1556. Eitner 1556.

—— Sextus tomus evangeliorum . . . quatuor, sex, et octo vocum . . . Nuremberg [1556?], Eitner 1556a.

—— Thesauri musici tomus quintus, et ultimus . . . quatuor vocum . . . Nuremberg, 1564. Eitner 1564d.

More, Thomas. Memoirs of Sir Thomas More; with a new translation of his *Utopia.* 2 vols. ed. and trans. by A. Cayley, the Younger, Esq. London, 1808.

—— The Utopia of Sir Thomas More; ed. by G. Sampson. London, 1910.

Moser, H. J. Die mehrstimmige Vertonung des Evangeliums. Leipzig, 1931.

Osthoff, Helmut. "Einwirkungen der Gegenreformation auf die Musik des 16. Jahrhunderts," in *Jahrbuch Peters.* Leipzig, 1934.

—— Die Niederländer und das deutsche Lied (1400–1640). Berlin, 1938.

Panofsky, Erwin. The Codex Huygens and Leonardo da Vinci's Art Theory. London, 1940.

—— Hercules am Scheidewege und andere antike Bildstoffe in der neueren Kunst. Leipzig-Berlin, 1930. "Studien der Bibliothek Warburg," XVIII.

—— Studies in Iconology; Humanistic Themes in the Art of Renaissance. New York, 1939. "The Mary Flexner Lectures on the Humanities," 7.

Panofsky, Erwin, and Fritz Saxl. "Classical Mythology in Mediaeval Art," *Metropolitan Museum Studies,* IV (1933), 2.

Petrucci, Ottaviano dei. Harmonice musices Odhecaton A. Venice, 1501; ed. by H. Hewitt. Cambridge, 1942.

Phalèse, Pierre. Liber I–VI cantionum sacrarum . . . quatuor vocum . . . Autore D. Clemente non Papa. 6 vols. Louvain, 1559.

—— Liber VII cantionum sacrarum . . . quatuor vocum . . . Autore Thomas Cricquillon. Louvain, 1559.

—— Liber I–VIII cantionum sacrarum . . . quinque, sex, septem & octo vocum . . . 8 vols. Louvain, 1554–1555. Eitner 1554g, h, i, k, l, m, 1555g, h.

Pirenne, Henri. Histoire de Belgique. 7 vols. Brussels, 1922–1932.

Plantin, Christophe. Concordantiae Bibliorum utriusque Testamenti . . . Antwerp, 1585.

Plato. The Works of Plato; trans. by B. Jowett. New York, no date.

Pomponatius, Petrus. De immortalitate animae. Bologna, 1525.

Pomponatius, Petrus. Tractatus de immortalitate animae; trans. by W. H. Hay II. Haverford College, 1938.

Porta, G. B. della. De furtivis literarum notis vulgo de ziferis libri quinque . . . Naples, 1602.

Praepositus, Jacobus. Ein schone vnd clegliche history bruder Jacobs probst Augustiner ordens . . . Basel?, ca. 1522.

Prose Fiorentine raccolte dallo Smarrito accademico della Crusca. 2d ed. 17 vols. Venice, 1716–1745.

Proske, Karl. Musica divina. Regensburg, 1853–1863.

Rabelais, François. The Works of Rabelais, n.p., n.d. "Bibliophilist Society."

Reese, Gustave. Music in the Middle Ages. New York [1940].

Reeser, Eduard. Drie oud-nederlandsche Motetten. Edition XLIV, Vereeniging voor Nederlandsche Muziekgeschiedenis. Amsterdam, 1936.

Reitsma, Johannes. Geschiedenis van de Hervorming en de Hervormde Kerk der Nederlanden. Groningen, 1916.

Renan, Ernest. Averroës et l'averroïsme. Paris, 1852.

Reusch, F. H. Der Index der verbotenen Bücher. 2 vols. Bonn, 1883.

—— Die Indices librorum prohibitorum des 16. Jahrhunderts. Tübingen, 1886.

Ripa, Cesare. Iconología di Cesare Ripa Perugino . . . divisa in tre libri. . . . Venice, 1669.

Roemer, H. Die Entwicklung des Glaubensbegriffes bei Melanchthon. Bonn, 1902.

Routh, E. M. G. Sir Thomas More and His Friends. London, 1934.

Rubsamen, W. H. "Kurt Huber of Munich," The Musical Quarterly, XXX (April, 1944), 226–233.

Ruegg, A. Des Erasmus "Lob der Torheit" und Thomas More's "Utopie." Basel, 1936. Gedenkschrift zum vierhundertsten Todestage des Erasmus von Rotterdam.

Ruffo, Vicenzo. Cantus di Vicentio Ruffo il secondo libro de madrigali a cinque voci . . . Venice, 1555. Eitner 1553m.

—— Cantus opera nova di musica intitolata armonia celeste . . . Vicentio Ruffo . . . Venice, 1558.

Sandberger, Adolf. Beiträge zur Geschichte der bayerischen Hofkapelle unter Orlando di Lasso. Vols. 1–3. Leipzig, 1894–1895.

—— Hubert Waelrant, in Allgemeine deutsche Biographie, Leipzig, 1875–1912.

—— "Mitteilungen über eine Handschrift und ein neues Bildnis Orlando di Lassos," in Ausgewählte Aufsätze zur Musikgeschichte, Munich, 1921.

—— Orlando di Lasso und die geistigen Strömungen seiner Zeit. Munich, 1926.

Schmidt-Görg, Joseph. Nicolas Gombert, Kapellmeister Kaiser Karls V: Leben und Werk. Bonn, 1938.

Schwartz, Rudolf. "Zur Akzidentienfrage im 16. Jahrhundert," in Wiener Kongressbericht, Vienna, 1909.

Shakespeare, William. The Works of William Shakespeare. The Shakespeare Head Press Edition. New York, 1938.

Smijers, Albert. "Van Ockeghem tot Sweelinck," in Algemeene Muziekge-schiedenis, Utrecht, 1938.

Smits, C. F. X. De Kathedraal van 'sHertogenbosch. Amsterdam, 1907.

Stelsius, Joannes. Concordantiae Bibliorum utriusque Testamenti . . . Antwerp, 1567.

Suida, W. E. Paintings and Drawings by Raphael. New York [1941].

Susato, Tileman. Liber i–xiv ecclesiasticarum cantionum quatuor & quinque vocum . . . 13 vols. Antwerp, 1553–1558. Eitner 1553, a, b, c, d, e, f, g, 1554d, 1555, a, 1557a, b.

—— Liber i–iv sacrarum cantionum quinque & quatuor vocum . . . 4 vols. Antwerp, 1546–1547. Eitner 1546d, e, 1547b, c.

Sweertius, Franciscus. Athenae Belgicae . . . Antwerp, 1628.

Symonds, J. A. Renaissance in Italy. 2 vols. New York, 1935.

Tasso, Torquato. Apologia . . . in difesa della sua *Gierusalemme liberata;* con alcune altre opere, parte in accusa, parte in difesa dell' Orlando furioso dell'Ariosto, della Gierusalemme istessa, e dell Amadigi del Tasso padre . . . Ferrara, 1585.

—— Gerusalemme liberata; ed. by A. Solerti. 3 vols. Florence, 1896.

Taylor, H. O. Thought and Expression in the Sixteenth Century. 2 vols. New York, 1920.

Tolnay, Charles de. Hieronymus Bosch. Basel, 1937.

—— Pierre Brueghel l'Ancien. Brussels, 1935.

Ueberweg, Friedrich. Grundriss der Geschichte der Philosophie. 5 vols. Berlin, 1923–1928.

Ulhard, Philipp. Cantiones selectissimae quatuor vocum. Liber II . . . Augsburg, 1549. Eitner 1549.

—— Concentus octo, sex, quinque & quatuor vocum . . . Augsburg, 1545. Eitner 1545.

Vasari, Giorgio. Lives of Seventy of the Most Eminent Painters, Sculptors, and Architects; ed. by E. H. and E. W. Blashfield and A. A. Hopkins. 5 vols. New York, 1926.

Venturi, Adolfo. Storia dell'arte italiana. 10 vols. Milan, 1901–1937.

Vicentino, Nicola. L'antica musica ridotta alla moderna prattica. Rome, 1555.

Villari, Pasquale. The History of Girolamo Savonarola and of His Times. 2 vols. London, 1863.

Vogel, Emil. Bibliothek der gedruckten weltlichen Vocalmusik Italiens. Berlin, 1892.

Volkmann, Ludwig. Bilderschriften der Renaissance. Leipzig, 1923.

Waelrant, Hubert. Liber I–II sacrarum cantionum . . . quatuor vocum ad veram harmoniam . . . 2 vols. Antwerp [1556?], Eitner 1556d, e.

—— Liber I–V sacrarum cantionum . . . quinque & sex vocum ad veram harmoniam . . . 5 vols. Antwerp, 1554–1556. Eitner 1554f, 1555e, f, 1556b, c.

Waetzoldt, Wilhelm. Hans Holbein der Jüngere. Berlin, 1939.

Warburg, Aby. Gesammelte Schriften. 2 vols. Leipzig, 1932.

Wauters, A. Seigneur de Grobbendonc (Gaspar Schetz), in "Biographie Nationale Belgique," Brussels, 1884–1885.

Wieder, F. C. De schriftuurlijke Liedekens. The Hague, 1900.

Willaert, Adrian. Gesammelte Werke I; ed. by H. Zenck. Leipzig, 1937. "Publikationen älterer Musik," IX.

Willey, Basil. Tendencies in Renaissance Literary Theory. Cambridge, 1922.

Wolf, Abraham, Friedrich Dannemann, and Angus Armitage. A History of Science. New York, 1935.

Worp, J. A. Geschiedenis van het Drama en van het Toneel in Nederland. Groningen, 1904.

Zacconi, Lodovico. Prattica di Musica . . . Venice, 1592.

Zarlino, Gioseffo. Istitutioni harmoniche. Venice, 1558.

Zenck, Hermann. Nicola Vicentino's "L'antica musica" (1555). Festschrift für Theodor Kroyer. Regensburg, 1933.

MUSIC EXAMPLES

ABBREVIATIONS USED IN THE MUSICAL ILLUSTRATIONS

6a vox	sexta vox
5ta p.	quinta pars
S.	soprano
A.	alto
C.	contratenor
T.	tenor
Vag.	vagans
B.	bass
meas.	measure

The accidentals provided by the author are put either above or below the note, or in parentheses. A circle around the note indicates the code note.

HUBERT WAELRANT, "Afflictus sum," meas. 46–50

cor me-um con - tur-ba-tum est

HUBERT WAELRANT, "Et veniat super me," meas. 30–33

Se-cun-dum e - lo-qui-um tu-um

HUBERT WAELRANT, "Et veniat super me," clausulas

meas. 33–34, T   II   meas. 59–60, S

III meas. 62–64, S   IV meas. 74–75, S   V meas. 49–50, S

HUBERT WAELRANT, "Et veniat super me," meas. 29–32 (cf. ex. 2)

S.
C.

ta
T

B.

a) CLEMENS NON PAPA, "In lectulo meo,"   b) CLEMENS NON PAPA, "Quare de vulva,"
     meas. 42–45   meas. 46–49

C.

et non   et non in-ve - ni   fu - is - sem qua-si non es - sem

. CLEMENS NON PAPA, "In lectulo meo," meas. 31–50

que - si - vi il-lum et non in- ve - - - - - - - ni (non   in ve - - -

S.
C.

que si-vi il-lum   que-si-vi il - et - - lum   et   non in - ve -
       que-   - si - vi il - lum et non   in - - ve -

T.
B.

que - si - vi il-lum et_____   non

-ni que - si - vi il - lum   et   non   in-ve - - ni)   et   non   in

-ni   que-si- vi   il-lum   que-si - vi   il - lum et   in-ve- ni   et   non   et
                                           ni   et non   non in-ve- ni   non   in

in - ve - - - - ni (et_____ non   in - ve - - - ni   et   non   in

-ve - ni   que- si - vi il - lum et non in -ve - - - - - - - - ni)

non in-ve-   ni que-si-vi   il - lum et   non in-   ve -   ni)
-ve-   ni que-si-vi   il-lum   et   non   in-ve -

in - ve - ni_____   (et non in-ve -   ni)

7. CLEMENS NON PAPA, "Quare de vulva,"
meas. 41–53

8. HUBERT WAELRANT, "Videntes autem stellam,"
meas. 1–3

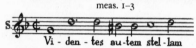

9. a) HUBERT WAELRANT, "Recumbentibus,"
meas. 1–3, S´   b) Part II, meas. 7–8, S   c) Part II, meas. 8–10, T

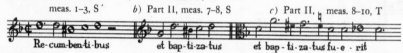

10. a) BENEDICTUS APPENZELLER, "Peccantem
me," meas. 33–37

b) meas. 70–73

11. THOMAS CRECQUILLON, "Ingemuit Susanna,"
Part II, meas. 17–24

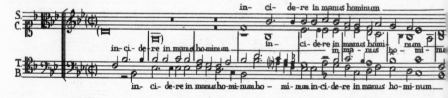

CLEMENS NON PAPA, "Domine non est exaltatum,"
    meas. 35–42

CLEMENS NON PAPA, "Conserva me," meas. 89–95

a) CLEMENS NON PAPA, "Caligaverunt oculimei,"
    meas. 41–44   b) Meas. 55–58

CLEMENS NON PAPA, "Vox in rama," meas. 29–32

5. CLEMENS NON PAPA, "Ne abscondas me," Part II,
    meas. 39–close

17. CLEMENS NON PAPA, "Venit ergo rex," meas. 50–59

18. CLEMENS NON PAPA, "Tristicia et anxietas,"
    meas. 75–80

19. HUBERT WAELRANT, "Si peccaverit frater tuus,"
    meas. 24–30

20. CLEMENS NON PAPA, "Fremuit spiritu Jhesu,"
    Part I, meas. 62–74

21. CLEMENS NON PAPA, "Fremuit spiritu Jhesu,"
    Part II, meas. 21–32

22. CLEMENS NON PAPA, "Fremuit spiritu Jhesu,"
Part I, meas. 1–14

23. JOSQUIN DES PREZ, "Absalon fili mi," meas. 60– close

24. CLEMENS NON PAPA, "Rex autem David," Part I,
meas. 6-7

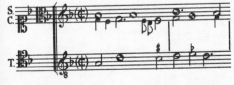

¹ This sharp is reproduced exactly according to the original.

25. CLEMENS NON PAPA, "Rex autem David," Part I,
meas. 20–34

26. CLEMENS NON PAPA, "Rex autem David," Part I,
meas. 39–45

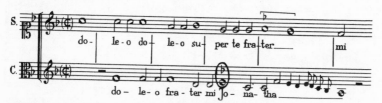

27. CLEMENS NON PAPA, "Rex autem David," Part II,
meas. 12–17

28. CLEMENS NON PAPA, "Rex autem David," Part II,
meas. 23–27

CLEMENS NON PAPA, "Jesus Nazarenus," Part I,
meas. 1–15

b. CLEMENS NON PAPA, "Jesus Nazarenus," Part I,
meas. 23–29

1. CLEMENS NON PAPA, "Jesus Nazarenus," Part I,
meas. 35–46

32. CLEMENS NON PAPA, "Jesus Nazarenus," Part I,
meas. 70–77

33. CLEMENS NON PAPA, "Jesus Nazarenus," Part II,
meas. 23–29

34. CLEMENS NON PAPA, "Vox in rama," meas. 54–close

CLEMENS NON PAPA, "Job tonso capite," meas. 12–27

¹ This sharp is reproduced exactly according to the original.

36. CLEMENS NON PAPA, "Job tonso capite," meas. 51– 69

37. CLEMENS NON PAPA, "Qui consolabatur me"
   Key-signature in Susato's edition

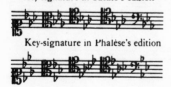

   Key-signature in Phalèse's edition

38. CLEMENS NON PAPA, "Qui consolabatur me" N.B.

   a) Bass   *b*) Contratenor

N.B. The signature in the bass is to be
found only in the first line of the Phalèse
edition; in the following lines we find
instead of an A flat a B flat—an obvious
error of the printer.

9. CLEMENS NON PAPA, "Qui consolabatur me,"
   meas. 37–close

The upper row of accidentals contains Commer's proposed accidentals
(C.); the lower row contains those proposed by the writer (L)

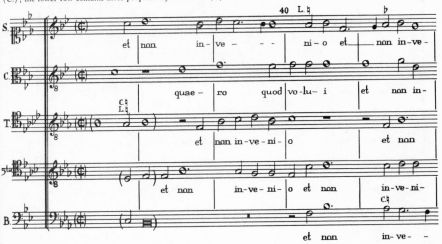

40. ADRIAN WILLAERT, "Quidnam ebrietas,"
meas. 20–22

41. ADRIAN WILLAERT, "Quidnam ebrietas"

42. ADRIAN WILLAERT, "Quidnam ebrietas"

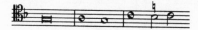

43. CLEMENS NON PAPA, beginning (superius) of ADRIAN WILLAERT, end (tenor) of "Quidnam
"Qui consolabatur me"   ebrietas," in retrograde motion

44. ADRIAN WILLAERT, "Quidnam ebrietas,"
meas. 12–21

45. THOMAS CRECQUILLON, "Domine Deus exercituum," Part II, meas. 39–close

46. THOMAS CRECQUILLON, "Domine Deus exercituum," Part I, meas. 67–close

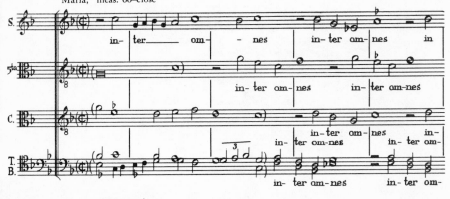

47. NICOLAUS GOMBERT, "Suscipe verbum virgo
Maria," meas. 60–close

48. HUBERT WAELRANT, "Afflictus sum," meas. 14–22

49. HUBERT WAELRANT, "Et veniat super me,"
meas. 53–58

50. HUBERT WAELRANT, "Et veniat super me,"
meas. 29-46

51. HUBERT WAELRANT, "Venit fortior post me,"
Part I, meas. 1-36

HUBERT WAELRANT, "Recumbentibus," Part I,
meas. 1–14

3. HUBERT WAELRANT, "Recumbentibus," Part I,
meas. 44–close

54. HUBERT WAELRANT, "Recumbentibus," Part II,
meas. 24–34

55. ADRIANUS PETIT COCLICO, "Non derelinquet
Dominus"

From M. V. Crevel, *Adrianus Petit Coclico*," The Hague, 1940. p. 281

ca- to- rum su- per sor- tem ju- sto- rum vir - gam pec- ca- to- rum su-

vir - gam pec- ca - to- rum su - per sor- tem ju- sto- rum vir - gam pec-

gam pec- ca - to- rum su- per sor- tem ju - sto- rum vir - gam pec- ca- to-

rum vir - gam pec- ca - to- rum su- per sor- tem ju- sto- rum su- per

per sor- tem ju- sto- rum ut non ex- ten - dant

ca- to- rum su - per sor- tem ju- sto- rum ut non ex-

rum su- per sor- tem ju- sto- rum ut non ex- ten-

sor- tem ju- sto- rum ut non ex- ten- dant ju-

6. EXEMPLUM CANTUS FICTI, LISTENIUS,
   Musica, 1547

INDEX